The Psychoanalytic Century

The Psychoanalytic Century

Freud's Legacy for the Future

Edited by

David E. Scharff, M.D.

Other Press
New York

Permission to reprint excerpt from "In Memory of Sigmund Freud" from *W. H. Auden Collected Poetry* by W. H. Auden is gratefully acknowledged. Copyright © 1940 and renewed 1968 by W. H. Auden. Reprinted by permission of Random House, Inc.

Copyright © 2001 David E. Scharff

Production Editor: Robert D. Hack

This book was set in 11 pt. Goudy by Alabama Book Composition.

10 9 8 7 6 5 4 3 2 1

All rights reserved. No part of this publication may be reproduced or transmitted in any form or by any means, electronic or mechanical including photocopying, recording, or by any information storage and retrieval system without written permission from Other Press, LLC, except in the case of brief quotations in reviews for inclusion in a magazine, newspaper, or broadcast. Printed in the United States of America on acid-free paper. For information write to Other Press, LLC, 377 W. 11th Street, New York, NY 10014. Or visit our website: www.otherpress.com.

Library of Congress Cataloging-in-Publication Data

The psychoanalytic century : Freud's legacy for the future / edited by David E. Scharff.
    p. cm.
  Includes bibliographical references and index.
  ISBN 1-892746-54-9
  1. Psychoanalysis—History—20th century—Congresses.
  2. Freud, Sigmund, 1856–1939—Congresses. I. Scharff, David E., 1941–

BF173 .P78 2000
150.19'5'0904—dc21

00-055076

Contents

Acknowledgments	ix
Contributors	xi
Introduction: The Analytic Century *David E. Scharff*	xv

Part I
History and Psychoanalysis — 1

1. Falling into History: Freud's Case of Frau Emmy von N. — 5
   Michael Roth

2. Freud, Freudians, Anti-Freudians: Whose Freud Is It? — 21
   Ernst Falzeder

Part II
Theory Reconsidered — 37

3. Freud Conserved and Revised:
   An Interview with David Scharff — 41
   Otto F. Kernberg

4. The Right Brain As the Neurobiological Substratum
   of Freud's Dynamic Unconscious 61
   Allan N. Schore

5. Modern Revisions of Freud's Concept of Transference 89
   Steven Ellman

6. Freud and Object Relations Theory 103
   Jill Savege Scharff

Part III
Learning from Hysteria 123

7. Dora: Freud's Pygmalion? 125
   Imre Szecsödy

8. Finger-Twisting and Cracked Voices:
   The Hysterical Symptom Revisited 139
   Iréne Matthis

9. Setting Freud and Hysteria in Historical Context 159
   Harold Blum

10. Panel Discussion: Relating 100 Years of Psychoanalysis
    to Clinical Practice 165

Part IV
Art and Literature 179

11. The Mind and the Book: Past, Present, and
    Future Psychoanalytic Literary Criticism 181
    Norman N. Holland

12. Freud and the Visual Arts 195
    Donald Kuspit

Part V
Freud and Love 213

13. What Freud Taught Us about Passionate Romantic Love 215
    R. Curtis Bristol

14. Freud's Theories of Love and Their Application to
    Treatment of Love Conflicts   231
    Stefan A. Pasternack

Part VI
Race, Ethnicity, and International Relations   247

15. Race and Countertransference: Two "Blind Spots"
    in Psychoanalytic Perception   251
    Dorothy Evans Holmes

16. Our Moral Universe   269
    Michael Moskowitz

17. Psychoanalysis and Diplomacy:
    Potentials for and Obstacles against Collaboration   279
    Vamık D. Volkan

18. Closing Panel: Psychoanalysis, Culture, and Society   297

19. Epilogue: Freud in Our Time   307
    David E. Scharff

Index   309

Acknowledgments

This book records the conference given at Georgetown University in October 1998. It coincided with the opening of the exhibit of material from the Freud Archives at the Library of Congress. There are many to whom I am grateful for their help with the conference, and in bringing this book to fruition. The staff of the Library, and particularly Irene Chambers and Cheryl Regan, of the Interpretive Programs Office, along with Michael Roth, the exhibit's curator, were enormously cooperative in getting our project off the ground, and they all participated enthusiastically in the conference itself. Harold Blum, Executive Director of the Freud Archives, lent his generous support and also participated.

The institutions that cosponsored, and the individuals who acted as liason, were instrumental in getting the conference—and therefore this book—off the ground. Stefan Pasternack and Curtis Bristol of the Advanced Studies Program in Psychiatry and Psychoanalysis, Department of Psychiatry, Georgetown University, were particularly supportive, urging us on before we were sure the conference could be done. I thank Steve Ellman of the Institute for Psychoanalytic Training and Research in New York; Robert Ursano of the Department of Psychiatry at the Uniformed Health Services University of the Health Sciences in Bethesda, Maryland; Joseph Lichtenberg of the Institute of Contemporary Psychotherapy and Psychoanalysis in Washington, DC; and David Joseph of the Washington Psychoanalytic Society.

At the inception of the project, Christopher Bollas cheered me on and assisted at several crucial points when the conference seemed impossible. Erica Davies and Michael Molnar, of the London Freud Museum, and Ingrid Scholz-Strasser, of the Vienna Freud Museum, lent valuable support to the conference and to this book.

My colleagues at the International Institute of Object Relations Therapy, its students, and its Board of Directors were marvelously supportive throughout the planning and running of the conference, teaching, working behind the scenes, and in every way possible. The most important support there was—and remains—was that of our administrators, Anna Innes and Mary Thomas, who made both the conference and the book possible through their selfless support.

I am grateful to Michael Moskowitz of Other Press and Karnac Books for his interest in publishing the proceedings, and to Bob Hack at Other Press for his stalwart and careful editorial work during its production.

Last and most, I thank Jill Savege Scharff. The idea for the Freud Conference was hers. A lion's share of the work—usually in the background—fell to her. Her often tested, unfailing support made both the conference and this book possible.

Contributors

Harold Blum, M.D. Executive Director, the Sigmund Freud Archives; Clinical Professor of Psychiatry and Training and Supervising Analyst, Department of Psychiatry, School of Medicine, New York University; former Editor-in-Chief, *Journal of the American Psychoanalytic Association*.

R. Curtis Bristol, M.D. Clinical Professor of Psychiatry and Co-director, Advanced Studies Program in Psychiatry and Psychoanalysis, Georgetown University; Baltimore-Washington Psychoanalytic Society; Institute of Contemporary Psychotherapy.

Steven Ellman, Ph.D. Institute for Psychoanalytic Training and Research; Professor, Clinical Psychiatry, City University of New York; Professor, Psychoanalysis and Psychotherapy, New York University Postdoctoral Program in Psychoanalysis.

Ernst Falzeder, Ph.D. Research Fellow, Woodrow Wilson Center for Scholars; Foundation Louis Jeantet (Geneva); Coeditor, *Freud/Ferenczi Correspondence* and *Freud/Abraham Correspondence*.

Norman N. Holland. Published eleven books exploring literature and psychoanalysis and one detective story. Marston-Milbauer Eminent Scholar at the University of Florida; Founder, Institute for Psychological Study of the Arts, University of Florida.

Dorothy Evans Holmes, Ph.D. Training and Supervising Analyst, Baltimore-Washington Psychoanalytic Institute; Professor of Clinical Psychology, George Washington University Psy.D. Program.

Otto F. Kernberg, M.D. President, International Psychoanalytic Association; Director, Personality Disorders Institute, New York Hospital-Cornell Medical Center.

Donald Kuspit, Ph.D. Professor, Art History and Philosophy, State University of New York at Stony Brook; A. D. White Professor-at-Large, Cornell; Contributing Editor, *Artforum*.

Iréne Matthis, M.D., Ph.D. Stockholm Psychoanalytic Society; Training Analyst and Supervisor, Swedish Psychoanalytic Institute.

Michael Moskowitz, Ph.D. Adjunct Professor, City University of New York Clinical Psychology Program.

Stefan A. Pasternack, M.D. Clinical Professor of Psychiatry and Codirector, Advanced Studies Program in Psychiatry and Psychoanalysis, Georgetown University; Baltimore-Washington Psychoanalytic Society; Institute of Contemporary Psychotherapy.

Michael Roth, Ph.D. Associate Director, Getty Research Institute; Curator, the Freud Exhibit, Library of Congress.

David E. Scharff, M.D. Codirector, The International Institute of Object Relations Therapy; Clinical Professor of Psychiatry, Georgetown University and Uniformed Services University of the Health Sciences; Washington Psychoanalytic Society and Institute.

Jill Savege Scharff, M.D. Codirector, The International Institute of Object Relations Therapy; Clinical Professor of Psychiatry, Georgetown University; Washington Psychoanalytic Society and Institute.

Allan N. Schore, Ph.D. Assistant Clinical Professor, University of California at Los Angeles School of Medicine; Faculty, Institute of Contemporary Psychoanalysis and Southern California Psychoanalytic Institute, Los Angeles; Editorial Board, *Neuro-Psychoanalysis*; Special Editor, *The Infant Mental Health Journal*.

Imre Szecsödy, M.D., Ph.D. Stockholm Psychoanalytic Society; Training Analyst and Supervisor, Stockholm Psychoanalytic Institute.

Vamık D. Volkan, M.D. Professor of Psychiatry and Director, Center for the Study of Mind and Human Interaction, University of Virginia, Charlottesville, Virginia; Training and Supervising Analyst, Washington Psychoanalytic Institute, Washington, DC; International Negotiation Network, the Carter Center, Atlanta, Georgia.

Introduction:
The Analytic Century

David E. Scharff

In the last century of the second millennium of the Common Era, Freud's thought and writings transformed the intellectual life of Western culture. Late in the nineteenth century, his first psychoanalytic book with Josef Breuer, *Studies on Hysteria*, which appeared in 1895, and the writings that followed began to influence a small band of colleagues and students, most of whom were in medicine. But it was in the dawn of the twentieth century, with the publication of *The Interpretation of Dreams* in 1900—and despite the fact that it initially only sold 800 copies—that Freud had not only stumbled upon free association, the technical mainstay of the psychoanalytic method, but had discovered the essential secrets hidden in the realm of dreams: a way of thinking that differed radically from logical thought, the principles of unconscious motivation and self-analysis. His theory of the biological basis of mind was first developed in 1895 in the unpublished *Project for a Scientific Psychology*. First appearing in print in Chapter 7 of *The Interpretation of Dreams*, it, too, has proved surprisingly prescient in many respects, despite major revisions required by the evolution of scientific paradigms and the availability of new research in the subsequent 100 years.

Freud's work has never been without its critics, from those who, as we can see in retrospect, conducted personal and groundless attacks, to those with thoughtful scientific disagreements. Today we still have critics of psychoanalysis who seem to lie in both categories. Freud: Conflict and Culture, the Library of Congress exhibit of material from the Freud Archives, complemented by artifacts and scholarship from the Sigmund Freud Museums of London and Vienna, opened in October 1998, after two years of delay. Although the Library cited issues of funding, skeptics remained convinced it was the outcry from Freud detractors that forced the delay. The design of the exhibit—when it finally made its debut—gave voice to the critics who have spoken throughout the century, and that voice was given more prominence in exhibit curator Michael Roth's accompanying volume, *Freud: Conflict and Culture* (1998).

The exhibit at the Library of Congress was a landmark event. To celebrate it, and to examine the evolution and implications for our field at the century's and millennium's end, the International Institute of Object Relations Therapy in Washington, DC, supported by five co-sponsors,[1] organized a conference held at Georgetown University to examine Freud's contribution and legacy. We wanted a forum that could ask, "What is still relevant of the core of Freud's legacy?" and "How have things changed in theory, practice, and in applied psychoanalysis?" The conference was designed to demonstrate the scope of his impact on psychoanalysis, psychotherapy, society, and culture. We hoped it would provide a vehicle for reexamination and updating of psychoanalysis 100 years into its history, and more specifically, would examine which of Freud's contributions have stood the test of time, and which have benefited from extensive revision during the twentieth century.

---

1. The co-sponsors of the Freud at the Millennium conference were: The Advanced Studies Program in Psychiatry and Psychoanalysis, Department of Psychiatry, Georgetown University (where the conference was held); the Institute of Contemporary Psychotherapy and Psychoanalysis, Washington, DC; the Institute for Psychoanalytic Training and Research (New York City); the Department of Psychiatry, The Uniformed Services University of the Health Sciences (Bethesda, Maryland); and the Washington Psychoanalytic Society (Washington, DC).

Two decades of cultural attack in England and America would consign Freud and psychoanalysis to the historical scrap heap. Through the exhibit and the conference, we began to see how this attack could also serve as a goad, forcing us to reevaluate the assets and liabilities of our tradition. If the Psychoanalysis Is Dead! movement succeeded, it would relegate Freud and analysis to the status of curious anachronisms and mere historical artifacts.

It is up to our field to reevaluate our science and art regularly and rigorously. The papers gathered here provide ample evidence that psychoanalysis is still a trove of ideas that adds up to more than the sum of its parts. While many specifics of Freud's early vision have been supplanted, taken as a whole the analytic point of view is vitally embedded in Western culture.

Freud's fundamental theories—that an unconscious life guides us, that psychological development beginning in infancy imparts meaning to our lives, that the thinking embedded in dreaming and the unconscious is fundamentally different from so-called logical thinking, that clinical narratives are revealed through transference—all these have become accepted common sense. His technical inventions of free association, free-floating attention, interpretation, and reconstruction have stood the test of time and remain stalwarts of our clinical armamentarium, although technique has evolved beyond them to include a new focus on countertransference and the relationship between therapist and patient.

James Michener, in his wonderful book about Israel, *The Source*, describes how archeologists examine a tell—a site that formed a hill as it was inhabited sequentially by different civilizations building one on top of the other during thousands of years. Archeologists begin by taking a slice from top to bottom, examining artifacts as they go. Thus they see the relatively modern artifacts first, only gradually unearthing the historical and prehistorical record, a sequence not unlike the route we often must take with a patient in analysis. The display of papers, ideas, and artifacts at the Library of Congress allowed those who attended to become, briefly, historians and archeologists, getting right to the bottom of things by viewing the ancient papyrus which holds the origins of our own branch of modern civilization. The papers that begin this volume by Michael Roth and Ernst Falzeder demonstrate the fruits of their research at the Freud Archives in the Library of

Congress. Digging through the archeological record, they have explored and documented the historical record Freud left.

Freud was exceedingly fond of archeology and its artifacts. On the first day of the conference, Erica Davies, Director of the London Freud Museum, described Freud's fascination with archeology, and the traces of its legacy in psychoanalysis. At age 29 Freud wrote to his fiancée, Martha Bernays, of his first visit to the Louvre: "There were Syrian kings tall as trees and holding lions for lapdogs in their arms; winged human animals with beautifully dressed hair, cuneiform inscriptions as clear as if they'd been done yesterday; and then Egyptian bas reliefs decorated in fiery colors; veritable colossi of kings, real sphinxes—a world as in a dream!"

Ms. Davies described how Freud followed the example he discovered in his visits to Charcot's house while in Paris, by developing a lifelong passion for collecting antiquities, which he compared to his addiction to cigars. The American poet, H. D., later described Freud "like a curator in a museum, surrounded by his priceless collection of Egyptian and Chinese treasures." Ultimately, his wonderfully diverse acquisition of more than 2,000 items included among its many Egyptian items others from the Near East, Mediteranean classical sites, China, and a few from the Americas—a collection that ranged from Greek pots and Egyptian artifacts to Far Eastern Buddhas. These embodied his extensive interest in ancient civilizations and their mythology, and served as reminders of his travels while he was at home working, and later when he was too ill to continue his travels. They came to form a museum of his own creation in which he worked every day, surrounded by mementos of ancient mythology and diverse systems of belief and thought. They reminded him of the archeological heroes with whom he identified. It inspired the powerful metaphor for psychoanalysis he described to the Wolfman: Psychoanalysis, like archeology, must go through layer after layer in order to arrive at the essential core.

With the help of friends and supporters, Freud was able to leave prewar Vienna with his collection intact. He died surrounded by his antiquities in the London house that is now the site of the London Freud Museum where the collection is displayed. Now Freud's private muse remains to inspire the world—truly a world as in a dream!

These artifacts spoke from the centuries to Freud as symbols of humanity's attempts to capture the core of psychology in myth and art.

Introduction: The Analytic Century / xix

Sigmund Freud at his desk with part of his collection. By permission of A. W. Freud et al./Mark Paterson and Associates.

So, for us, the pictures and reconstruction of Freud's Vienna house and office, described at the conference by Ingrid Scholz-Strasser, Director of the Vienna Freud Museum, become an archeological symbol of the origins of psychoanalysis—even as the temples and ruins of ancient Greece and Rome were symbols for the eighteenth century, and still for Freud, of the origins of Western culture.

In the same way that the artifacts of Freud's house and collection physically mark our beginnings, the artifacts and documents of the Freud exhibit mark the beginnings of our ideas. Exhibit directors Irene Chambers and Cheryl Regan of the Interpretive Programs Office of the Library of Congress gave an orientation to the exhibit that enhanced participants experience of the exhibit. Through a technique known as "exploded manuscripts," they mounted a physical exhibit that brought examples of Freud's texts to life, translating them not only into English, but into understandable prose, providing the context for the development of his ideas, marking Freud's evolution from neurologist to psychoanalyst, from founder of a movement to cultural philosopher and icon. The exhibit provided evidence of the pervasive cultural influence of Freud and psychoanalysis through

xx / Introduction: The Analytic Century

A room of the Sigmund Freud House and Museum, Vienna. Courtesy, the Vienna Freud Museum.

television monitors placed throughout the exhibit playing clips of analytic ideas in movie and television exerpts—some funny, some serious. Leaving the exhibit, we were faced with a wall of magazine covers featuring Freud and psychoanalysis in the popular press.

In these ways, the conference, and now this volume in which the papers and discussions are printed, demonstrate a process of evolution, modification, study, and reevaluation that has continued since Freud. The psychoanalytic tradition should not—and could not—remain solely based on Freud's personal contribution. Psychoanalytic concepts have experienced vigorous evolution during the second half of the twentieth century. It is the subsequent modifications and revisions—often in response to the criticism and controversy that have marked the entire history of psychoanalysis—that have made it into a sturdy, well-tempered instrument for understanding the human condition.

In this volume we celebrate Freud's legacy, and explore the scope of his impact on psychoanalysis, psychotherapy, society, and culture. The contributions of many distinguished colleagues follow the evolution of analysis as his ideas move beyond historical artifact to become

Artifacts and display, The Vienna Freud Museum. By permission, The Sigmund Freud Museum of Vienna.

living internal objects, embedded in Western culture. We begin with history, with the origins of psychoanalysis and the way those origins are treated now, and with an examination of the relationship between psychoanalysis and history. The following sections examine the role of analytic theory in furthering our quest, Freud's clinical contribution, and the ways in which Freud's work influenced the development of modern ideas of the interaction of brain and mind on the one hand, and of modern object relations theory on the other. Then we branch out to examine Freud's influence on culture and society: in art, literature, on ways of understanding love, race, social relations, and international relations.

It has been an exciting task hearing and then assembling these papers. I hope the reader will find them a useful key to opening new paths for psychoanalysis in the twenty-first century.

PART I

HISTORY AND PSYCHOANALYSIS

The first papers in this collection both deal with the history of psychoanalysis and the effect of psychoanalytic thought on the writing of history. **Michael Roth's** paper, "Falling into History: Freud's Case of Frau Emmy von N.," focuses on Freud's discovering—or rather his "falling into"—the analytic method of listening, as a paradigm for understanding history. Roth also explores the discovery of the analytic space in which the psychotherapist no longer dismisses or attempts to redefine an hysteric's past, as Janet and Charcot had done. Freud's patient Emmy von N., whose story is a mainstay of *Studies on Hysteria*, told Freud to let her finish her story before he tried to soothe her, leading Freud to say he "fell in with this." He thereby joined her attempt to learn from her story rather than imposing his ideas on her, and in so doing, he began to "fall into" psychoanalysis. Roth uses this example to draw a lesson for the discipline of history: nineteenth-century historians attempted to remain outside the past they described, denying their own involvement in the story. Modern historians, like modern analysts, recognize their involvement—their "desire"—for the history they describe just as psychoanalysis now recognizes the involvement of the analyst in the story of a past that is jointly reconstructed as a part of the patient's present. While this interaction between observer and observed is unavoidable—in history and in psychoanalysis—it can be reorganized and taken into consideration. The reality of the relationship that brings personal and social history to current life becomes an essential part of the story. This is the analytic space that Freud began to "fall into" in his early treatments as he moved from suggestion and hypnosis to listening to his patients' stories.

Ernst Falzeder's paper "Freud, Freudians, Anti-Freudians: Whose Freud Is It?" follows Roth thematically. In a brilliant gathering of evidence, he shows how the historical record documents the personal and political relationships and battles that characterized the early history of psychoanalysis. He then shows how the same process of partisan depictions of analysis—the frequent partisan rewriting of its history in order to support a point of view—is a process that continues in the current Pro-Freud/Anti-Freud battle of recent years, one that resurfaced most recently in the battle over whether there should even be an exhibit on Freud at the Library of Congress. "Writing the history of psychoanalysis has become instrumentalized, and has been used as a weapon in a very contemporary battle," Falzeder writes. The argument of contemporary Freud-bashers that the past and the accuracy of memory do not matter—their refutation of Freud's early central tenet that hysterics suffer from what they remember—is refuted by the very effort of the Freud bashers to establish the historical truth as they see it. Their insistence on a historical truth and its importance is the exact crime of which they accuse Freud.

Falzeder depicts history as a personal and political battlefield. Whosoever owns the past can own the present. The hysteric's complaint is that someone or something else—the trauma or the person who inflicted it—owns the past. Therefore, the discovery of her history is a battle for ownership of her life in the present of the treatment. In an analogous way, political historical battles are fought over ownership of the current state of the field. There are important continuing implications of this theme concerning the place of psychoanalytic theories of ideas and of people. Analysts are especially interested in the place of Freud as the central character in the drama of psychoanalysis. Falzeder's research establishes a principle: Analytic contributors have to be understood in context of their historical relationship to Freud.

The two papers offered by Roth and Falzeder form a contemporary statement of the complex philosophical problem about how we know, what we think we know, and about the transience both of contemporary understanding of history and of our understanding of our patients' dilemmas.

1

Falling into History: Freud's Case of Frau Emmy von N.[1]

Michael Roth

> I made it impossible for her to see any of these melancholy things again, not only by wiping out her memories of them in the *plastic* form but by removing her whole recollection of them, as though they had never been present in her mind. [p. 61]
>
> —Sigmund Freud

    Studies on Hysteria is a curiously hybrid text. It belongs to the prehistory of psychoanalysis, and one of the interests it has for us is that in it we can see Freud in the process of breaking away from a variety of influences even as he is nourished by them: Meynert, Charcot, Breuer, and Bernheim, to name just a few. We can also see

---

    1. "Case Two of Josef Breuer and Sigmund Freud," *Studies on Hysteria*, in *The Standard Edition of the Complete Works of Sigmund Freud*, trans. and ed. James Strachey (London: Hogarth Press and The Institute of Psycho-Analysis, 1955), 48–105. All subsequent references to this work will be given parenthetically in the text.

Freud staking out a terrain for psychoanalysis: the effects of the remembered past, mediated through desire, on the present.

The "effects of the past" that concerned Freud and Breuer were, of course, the symptoms of hysteria. Hysteric patients suffer mainly from reminiscences, they wrote, and their investigations in the 1890s were aimed at removing the potency of the past. Breuer and Freud were committed to the view that the reminiscences that caused hysterical suffering were historical in the sense that they were linked to actual past traumas in the patient's life. The affect associated with the past trauma provokes no balancing reaction, and it remains unacknowledged; the amnesia (or paramnesia) results from the force of that affect being dammed up. They wrote that "the injured person's reaction to the trauma only exercises a completely cathartic effect if it is an *adequate* reaction" (p. 98). The past that continues to wound is the past that originally found no outlet. Denied an "appropriate" response, the ghost of past experience continues to haunt the hysteric: "The ideas which have become pathological have persisted with such freshness and affective strength because they have been denied the normal wearing-away process by means of abreaction and reproduction in states of uninhibited association" (p. 11).

In the Whiggish histories usually written by partisans of psychoanalysis, *Studies on Hysteria* is read as Freud's recognition of the value of "uninhibited association" for coming to terms with the past, and especially of the role of sexuality in that past and our present relation to it. The uninhibited Freud, the conquistador as he liked to say, was ready to go where no one had gone before—or at least where very few doctors were willing to linger. Where abreaction was, there association would come to be. In the demonic accounts of Freud's nefarious effects on our century, *Studies on Hysteria* is read as the tale of the psychoanalyst's first learning to listen to his female patients, but of his coming to ignore the realities of what they were telling him. According to this account, in *Studies on Hysteria* the patriarchal, authoritarian Freud was about to lose his nerve when confronted with the testimonies of women who were often the victims of male sexual violence.

The Whiggish and demonic emplotments of the history of psychoanalysis neglect both Freud's precursors in this terrain of release/understanding through association, as they simplify Freud's own reluctance to move into what was for him frighteningly uncertain ground. Conquistadors are not supposed to be dragged into the new territory by the natives. But in Freud's case, the natives of neurosis were the ones who best knew the terrain of dammed desire, and he had to learn to follow them. But like his patients, Freud was full of resistances: doctors were not supposed to learn from their patients, they were supposed to *make them better*. The doctor was the scientist, the man of reason, and the neurotic patient had to be brought onto *his* terrain: and it should be firm ground in contrast to the swamp of (feminine) hysterical desire. But who would conquer whom?

The case of Emmy von N. presents a complex Freud, neither hero nor villain, a theorist undecided about the relation of memory to real events, and a doctor not yet convinced that the "normal wearing-away process" is best achieved through a talking cure that allowed the patient to acknowledge the past as a way to escape its domination. When Freud began treating Fanny Moser (Emmy von N.'s real name) in 1889, he was intrigued by the possibility of simply removing the reminiscence that cause the hysterical suffering. Hypnosis, Freud had learned in France, could be used as an "amnesic technique," a tool for removing the past from patients so that they could get on with their lives. Amnesic techniques gave the doctor enormous authority, the possibility of remaking the identity of the patient. But in order to become a real Freudian, Freud would have to dispense with the dream of removing the past in favor of a model of recollection, of constructing a past with which one could live.

In this paper I will discuss the school of forgetting against which Freud would define psychoanalysis. This school is most familiar to us as the group of researchers and clinicians around Charcot. Although Charcot and his colleagues at the Salpêtrière were locked in an intense rivalry with Bernheim and his students at Nancy, for Freud their use of hypnotism and suggestion linked them as a common temptation and as an "Other" against whom he would define himself. In the "Case of Emmy von N.," Freud was still trying out his French lessons as he attempted to assume the authority of suggestion and to wield the power of erasing the past. In this case study we see him working through the French forgetters, as he began to make the problem of suggestion an issue for any attempt to make sense of the past—not just as a price for erasing it. This issue—how can we actively recover the past for the present without simply inventing the past—would remain at the core of psychoanalysis and of modern historical thinking generally. It is not an issue that can be driven away through suggestion nor through the attack on suggestion. Modern historical thinking and psychoanalysis acknowledge the problem of suggestion, which is a version of the problem of epistemological contamination: there is not a pure place from which one can know the past. Though they acknowledge suggestion as a possibility, neither psychoanalysis nor historical thinking claim this possibility as a reason for embracing the position of the skeptic, of the person who would reduce insight to imitation, knowledge to persuasion. Whether the position of the skeptic is ultimately a hysterical position is a question beyond the scope of this essay.

For Charcot and his school, hysteria could often be traced back to a shock to the nervous system that disrupted subsequent memory. An original trauma continued to produce a psychical piercing, or a dynamic lesion of the nervous system, and could be healed through forgetting. A good example of this psychical piercing can be found in the strange case of Mme. D.'s hysterical amnesia, which was discussed by Charcot, Janet, and other physicians of the 1880s.[2] Mme. D. was told by a stranger that her husband was killed at the job, and that she should "prepare a bed" for they would soon be bringing back the body. But the story was a practical joke. The "shock" came when she saw him still alive. Since the initial shock of this odd prank, she did not remember anything back to the previous July 14, nor did she seem to have any new memories. The trauma, when combined with a predisposition to hysteria, led to hysterical "retro-anterograde" amnesia. Charcot used the word "elaboration" to describe the process through which an idea or remembered event acquired hysterical potency over time. Through elaboration, or autosuggestion, the trauma accumulated force and became the root of the hysterical symptoms. Like hypnotic suggestion, elaboration was a process that took place in the brain but not one that involved any conscious awareness. In the case of Mme.

---

2. See Charcot, "Sur un cas d'amnésie rétro-antérograde: Probablement d'origine hysterique." *Revue de médecine*, xii (1892), 81–96. Janet, *Névroses et idées fixes: Etudes expérimentales sur les troubles de la voluntém de l'attention, de la mémoire, sur les émotions, les idées obsedantes et leur traitement* (Paris, 1898), 109ff. A. Souques, "Essai sur l'amnésie rétro-antérograde dans l'hysterie, les tramatismes cérébraux et l'alcoholisme cronique," *Revue de médecine*, xi. (1892), 366–401; 867–881. I discuss this case in "Hysterical Remembering," in MODERNISM/MODERNITY, 3, no. 2, (1996).

D., the shock of hearing of her husband's death and then seeing him continued to block her capacity to remember (and thus to experience) any new events.

The concept of elaboration depended on a new and complex notion of the brain and of memory. An original event is remembered by the subject in ways that are independent of consciousness. The subject, or perhaps we can say "part of the subject," registers the event neurologically, and its representation is stored in the brain. That stored event continues to have effects on the workings of the nervous system, even if the event itself can not be recalled consciously by the subject. This process, of course, is very familiar (if still controversial) for us, but in the late nineteenth century the idea of memories having effects independently of consciousness was new and disturbing. Curiously, Charcot paid almost no attention to the significance of the stored event. The initial experience was treated like an electrical charge that continued to have consequences on the nervous system, not as an event that was cognitively or emotionally unbearable for the conscious subject.

Charcot saw the phenomenon under what he imagined as controlled conditions in hypnosis. Under hypnosis subjects are given access to a different set of memories than they would recall in their normal personalities. This access can often be remembered, with the proper hypnotic suggestion, so as to integrate the different faculties of memory. In other words, once a forgotten event is remembered under hypnosis, it can often be opened to the normal faculties of recollection. Paradoxically, once it is part of these normal faculties of recollection, it can be forgotten—the normal wearing away process, as Freud put it. Alternatively, that which happens during the hypnotic trance can, through suggestion, be closed off from remembrance in the normal state. "You will remember nothing of what has happened here after I awaken you."

These techniques were long familiar to mesmerists and more mainstream scientific investigators by the time Charcot announced his serious interest in hypnosis in 1882.[3] But when Charcot leant his

---

3. Adam Crabtree regards Charcot's paper delivered to the Académie des Sciences on February 13, 1882 as decisive. This was published in 1882 as "Sur les divers états nerveus déterminés par l'hypnotisation chez les hystériques," *Comptes-rendus hebdomadaires de séacnes de l'Académie des Sciences*, 94:403–405. Charcot had

prestige to the study of hypnosis and related states, it seemed to make new phenomena visible and old explanations suddenly worth taking seriously. Charcot took a narrow view of his subject, one that legitimated his own expertise. There was nothing mysterious about the phenomena, no invisible fluids or forces from the beyond. Hypnotism was a series of several "nervous states," which, like the stages of hysteria, could be isolated and described in detail. As Anne Harrington notes, "Charcot manages, in one fell swoop, both to give an aura of medical respectability to a formerly shunned and suspect subject, and simultaneously to stake a clear claim to the medical profession's exclusive competency to deal with this subject."[4] For him, hypnotism was an artificially created hysteria, and thus could be used to investigate cases of the spontaneously generated disease. One of the ways the master did this was by hypnotizing female hysterics and suggesting to them that they mimic the symptoms of male hysterics. His best patients performed splendidly.

In the case of Mme. D., hypnosis proved very valuable indeed. First, it allowed Charcot to determine that the woman was indeed registering her experiences, even though she could not recall them:

> This woman, who we have been able to hypnotize, rediscovers in her hypnotic sleep the memory of all the facts that have transpired until the present, and all these memories thus unconsciously recorded are revived in hypnosis, associated, uninterrupted, so as to form a continuous course and as a second self, but a latent, unconscious self, which strangely contrasts with the official self with whose profound amnesia you are acquainted.[5]

Hypnosis thus revealed a "second self" that did not suffer the effects of the trauma that afflicted her conscious self. The traumatic

---

already published *Contribution à l'étude de l'hypnotisme ches les hystériques* (Paris: Progrès médical, 1881). See Crabtree, *From Mesmer to Freud: Magnetic Sleep and the Roots of Psychological Healing* (New Haven, CT: Yale University Press, 1994), 166–167.

4. "Hysteria, hypnosis, and the lure of the invisible: the rise of neo-mesmerism in *fin-de-siècle* French psychiatry," in *The Anatomy of Madness: Essays in the History of Psychiatry*, vol. III, ed. W. F. Bynum, Roy Porter, and Michael Shepherd (London and New York: Routledge, 1988), 277.

5. Jean-Martin Charcot, "Sur un cas d'amnésie rétro-antérograde: Probablement d'origine hysterique," *Revue de médecine*, xii (1892), 85.

idea—the false report of her husband's death—had acted as a form of suggestion, cutting off a faculty of memory as did hypnotic sleep. For Charcot, the nervous system of the traumatized subject functioned much like the nervous system of the hypnotized subject. They were hysterical. The task for Charcot in the case of Mme. D. was to use hypnotism to overcome the disjunction between the first and second selves. Hypnosis functioned both as the sign of the pathology and the possibility of curing it. If the patient was willing to follow the hypnotic suggestion to remember, then the wound of the trauma could be healed.

But remembering for Charcot did not have any of the connotations of integrating the self or facing one's desires that it would come to have in the twentieth century. Remembering was a behavior that Charcot wanted to promote, a behavior currently inhibited by a (probably degenerate) nervous system that had not recovered from a shock (a trauma) it had received. Marcel Gauchet has emphasized Charcot's indebtedness to the neurophysiologists who, by 1870, had established that "the totality of the nervous system can and should be analyzed in terms of unities similar in structure and function; that is to say, in terms of sensori-motor connections and reflex processes."[6] The reflexive reactions of a degenerate nervous system following a trauma leave it vulnerable to suggestion—that is one of the key reasons for the production of symptoms. Suggestion can be used to get the system back on track.

From Pierre Janet's perspective, elaboration led to what he saw as the root of hysteria: the dissociation—the breaking apart into isolated fragments—of the personality. But how was the doctor to provide the hysteric with renewed capacities for psychological synthesis? One of the chief obstacles was the now elaborated memory of the trauma. Thus, forgetting was essential to cure: "One of the most precious discoveries of pathological psychology would be that which would give us the certain means to provoke the forgetting of a specific psychological phenomenon."[7] Since Janet regarded the memory of the report

---

6. Marcel Gauchet, *L'Inconscient Cérébral* (Paris: Seuil, 1992), 65. See also "Suffering and the Origins of Traumatic Memory" by Allan Young in *Social Suffering*, A. Kleinman, V. Das, and M. Lock, eds. (Berkeley, CA: The University of California Press, 1997).

7. *Ibid*, 404.

of her husband's death as Mme. D.'s *idée fixe*, after some months of failing to get her to make it a conscious memory, he concentrated his efforts on "suppressing" it, or at least at reducing its potency. The strength of the memory was such that it could not be removed, so Janet "modified it" by "transforming" the idea to make it less frightening. Instead of a stranger entering the house, during hypnosis Janet "modified his features" so that it was the psychologist himself who knocked at Mme. D.'s door! And instead of announcing the terrifying news, Janet's image said only: Mme. D., prepare a bed because I would like to sleep at your house in M."[8] Now, when Mme. D. had the recurrent dream about the incident, it aroused much less emotion, thus allowing her personality to integrate the various segments of the past into her personal memory. Janet deelaborates the memory and thus removes its potency. In Charcot's terms, by manipulating the image he destroys its ability to continue to affect the nervous system. The past is in the way. By changing the past, the psychologist opens the possibilities of new memory for Mme. D. "In a word, after the disappearance of the obsessional idea (*idée fixe*), the unity of the spirit is reconstituted."[9]

The problem with hysterics, it seems, was that they neither remembered nor forgot—that is, they could not bring to mind consciously (by an act of will) the element in their past that disturbed them, or when they did so it was without any of the affect that seemed to have been linked to the memory. But the therapeutic task was not simply to help the patient forget or ignore the pathogenic past. Hypnotism was thought to be a way of giving the hysteric access to this past; but whatever happens during the hypnosis was often forgotten upon awakening. Thus, only during hypnotism did some of Janet's patients feel connected with the past that otherwise haunted the present. As a result, a dependence on hypnotism and on the hypnotist often developed. Janet's patient, Marceline, would need to be hypnotized every two to three weeks (in secret, since her employers knew nothing about this) in order to avoid a relapse into a catatonic, anorectic state. Blanche Witt, a severely hysteric patient from the Salpatrière, grew even more dependent on Janet. "Blanche will now

---

8. *Ibid*, 146.
9. *Ibid*, 405.

speak only to me, will only be touched by me. She does not pay any attention to the words addressed to her by the other people present."[10]

The hypno-psychologist may complain about dependence (or "*electivitè*," as Janet called the attraction to the doctor), but this did not stop him from remaking the personality of his patient. In Blanche's case, he even named his new creation!

> I asked her what she thought of this new state (of hypnosis), she would tell me that she still feels herself to be Blanche Witt; but, on the other hand, she discovers a personality, inclinations and properties so different that she has difficulty believing that she is still the same. She accepts, therefore, very willingly the name "Louise" which I propose she take.[11]

Finding the right balance between memory and forgetting was very difficult. Who would define what the balance should be? In the case of the hysteric patient, Irene, she remembered the *fact* of her mother's death, but displays none of the affect "appropriate" to the event. But in this age of mediums and spiritist reconnections with the dead, what *should* she have felt? How can the memory be brought into relation with the emotions "proper" to it? In the end, when Janet considers the great body of his own and his colleagues cases, he chooses another solution. The final sentence of his weighty book, *L'Etat Mental des Hysteriques*, runs as follows: "In conclusion, the biggest favor that the doctor can do for his patient is to direct his mind."[12]

If some form of autosuggestion or hypnoid state is at the root of hysteria, then a cure would be to replace the poisonous claim of the traumatic past with the hygienic claim of the benign physician. Suggestion through reason, or reason through suggestion, but if the idea of reason includes the independence of mind, how can it be achieved through suggestion? The replacement of *elaboration* by the direction of the physician would *not* cure hysterics of their vulnerability to suggestion. Indeed, the need for, demand for suggestion was one

---

10. Jules Janet, "L'hystérie et L'hypnotisme, d'après la théorie de la double personnalité", *Revue Scientifique*, no. 20 (1888), 618.

11. *Ibid.*

12. *L'Etat Mental des Hysteriques*, 618. "En resumé, le meillure service que le médecine puisse rendre à un hysterique, c'est de diriger son espit."

of the byproducts of the treatment. Janet called this the *passion somnambulique*: "The hysteric who awaits somnambulism resembles in many ways the morphine addict who awaits his shot, even though his anxiety has perhaps a more moral and less physical character."[13]

Although Janet seemed uneasy at times with the power these patients were willing to give him, as he wondered what it said about "the dependence which exists naturally among people,"[14] he did not think through what it would mean to "cure" the hysteric of his or her need for suggestion, direction, or authority. After all, hysteria was an ancient illness perhaps always triggered by the power of suggestion, and hypnosis seemed to put this power into the (well-scrubbed) hands of the physician. The authority was immense, but in the hands of a truly scientific doctor it need not be infallible, only self-correcting. Pontalis quotes Charcot as saying: "What one does one can always undo."[15] Suggestion from the past was malignant; suggestion from the doctor as the voice of progress and reason was benign. Janet put the well-worn appeal to the weak predisposition of the patient in a new form: "Some minds more than others, have the need for perpetual imitation."[16] The problem was a technical one. How could the physician be present enough for the hysteric in constant need of direction? Janet states: "The true treatment of hysteria, Briquait said, is happiness. I have tried to understand what was this happiness which is proper to hysterics; it is, in my view, simplicity, almost the monotony of a simple existence which reduces the effort at adaptation."[17] The monotony of a simple existence would mean that hysterics would have less need for suggestion; little variety would mean they could continue imitating the tried and true models provided by the physician. Reason, when imitated, created normality: this happiness, which is proper to hysterics, is what Freud called "common unhappiness."

In addition to Bernheim's hypnotic techniques, Charcot and Janet's views on suggestion and hysteria had a decisive impact on Freud's understanding of the etiology of hysteria and of the possibilities

---

13. *Ibid*, 429.
14. *Ibid*, 423.
15. J. B. Pontalis, "Le Sèjour de Freud à Paris," *Nouvelle Revue de Psychanalyse*, 8 (1973), 236.
16. *L'Etat Mental des Hysteriques*, 479.
17. *Ibid*, 478.

for cure. Freud, like Charcot, was intensely concerned with the process through which a memory could become a psychological wound; that is, a trauma. In his early work (writings that precede, roughly, *The Interpretation of Dreams*) Freud strove to remove the memory's potency, not through forgetting like Janet but through the discharge of energy through a particular form of recollection. Freud came to develop psychoanalysis as a mode of interpretation that would create a past that one could live with. Psychoanalysis emerged out of mourning, out of the work that enables a person to detach him or herself from the past even while retaining some (narrative) connection to it. The talking cure demands that one situate oneself (or one's desires) in relation to the past, not that one reconstruct *the* actual past in the present. The role of trauma has been of decisive significance in the history of psychoanalysis, and as Freud emerged from mourning for his father he also radically altered the place of childhood trauma in the theory of hysteria. This has led some writers to claim that Freud was either fleeing from an insight into the persecution of (especially female) children, that he was covering over his and his friend Fliess's gross incompetence, or that he was protecting his own abusive father. I shall not discuss these claims here, but want to emphasize that Freud created psychoanalysis as a mode for connecting with and representing the past that has important affinities to mourning, in contradistinction to neurosis. He developed a hermeneutics of memory rather than a tool for some unmediated expression of the past (whatever that might be) that would pretend to get free of it. That is, Freud developed psychoanalysis as a way of using the past rather than revolting against it.[18]

But in *Studies on Hysteria* psychoanalysis had yet to emerge, or rather its early modes of inquiry and application were in competition with other approaches to dynamic psychology. One of the most fascinating aspects of Freud's treatment of Emmy von N. is his attempt to play the role of the powerful physician wielding the latest tool of science—hypnosis—to direct the mind of his patient, who happened to be one of the richest women in Europe. And when hypnosis didn't

---

18. On these general themes in psychoanalysis see my *Psycho-Analysis as History: Negation and Freedom in Freud* (Ithaca, NY, 1987, 1995) and "Freud's Use and Abuse of the Past," in M. Roth, *The Ironist's Cage: Memory, Trauma and the Construction of History* (NY: Columbia University Press, 1995), 186–200.

work, he reverted to overt command: If you don't accept my explanation for your stomach pains by tomorrow, I will ask you to leave. You'll be on your own and in need of another doctor. The normally independent woman returned docile and submissive (p. 82), we are told. Freud is clearly pleased with what he seems able to do (for a change), but he is also uncomfortable with the feeling, the illusion of power and authority. He is at best awkward in making his patient forget too much, and at worst irresponsible as he gives her a suggestion as a joke. Freud, who has great ambition for, but little confidence, in what he is doing, always feels about to be judged, perhaps dismissed by this "normally independent" and abnormally powerful woman. Emmy's adherence to his authority, when he has it, is itself a hysterical symptom of the patient's inability to live with the powers of the past. Freud's dilemma is how to use this authority without merely producing new symptoms or acting out his own and the patient's fantasies.

Under hypnosis, Emmy described scenes from her past, and after she had done so, Freud would remove the fear of the visions associated with them: "My therapy consists in wiping away these pictures of [frightening episodes from the past], so that she is no longer able to see them before her. To give support to my suggestion I stroked her several times over the eyes" (p. 53). The therapy goes well as the patient "unburdens herself without being asked to. It is as though she had adopted my procedure and was making use of our conversations, apparently unconstrained and guided by chance, as a supplement to her hypnosis" (p. 56). While in hypnotic sleep, she would punctuate her stories of frightening memories with the "protective formula": "Keep still!—Don't say anything!—Don't touch me!" (p. 56). Emmy is afraid, she explains, that if her reminiscence is interrupted, then "everything would get confused and things would be even worse" (p. 56).

Freud listened to these stories and tried to piece together their significance. At the same time, he used the power of hypnotic suggestion to change the content of the memories that had given rise to the stories in the first place. Thus, there is a deep tension in the case between Freud's aggressive use of his authority through hypnosis to change his patient's relation to her past, and his recognition that before the memory of the past could be successfully altered it had to be constructed in a conscious, possibly narrative form. "I cannot," Freud complained, "evade listening to her stories in every detail to the very end" (p. 61). This tension is most evident when Emmy complained about Freud's eagerness to erase her memories before she had had the chance to recount them for him: "Her answer, which she gave rather grudgingly, was that she did not know. I requested her to remember by tomorrow. She then said in a definitely grumbling tone that I was not to keep on asking her where this and that came from, but to let her tell me what she had to say. In fell in with this, and she went on . . ." (p. 63).

In this passage we can see the conquistador stopped (at least for a moment) in his tracks. It is the patient who sets a limit, or at least a context, for his authority. *Let me speak these memories before you try to explain them or wipe them away with the tool of hypnotic suggestion. Fall in with me before you use that authority to which I am supposedly so susceptible.* Freud described himself not as giving definitive explanations nor as wiping away the past with the tool of hypnotic suggestion but as "falling in" with the patient's chosen procedure. (*Ich gehe daruf ein* . . .) Like Anna O. (at least in the stories told about her), Emmy teaches her doctor to listen.

By "falling in" with Emmy's stories, Freud was falling into psychoanalysis and falling away from Charcot, Bernheim, and the road taken from them by Janet. What is the significance of this fall, for psychoanalysis and for thinking about history generally?

The significance for psychoanalysis is well-known, if still controversial. By falling in with the patient's stories, the analyst becomes part of a relationship, a component in a process in which he or she has only limited (albeit important) control. Freud certainly recognized the phenomenon that so impressed the Janets: patients make an enormous—sometimes bottomless—investment in the relationship to the doctor; they reproduce their illnesses in this relationship. But whereas this phenomenon contributed to therapeutic pessimism about the capacities of the hysteric to lead a normal life, it also became a therapeutic opportunity for the psychoanalyst. That is, the "need for suggestion" and the "perpetual imitation" evinced by patients within the therapeutic process were exposures of the history of the illness, a revelation of the etiology of its symptoms, if only the analyst were prepared to read it properly. Freud would later understand this exposure through the concept of transference, and the psychoanalytic investigation of the therapeutic relationship itself became one of the defining elements of this new approach to the mind and to mental illness.

The concept of the transference also describes the power of the analyst in treatment. This power is a function of the unconsciously repetitive elements of the transference itself. How can analysts use this power without sinking patients further into the dynamic that is itself at the root of their problems? How to use one's authority to expose one's authority as neurotic? These questions were already apparent in *Studies on Hysteria*, and would remain crucial for the criticism and defense of psychoanalysis as a clinical enterprise. By falling into Emmy's stories, Freud was falling into the domain demarcated by these questions.

Since Freud's time, psychiatrists and therapists have tried to escape this domain in two very general ways: (1) by denying they really have authority; (2) by denying that the basis of their authority is neurotic. Those who favor the first option often underline the *relational* aspects of the psychotherapeutic situation (as if these were not always present in Freud's work) apparently with the happy thought that by telling clients they are in an equal relationship they suddenly acquire equality. The power of suggestion obviously remains strong. The second option assumes that the legitimacy of the therapeutic practice (whether analytic, psychopharmacological, or both) somehow naturalizes and neutralizes the dependence that the client comes to have on the doctor. After all, so this reasoning goes, they *should* be dependent! This was the route Janet himself took when he defined the kind of happiness appropriate to the hysteric and attempted to provide that kind of happiness. Since the dependence is on a reasonable person—a source of reason and progress—it is suddenly no longer a symptom.

The domain demarcated by the transference is dangerous ground on which to stand because it is always in danger of shifting under one's feet. As critics of psychotherapy regularly remind us, there is no firm (epistemologically clean) place to stand in this domain. The analysand makes multiple investments in the possibilities for insight through the analytic relationship, and doing so is part of the conflicted history that leads the person to desire change; yet doing so is also part of that history, which in the present makes any change extremely difficult. The conflicted history of the person *is* the present, and any change that can occur must occur *through* that history. The French theorists of *amnesics*, who Freud was still trying to follow in the case of Emmy von N., were developing techniques that would remove the troublesome parts of the patient's history, or that would transform the reminiscences causing suffering in the present. They wanted to act on the person's contaminated past *from outside that past*, thereby protecting their intervention (and themselves) from contamination. In falling into Emmy's stories, Freud was falling into her history; there was no longer an intervention possible from a point outside it.

Freud's fall has been suggestive, if I can use that word, for theorists of history trying to understand the stories that are left to us from the past. Since the professionalization of history-writing in the mid-nineteenth century, there has been an effort to ensure that historians stand outside of—or at a distance from—the events that they are attempting to explain or interpret. The standpoint of objectivity was supposed to ensure that the authority of the historian was derived from established scientific criteria in the present, not from some personal, biased connection to the material from the past being described.

Recent theorists of history have called into question the picture of the neutral, disconnected historian relating past events from the outside. The point of this questioning is not that all interpretations of the past are equally valid, but that it is important to interpret the complex ways historians establish connections between their own present and the past they are bringing to it. Some of these connections can, as Dominck LaCapra has stressed, be usefully described as transferential since they facilitate the unconscious repetition of past patterns in the present.[19] Historians represent the past, and often in doing so also act out their unconscious or hidden investments in the objects of their research, which are often objects of complex longing and loathing. An acknowledgement of the transferential relations between historians and the pasts we construct enables us to attend to the processes of mediation and unconscious repetition that contribute to any historical representation.

By falling in with Emmy's stories, Freud was beginning to develop psychoanalysis as a form of historical consciousness that focused on the role of desire vis-à-vis the past. How does our relationship to a

---

19. See, for example, the essays in *Representing the Holocaust*, D. LaCapra, ed. (Ithaca, NY: Cornell University Press, 1994).

remembered past, or to the past which we imagine is inaccessible to us, serve particular desires in the present? And how does serving *those* desires make it impossible to serve others? These are questions Freud was already beginning to pose in *Studies on Hysteria*, and they would become crucial to the domain of psychoanalysis as a theoretical and clinical enterprise. I have argued in *The Ironist's Cage* that they are also central to the construction of history as a theoretical and practical enterprise. Historical representations attempt to satisfy or stimulate certain desires, and it is usually impossible for them to do so without denying others. Recent controversies surrounding the commemorations of World War II provide many examples in this regard. But the retreat from the transferential attempts to have uncontroversial museum exhibits, cool detached histories, or neat positive therapeutic experiences, are merely denials, not solutions of the problem. One can hope to make the workings of transference in historical representation more apparent, but one can not avoid this dynamic through some properly hygienic stance towards the past.

How does the remembered or imagined past draw one to it? How does the traumatic past compel our attention, care, or obsession, even as it seems to demand acknowledgement that one can never comprehend what happened there? These questions are as important for psychoanalysts as they are for historians. The models of Charcot and Janet pointed in a different direction. They are alien to modern historical discourse and to psychoanalysis because they are unconcerned with the investment one has in the past. Charcot and Janet employed technologies of memory or forgetting, but neither had conceptual space for the desire that one has for the past—a desire that results in an effort to narratively link present and past.

This conceptual space was what Fanny Moser opened up for Freud in "The Case of Emmy von N." It remains the space of modern historical consciousness, which understands freedom as the result of acknowledging one's past in a present containing possibilities for change. It is the space into which Freud was beginning to fall in *Studies on Hysteria*.

2

Freud, Freudians, Anti-Freudians: Whose Freud Is It?

Ernst Falzeder

> *Dedicated to Peter Heller, mentor and friend*
>
> Freud and psychoanalysis are not about nothing. . . . [Freud] did open up for exploration a realm of the psyche—for better *and* worse. . . . The trouble with the orthodoxists and faddists of psychoanalysis was and is that they might well promote the very opposite of what they intend. For by making excessive and fraudulent claims on behalf of psychoanalysis they may discredit it to the point where it loses all credibility and is discarded as rubbish, which it is not. . . . Americans go for simple alternatives. They like to be all for or all against things. But things are rarely that simple. Freud and psychoanalysis are a mixed bag—not to be put in a shrine nor to be thrown on a garbage dump.
>
> —Peter Heller (1994)

THE RISE AND DECLINE OF PSYCHOANALYSIS

It has become commonplace to say that Freud and psychoanalysis have had an enormous influence on Western culture and society of the

---

This contribution has been given final editing by David Scharff.

twentieth century, and that hardly any tendency in our life has escaped their impact. Speaking of Freud, Richard Wollheim remarks that "[i]t would be hard to find in the history of ideas, even in the history of religion, someone whose influence was so immediate, so broad and so deep" (Wollheim 1971, p. 9). And talking about the success of psychoanalysis in general, the sociologist Ernest Gellner maintains that "[t]here has been nothing like this since the spread of the potato and of maize, and this diffusion was even faster and may have deeper implications" (Gellner 1985, p. 11).[1]

It may be questioned whether Freud actually has influenced the development of culture to such a great extent, or if his name rather stands for changes that would have occurred anyway, with or without him. However this may be, Freud has become a "whole climate of opinion," as W. H. Auden called it (Jones 1957, p. 432),[2] or, in the words of the literary critic Harold Bloom (1986), "the central imagination of our age."

There is no doubt, however, that classical psychoanalysis, as a mode of treatment, is gradually disappearing from the therapeutic landscape, and that vital parts of psychoanalytic theory have increasingly been challenged or attacked. "The past decade, in particular, has seen a dramatic decline of psychoanalysis and simultaneously a triumph of biological psychiatry, of psychopharmacology, genetics, electrical and biomolecular investigations of the brain, and also of behaviorial, cognitive, and developmental psychology. It seems that a behavioristically empirical and pragmatic concept of science prevails at the end of the millenium. The trend is against anything speculative or philosophical, doubtlessly at the cost of a more differentiated view of human beings" (Haynal, 1998).

---

1. Freud is also the most heavily cited author in indices for social sciences, arts, and the humanities (Megill 1982). "The documentation on Freud is said to surpass in specificity and depth of insight the extant material on any other human being in history" (Henry Murray, in Mahony 1987, p. 1).

2. ". . . if often he was wrong and, at times, absurd, / to us he is no more a person / now but a whole climate of opinion" ("In Memory of Sigmund Freud"; reprinted in *International Review of Psycho-Analysis*, 1974, 1:4).

OUR CHANGING IMAGE OF FREUD AND THE ROLE OF HISTORIOGRAPHY

Part of this general trend is our changing image of Freud. There is an ever-growing literature trying to prove not only that psychoanalytic theory is fundamentally wrong, but also that Freud was a dubious character—not only that psychoanalysis is a "hoax," but also that Freud was a "quack." Naturally, psychoanalysts and other adherents of psychoanalysis counter these allegations, but they are clearly on the defense.

Historical research plays a central role in these discussions. Biographical research on Freud and his circle unearths more and more details, adding to our picture of Freud the man and scientist. Furthermore, a combination of psychobiography and intellectual history is pivotal for an epistemology of psychoanalysis and for the "context of discovery" of its theory. It helps, probably better than anything else, to understand the coming into being, the contents, the meaning, and the connotations of a concept. While such a detailed historical investigation does not tell us anything about the *validity* of ideas, or about their "context of justification," it can provide us with the links between the theoreticians and their theories. These links are particularly important in a science such as psychology, where the subject of investigation is also its object, and where, instead of trying to eliminate the autobiographical element, it can be better controlled by systematically taking it into account.

Perhaps even more important, history "sets the record straight and enables us to see what the relations between the empirical facts and the theoretical constructs really were" (Macmillan 1991). Macmillan (in a prelude to his devastating critique of Freud and psychoanalysis) quotes the example of a theory where the attempt to confirm it fails, and continues: "By itself, the failure provides no guide as to where the fault lies. Perhaps the original facts were inaccurately described or the original theoretical terms inadequately formulated. Would it not be sensible to see how those terms or statements were arrived at? Was there a worthwhile theory to begin with? Until the relation between fact and construct is clarified, we cannot tell whether the theoretical ideas were required by observation alone, by theory alone, or by some combination of theory and observation. In brief, historically based evaluations help us establish what has to be explained and whether any explanatory effort is justified." In my view, this argument—that history and logic may complement each other—not only holds true in the case of a wrong theory (such as psychoanalysis, in Macmillan's view). It is perhaps even more applicable in the case of a highly sophisticated, partly contradictory, multilayered, and stratified theory, containing formulations in differing degrees of abstraction, a theory that has been partly confirmed, partly proved wrong, and has been found in general to be extremely stimulating for a host of disciplines (including Freud-bashing), as I see psychoanalysis.

Historians, however, have not yet reached an agreement on their evaluation of Freud. For some, he is the hero of a legend; for others, the villain of the piece. He can be the relentless, heroic searcher for truth, or the inveterate liar and falsifier of case histories. We have heard nearly everything about Freud: that he was the greatest psychologist ever, or the criminal, who attempted to murder his best friend; that he was a superhuman being who achieved what no other living creature before him had achieved—descending into his own deepest depths, wrestling with the angel of darkness, and thereby healing himself, transforming himself into a different man, or that he was a drug addict whose "theory" is nothing but wild speculations made "under the influence." Was he an ascetic bourgeois, or someone obsessed, be it with "masturbation" (Crews 1995, p. 124), or be it "with copulation from the rear" (ibid., p. 48), frequenting prostitutes, and sleeping with his sister-in-law? Was he a wise and successful therapist, or did he botch nearly all of his cases? Was he a mild-mannered, tolerant, benevolent friend, or a bitter, acerbic person, whose friendships all ended in breakup? Was he a model husband and father, or a family tyrant? Was he a revolutionary, paving the way for sexual liberation, anti-authoritarianism, pacifism, and women's lib, or was he counterrevolutionary, reactionary, phallocratic, undemocratic, and adamantly opposed to women's emancipation—indeed "the male chauvinist par excellence" (ibid., p. 206)? Perhaps the most important of these controversies is fought over the question whether Freud was a trustworthy, reliable scientist, or someone who lied, cheated, and falsified or invented his case histories, who changed reality to suit his theory, someone, in short, who sacrificed truth for fame.

Reality, however, is more complex than this picture in black and white. Would it not be time to go beyond these pseudodichotomies, and to develop a truly *historical* perspective and evaluation, empathic but as unbiased as possible, trying to understand without idealizing or condemning, showing the roots of a theory and movement that changed the face of the century?

CONFLICTS AND STRATEGIES

In times of conflict, early psychoanalysts, including Freud, often had recourse to a strategy that countered differing views by character assassination, pathologizing, or *Totschweigen* (killing by silence) of their proponents. If it was true that Freud had discovered the truth, as he and his followers were convinced he had,[3] and if it was true that Freud "emerged" from his self-analysis "serene and benign . . . , free to pursue his work in imperturbable composure" (Jones 1953, p. 320), free from neurosis and any trace of personal dependence (Jones 1957, p. 44), any opposing or differing views could only be neurotic, "just resistance" (Freud to Abraham, October 21, 1907): "Had I only experienced one single case of deviation without prior personal motivation!", as Freud wrote to Eitingon (August 24, 1932, Sigmund Freud Copyrights, Wivenhoe, England).

In a chilling summary, Marina Leitner has recently given a list toward whom and how Freud applied this self-immunizing strategy: among others, Adler was called "paranoid," Stekel "infantile-perverse" and a "perfect swine," Jung was "mentally deranged to a serious extent," Tausk was a "meschuggener," Oberholzer a "*severe* neurotic," Otto Gross "quite paranoiac," Oberndorf a "strongly neurotic person," Storfer "a pathological personality," Rickman's "underlying psychosis must be regarded as incurable," Hárnik's "paranoia . . . fully manifest," Wilhelm Reich's diagnosis of "schizophrenia" was spread by two of his training analysts, and so on. Even Freud's most stalwart and reliable followers did not escape their diagnoses: his *rocher de bronze*, Karl Abraham, had "a trace of a persecution complex," James Putnam suffered from "paranoic tendencies," Brill was supposed to be a "crazy Jew (meschugge!)," Sachs had a "brother complex," Reik was said to be "decidedly neurotic," and Jones's behavior was explained by

---

3. For example: "We are in possession of the truth; I am as sure of that as I was fifteen years ago" (Freud to Ferenczi, May 8, 1913; Freud and Ferenczi 1992, p. 483).

"*complex* related motives" (all quotes in Leitner 1999). Perhaps most instructive are the cases of Otto Rank and Sándor Ferenczi, whose character assassination has been described by Balint, Bonomi, Dupont, Falzeder, Haynal, Kramer, Leitner, and Lieberman, among others.

If today we have conflicting views about Freud, so had the early pioneers of psychoanalysis. Abraham had a Freud different from Ferenczi's, and so had Brill, Jones, Rank, Eitingon, or Pfister, and so on. But not only had those persons their peculiar perception, colored by their personality, role within the movement, intelligence, prejudices, and ambition—Freud himself offered himself in a different way to different disciples. Even more, he actively sought to establish alliances between some of them, to discourage cooperation between others. He had his favorites to whom he was chatty to the point of indiscretion. Part of the fascination of reading Freud's letters to various correspondents is his ability to tune in with the other so that each of these exchanges has its own particular tone and atmosphere. Freud at his best could write in a different way about one and the same event to different people, while still remaining accurate. But there is also Freud the strategist and politician, who very carefully chose what to disclose and what not, who frequently violated medical discretion and therapeutic principles in the interest of the "cause," and who took sides with one of his followers against the other.

Let me give you three examples.

My first example occurred in the spring of 1912, when a Swiss doctor wrote to Freud. His request can be deduced from Freud's reply of March 1, 1912: "I certainly approve of your plan, and will myself, in a publication, endorse that each analyst should have undergone an analysis himself. So if you think that you are in need of my help, I will be only too happy to give it to you." Freud even proposed interrupting the treatment of one of his patients to make a place free for his colleague. This is a very interesting case, as it already contains some key elements and problems that pertain to psychoanalytic training to this day. For instance, Freud raised the question of fees: "Unfortunately, I am . . . in the embarrassing situation that I have to ask for a fee also from colleagues, whom I would prefer to give my full interest without being paid for." In addition, there is the question of discretion, and of whether this analysis should or could kept secret: "Dr. Jung will not be informed . . . , nor will anybody else, although I think that your presence in Vienna can hardly be kept secret. But then, an analysis is nothing to be ashamed of among ourselves."

Three months later, the colleague started his analysis. To be sure, Freud did not only hasten to inform Jung of the analysis (letter of June 13, 1912, Freud and Jung 1974, p. 511), but also immediately reported to the colleague's wife, herself a budding analyst, who had sent Freud some further information about her husband. Freud had deliberately not read this information, because he had decided "to treat him as correctly, that is, as severely as possible—and for such an undertaking any information which does not come from the patient [sic] himself is interfering (*störend*)" (June 6, 1912, Library of Congress, Washington, DC). He further offered his opinion, which can have hardly been reassuring to the doctor's wife, that her husband would suffer from "very serious disturbances. Unfortunately, five weeks are not sufficient a time to bring about a change. What I can do is to stir him up as profoundly as possible. In the first session he has shown himself as very nasty, and thus has shown me many hidden things. But then in the second hour he was nice, which makes me fear that he will now hide his resistances from being discovered. But I promise to have a keen eye on him" (ibid.).

Seven years later, this former patient was about to become president of the Swiss Society. Freud was not in favor, and voiced his strong disapproval to Ferenczi, obviously drawing conclusions from what he had learned in the analysis: "The [supposed] president . . . as a *severe* neurotic, is very questionable to me. In Switzerland they certainly have a very special pure strain of fools" (January 24, 1919). Please note that, while Freud made no bones of his reservations against this analyst to Ferenczi and others, nothing of this can be found in his letters to the person himself.

Let me lift the veil. Emil Oberholzer (1883–1958) did become cofounder, in 1919, of the Swiss Society for Psychoanalysis (which is still in existence today),[4] and he did become its first president,

---

4. On February 10, 1919, in a circular letter, Pfister and Mira and Emil Oberholzer proposed the founding of a Swiss Society for Psychoanalysis. The organizational meeting subsequently took place on March 21; the first meeting, with guest lectures by Jones, Rank, and Sachs on "Psychoanalysis as an Intellectual Movement," took place on March 24; affiliation with the International Psychoanalytic Association (IPA) was also decided upon there. The First Chair was Emil

remaining in this office until 1927, when he and nine others split from it, founding their own purely medical psychoanalytic group. On that occasion, it became clear that the diagnosis of "neurosis" had become shared knowledge. Max Eitingon, for example, stated that it would have been "quite clear to all of us" that Oberholzer was "a completely untreatable neurotic" (circular letter of February 16, 1928; Archives of the British Psycho-Analytical Society).[5]

My second example takes place in the 1920s, when Freud consistently worked against Jones's becoming president of the IPA. To Ferenczi he wrote, for example: "Jones is in many respects a personality unsuited to be a leader" (January 25, 1923). As a matter of fact, Freud had not one good word for Jones, writing to Ferenczi: "Eitingon doesn't want to be president, and I absolutely don't want Jones to" (July 5, 1927). In 1932, Freud strongly supported Ferenczi's presidency ("I would like to insist on it for you"; May 1932), and only after Ferenczi *himself* had stepped down from running for it, the way was open for Jones. To whom Freud then wrote: "Thank you for your first letter as President! I was sorry that Ferenczi's obvious ambition could not be satisfied, but then there was not a moment's doubt that only you have the competence for the leadership" (Freud to Jones, September 12, 1932).

Finally, my third example will be one of a rivalry between two persons, of which hitherto only one side has been laid down. As is well known, Ernest Jones and Abraham A. Brill heavily competed with each other, be it for Freud's approval, for the leadership in the English-speaking countries, or for control over the Freud translations. Only Jones's version was written down, heavily influencing our perception of history. The Freud/Brill letters give us a fascinating counterpart to Jones's account and the facts as known from the recently published Freud/Jones correspondence. Brill was always much closer to Freud's heart than Jones. It is interesting to see how decidedly Freud took sides with Brill against Jones, how he told Brill so, and how veiled and guarded his pertinent remarks to Jones were. When,

---

Oberholzer, Second Chair, Hermann Rorschach; other members of the Board were Binswanger, Morel, and Pfister.

5. Oberholzer's group eventually dissolved after his emigration in 1938. He went with his wife, the child-analyst Mira, née Gincburg (1887–1949), to New York, where he became a member of the New York Psychoanalytic Society.

however, Brill for some time did not maintain as close a contact as Freud wished, Freud switched sides—although he was never as outspoken to Jones about Brill, as to Brill about Jones (all following quotes, if not mentioned otherwise, from the Library Congress, Washington, DC).

To Brill, Freud wrote, "regarding your disagreement with Jones I have to take your side most emphatically" (February 14, 1909). A few days later: "Before me there lie two letters . . . , yours and the latest from Jones, the one clear and honest, the other obscure and diplomatic, easy to see through with your help. . . . [Jones] has an inborn tendency for intrigues and crooked, diplomatic ways to which he succumbs in a playful way; but of course he is not nearly as satanic as he boasts of himself" (February 22, 1909). Freud even shared his correspondence with Brill and Jones with Jung, while reporting to Brill about it: "When Jung visited me at the end of March, I read to him the letters of Jones and yourself. He was also taken aback, but then decided to take them as neurotic and not to see a hostile intention behind them" (May 2, 1909).

During the First World War, and in the years afterwards, there was a serious conflict between Freud and Brill regarding the English-translation rights. Freud had previously authorized Brill to do all English translations of his works, so Brill was offended when other translations appeared, evidently with Freud's approval. Without going into detail, let me state that much of the resulting confusion was due to Freud's ignorance regarding American and British translation rights, and his sometimes inconsistent handling of his translations. He was eager to see his works appear in other languages, and tended to authorize the translator who promised to work fastest. Jones, of course, was thoroughly dissatisfied with Brill's translations, told Freud so, and worked hard to have other translations appear under his control. So Brill could write to Freud on October 27, 1914: "I . . . told you of my wish to translate [the *History of the Psychoanalytic Movement*] . . . I was hard at work preparing it when I met Jelliffe and he told me of Jonese's [sic] connection with it. I was baffled and I refused to believe it. It was very strange. . . . As a matter of fact Jones did have something to do with it. . . . I am convinced that Jones has been trying in all sorts of ways to bring this about and has not been honest with me about it." Brill felt hurt, and did not answer Freud's letters, which touched a deep cord in Freud: "I have got no answer to my last letter from you. Also Jones complains of your unexplicable silence. Can you be 'falling off?'" (December 9, 1919). Brill should overcome his neurotic tendencies in the interest of the cause: "Now as for Jones I guess your recriminations are justified, but we want him, we owe him a bit of tolerance (the same every one of ourselves stands in need of), he is a true friend and adherer of our cause, a powerful hand and it is important, that there should exist no personal enmity between our leaders" (January 19, 1920). "You ought to bury your jealousy against Jones and cooperate with him for the common cause" (October 26, 1920).

In this, as in many other examples, it becomes clear that personal motives, not theoretical differences, played the chief role in deciding whether someone was to be regarded as friend or fiend. When we have a look at the theoretical differences in the history of psychoanalysis, we are impressed to see how quick one could become a dissident or heretic. Splits in the psychoanalytic movement occurred over questions such as: How long should a session last? How many sessions per week? Does the Oedipus complex start at four years of age or earlier? Is the role of the mother as important, or even more important, than the one played by the father? Does the material produced during an analysis reflect more the present situation or the past? Is psychoanalytic group therapy permissible? Does aggression or love play the most important role in life and neurosis? In fact, it was "Jung's *behavior* towards [Freud], not his view of the libido [that] . . . destroyed the intimacy" between them, as Freud wrote to Otto Rank (August 22, 1912, emphasis added). From this standpoint, it is not surprising that Freud could maintain lifelong friendships with persons who put forward views very different from his (e.g., August Aichhorn, Lou Andreas-Salomé, Ludwig Binswanger, Oskar Pfister, and James J. Putnam), if they could only convince Freud of their allegiance to the "cause" and their friendship to him. Even Abraham, Jones, and Helene Deutsch, members of the inner circle and perceived as pillars of orthodoxy, voiced different opinions and had periods of strained relationships with Freud at one time or another, without ever falling outside.

MIRRORING CONFLICTS AND STRATEGIES

This is not the place to give a full account of all the controversies within the psychoanalytic movement, and of Freud's and his followers' sometimes questionable roles in them, but these examples may suffice to demonstrate the heated and secret atmosphere in a closely knit group, experiencing the outside world as hostile, and anxious to maintain coherence within. My point here is that many of the present controversies about the history of psychoanalysis duplicate precisely that history, rather than take a true historical stance.

Much of the historical literature has been partisan, has been written with an agenda, and has not escaped pseudodichotomies. Each of the parties or camps seems to have construed a "Freud" of its own. Writing the history of psychoanalysis has become instrumentalized, and has been used as a weapon in a very contemporary fight. The field has become a battleground, and we are faced with what has been called the "Freud Wars" (Forrester 1997) or the "Memory Wars" (Crews 1995).

Former colleagues and collaborators, friends even, fall out with each other over details of Freud's academic career or of his private life, over questions whose importance definitely does not impress the spectator—to the point that they refuse to speak at the same conferences. It would be nice to know, but is it really that important, whether Freud had a fling with his sister-in-law or not.

The hero worship of Freud by some historians is evident. They present Freud as some supreme, nearly superhuman being, and psychoanalysis as the pure and simple truth, while pathologizing their opponents. In doing this, the glorifying historians of psychoanalysis (Ernest Jones, Hanns Sachs, Theodor Reik, and recently, to some extent also Peter Gay[6]), duplicate the strategy applied by Freud and his followers.

In the third volume of his Freud biography, Jones labeled nearly all dissidents neurotic or psychotic, and their dissident theories as the outcome of psychotic thinking, notably in the cases of Ferenczi and Rank (Jones 1957, pp. 44–77; 176–179). There were only a few to publicly stand up against these allegations. Erich Fromm in particular objected to what he called Jones's "typically Stalinist type of re-writing history, whereby Stalinists assassinate the character of opponents by calling them spies and traitors. The Freudians do it by calling them

---

6. In whose monumental Freud biography the name of Wilhelm Reich is *not* even mentioned.

'insane.' . . . [I]ncidentally, Jones does not seem to be aware of the disservice he does to psychoanalysis. The picture he gives of the central committee is, then, that two members, and the most trusted ones, became insane. Of one, Dr. Sachs, he says that Freud said he should not have belonged in the first place. Of Eitingon he says that he was not too bright. There remain Abraham and Jones, who were, according to Jones' own testimony, constantly engaged in the pettiest quarrels with all the other members. A beautiful picture of the group of those who claim to represent the sanity which follows from psychoanalysis!"[7]

Jones's verdict, however, not only included the dissidents, but also fellow historians and analysts, who happened to see things in a different light. Listen to an astonishing blackmail letter Jones wrote to one of his critics: "I think it is sheer nonsense [sic] to talk of my having made an attack on Ferenczi simply because there are people who cannot bear the truth. The same of course applies to Freud, Rank, and so forth. I have all the letters Ferenczi wrote to Freud from 1907 till the end. They make most painful reading as displaying a thoroughly unstable and suffering personality whom I personally had always loved. But the evidence of the increasing deterioration is only too plain. Up to the end Freud wanted him to be President of the International Association, though he advised him to keep back the paper he had written for the last Congress [Ferenczi 1933] since it would harm his reputation.[8] The President of the Congress refused to admit such an obviously psychopathic paper, and it was only at my intervention that it was allowed. Naturally if anyone attacks me in public I shall have to produce some of the evidence I have taken care to suppress in Ferenczi's own interest."[9] Izette de Forest astutely commented, "one wonders why Freud, trying to prevent Ferenczi from giving the last paper at Wiesbaden, still constantly tried to get F. accept the Presidency of the Intern[ational Psychoanalytic Association]. Why would Freud want a man suffering from 'mental deterioration' to be Pres.? And why did Jones work to get the last paper published, if it was

---

7. Letter to Izette de Forest, October 31, 1957, Erich Fromm Archives.
8. This reference is to Ferenczi's paper "Confusion of tongues between adults and the child." In *Final Contributions to the Problems and Methods of Psycho-Analysis*. London: Karnac Books, 1980, pp. 156–167. [D.E.S.]
9. Letter to Dr. Magoun, November 28, 1957, ibid.

'psychopathic' and bad for Ferenczi's reputation and if he loved him so much?"[10]

On the other hand, there is a tendency among the so-called revisionist historians to sympathize, or identify, with the dissidents of the psychoanalytic movement. The past years, for instance, have seen a veritable Ferenczi renaissance, and their are signs that a similar renaissance is imminent for Otto Rank. Having contributed my own little share to rehabilitating both the personal integrity and the value of the theories of Ferenczi and Rank, I may perhaps be permitted to warn against a new, more or less anti-Freudian, Ferenczianism or Rankianism. As Axel Hoffer put it, there is a "Freud and Ferenczi within each of us" (Hoffer 1992, p. 2), and it makes little sense to champion the one at the cost of the other.

As to Freud's most severe critics, they, too, tend to repeat historical patterns. Just like some of Freud's contemporary critics, they regard the whole of psychoanalysis as rubbish, and their agenda is simply to relegate psychoanalysis "to history's ashcan" (Crews 1995, p. 223). As Forrester (1997) observed, they have a "heartfelt wish that Freud might never have been born or, failing to achieve that end, that all his works and influence be made as nothing." If Freud and his followers were convinced of being in possession of the truth, some contemporary scientists (such as Crews, Esterson, Macmillan, Webster, and others) are equally sure that, in Crews's (1997) succinct summary, "the 'clinical validation' of psychoanalytic ideas is hopelessly circular and . . . Freud's theories of personality and neurosis are woolly, strained, and unsupported" (p. 107), that they "amount to castles in the air" (ibid., p. 34), and that all of "his theoretical and therapeutic pretensions have been weighed and found to be hollow" (ibid., p. 107). They see it as their duty to warn the public against this pseudotherapy and pseudoscience.

Surprisingly, these polemics against Freud and psychoanalysis have something in common with the target of their venom. Both psychoanalysis and the writing of its history are about reconstruction of the past, indeed of an unknown, a forgotten, or—dare I say—a repressed past. Repression, in Freud's words "the cornerstone on which the whole structure of psychoanalysis rests" (1914, p. 16), naturally is

---

10. Letter to Erich Fromm, December 3, 1957, ibid.

also a main focus of its critics who claim that there is "not . . . a shred of evidence for the existence of such a mechanism" (Crews 1995, p. 122). In other words, the critics say, our lives are *not* largely determined by our past, it is *not* true that we all suffer, more or less, from unconscious reminiscences, from a falsification of our private history, and Freud is *wrong* in claiming that setting that historical record straight would strip our suffering from its neurotic surplus and reduce it to the "common unhappiness" (Freud 1895, p. 305) we all share as human beings. Yet, this is *precisely* what the revisionist historians claim for the history, not of the individual, but of psychoanalysis: that its past lies in the dark, that it has been suppressed by the superegos of the movement—the "official" historians—that this past has nevertheless strongly influenced the development of psychoanalysis and its offsprings, and that it is important to reconstruct and reveal it in order to bring about changes in the present.[11] Thus, ironically enough, Freud's harshest critics cannot help but bear witness to the ongoing, pervasive influence of his thinking. In a way, the present disputes about, and the plight of psychoanalysis are also part of Freud's legacy.

REFERENCES

Bloom, H. (1986). Freud, the greatest modern writer. *New York Times Book Review*, March 23, 1986, section 7, page 1.

Breuer, J. and Freud, S. (1895). The psychotherapy of hysteria. In *Studies on Hysteria. Standard Edition* 2:253–305.

Crews, F. (1994). The revenge of the repressed: part II. *New York Review of Books*, Dec. 1.

Forrester, J. (1997). *Dispatches from the Freud Wars: Psychoanalysis and Its Passions*. Cambridge, MA: Harvard University Press.

Freud, S. and Ferenczi, S. (1992). *The Correspondence of Sigmund Freud and Sándor Ferenczi, Volume 1, 1908–1914*. Brabant, E., Falzeder, E., and Giampieri-Deutsch, eds. Cambridge, MA: Harvard University Press, 1994.

---

11. In attacking psychoanalysis and its theory of repression for being the alleged godfathers of the present recovered-memory movement, Crews, by the way, consistently mistakes "repression" (of inner wishes) for "denial" (of outer reality).

Freud, S. and Jones, E. (1993). *The Complete Correspondence of Sigmund Freud and Ernest Jones 1908–1939.* A. R. Paskauskas, ed. Cambridge, MA: Harvard University Press.

Freud, S. and Jung, C. G. (1974). *The Freud/Jung Letters.* McGuire, W., ed. Princeton, NJ: Princeton University Press.

Gellner, E. (1985). *The Psychoanalytic Movement or The Cunning of Unreason.* London: Paladin.

Haynal, A. (1998). Tiefenpsychologie in der Schweizer Psychiatrie. Paper read at the conference *Schweizer Psychiatrie im Spannungsfeld der Geschichte,* Psychiatrische Universitätsklinik Zürich, October 22. Unpublished manuscript.

Heller, P. (1994). Letter to the author, January 1, 1994.

Hoffer, A. (1992). Asymmetry and mutuality in the analytic relationship: lessons for today from the Freud-Ferenczi relationship. Paper given before the Southern California Psychoanalytic Society, Los Angeles, January 12. Unpublished manuscript.

Jones, E. (1953). *The Life and Work of Sigmund Freud, Volume 1.* New York: Basic Books.

——— (1957). *The Life and Work of Sigmund Freud, Volume 3.* New York: Basic Books.

Leitner, M. (1999). Pathologizing as a way of dealing with conflicts and dissent in the psychoanalytic movement. *Free Associations* [forthcoming].

Macmillan, M. (1991). *The Completed Arc: Freud Evaluated.* Cambridge, MA: The MIT Press, 1997.

Mahony, P. (1987 [1982]). *Freud as a Writer.* New Haven and London: Yale University Press (expanded edition).

Megill, A. (1982). The reception of Foucault by historians. *Journal of the History of Ideas,* 48:117–141.

Wollheim, R. (1971). *Freud.* London: Fontana.

PART II

THEORY RECONSIDERED

Most psychoanalysts and psychotherapists center their interest on the clinical application of Freud's legacy. This section begins with an interview with **Otto F. Kernberg** given on December 17, 1997, in anticipation of the Freud exhibit and conference. In this interview, Dr. Kernberg, who was then President of the International Psychoanalytic Association (IPA), explored the staying power of Freud's theory and clinical contribution, highlighting those modern developments which appear to Dr. Kernberg to be among the most exciting and personally interesting. The interview is a testament to the breadth of psychoanalysis itself and to the breadth of vision of one of Freud's most visionary exponents. The interview makes clear that the paths of modern analysis no longer involve slavish repetition of Freud's word, but the continuing careful re-examination of his legacy in the light of evolving scientific research and philosophic development. A living craft and school of thought cannot be mummified. It must be continually updated and rejuvenated by fresh thinking, for the fear that we will spoil the pure gold by alloying it with revisionist ideas is the surest way to drain the life out of our art and science.

Allan N. Schore's paper, "The Right Brain as the Neurobiological Substratum of Freud's Dynamic Unconscious," elaborates specifically on several of Kernberg's ideas, and on the centrality of affect as the phenomenon that sits astride the boundary between biological aspects of brain and psychological aspects of mental experience. In easy-to-read language, Schore summarizes a great deal of technical neurobiology, much of which he has written about from a technical standpoint in other publications. (See his references 1994, 1999, in press b). He agrees with Kernberg that we are now in a position to study the neurobiological basis of psychoanalysis. Following John Bowlby's integration of behavioral biology and analysis twenty years ago, analysis has moved the center of early development to the affects central to the attachment relationship. Schore documents the primacy of the right brain, especially the right orbito-frontal lobe as the executive area for affective integration that dominates the first three years of life, storing and coding early attachment behaviors. The earliest, and therefore preverbal, highly affective relationships between infants and their primary caregivers are read by the facial expression, the tonality and rhythm of speech, and other stimuli that have the standing for the right brain comparable to that which speech later has for the left brain. The optimal situation for the development of the infant's right brain is a positively toned affective relationship with dedicated caregivers during the development of early attachment. Throughout life, the right brain receives and decodes these phenomena underneath conscious awareness, an inheritance of the way a mother and her infant have experienced their right brains as "entrained" with each other before speech. This mode of communication continues to exist throughout life and is the basis of the heavily affective mode of thinking Freud grouped together as "primary process thinking." It determines the organization and activity of unconscious thought, and complements the more linear, logical processes of verbal thought that occur in the left hemisphere. The coupling of two affective experiences that proceeds between mother and infant as if directly between one right brain and another, is also the basis for what we now often call "intersubjectivity," the empathic connectedness between people in intimate relationships, including psychotherapy.

Schore also applies aspects of "dynamical systems theory" or "chaos theory" to understand the way the intersubjective processes between mother and infant organize early affective exchanges. In the process of complex and continuing feedback between parent and infant—or iteration of experience in the language of chaos theory—

the minds of the two become linked or entrained over time, and proceed to organize each other neurologically and emotionally. This entrainment of the brains and minds of the two is also embedded in a wider and even more complex social context. The organization of the infant's mind is not a simple, linear, or predictable one, but rather one that follows the principles of self-organizing systems in which order emerges out of chaos. Systems organized in this way are maximally suited to maintain adaptive possibilities within inherently complex environments.

Schore's argument leads us to the question of how to view Freud's model of the mind. The picture Schore gives follows Winson (1990) who views the unconscious as a cohesive mental structure that acts throughout life according to its principles of interpretation. His picture of the central role of positively toned affect revives Freud's pleasure principle, although in a form that needs reevaluation and modification in light of contemporary research. Finally, he redefines Freud's model of energy. He sees mental energy as consisting the role of affect in organizing the mind emotionally and therefore the brain's underlying neural structure.

Looking back, we can understand that Freud could not know the difference between deterministic chaos and its principles of emergent organization, and idea of random chaos that he thought characterized primal urges and bodily imperatives. In dynamic systems, order emerges as a fundamental property of the disordered complexity. When Freud separated ego from id, he could not know the fundamental interrelatedness of separate areas of mind that are becoming clearer today. More ordered "ego function" exists in a life-long oscillation between its imposed order which is more nearly linear, and the affectively ordered unconscious. Many organizing principles interact in an exceedingly complex system. We may or may not retain the term "id" for the region that is organized in terms of chaos theory, but if we retain it, it has to be redefined. Freud seems to have been right that there are areas of mind attuned to bodily processes, but he did not quite understand that many of these same parts of mind are exquisitely attuned to the early affective experiences that, throughout life, are organized differently from left brain, predominantly verbal thinking. Freud understood that affective and verbal thinking both operated throughout life. But since the unconscious is the repository of early affective experience, we can now see its continuing importance for monitoring affect throughout life. Clinically, an area of our intense interest lies in the microcosmic interactions of transference and countertransference that, like the early mother-infant relationship, pass between therapist and patient as right brain-to-right brain transactions.

Steven Ellman's contribution explores the evolution of Freud's concept of transference. He notes that Freud began by considering transference as the imposition of old situations onto the analysis, and regarded them as a nuisance, an interference with his work. But while writing the Dora case, he seems suddenly to have recognized that which analysis has taken as axiomatic ever since: transference is the expression of old problems in the current setting. Ellman cites other tendencies in Freud's later writing that introduce modern ways of viewing transference, and then considers the revisions introduced in the last twenty-five years by various schools, ending with his own vision of the centrality of transference and of our debt to Freud.

In the final essay in this section, **Jill Savege Scharff** compares Freud's theory of mind with object relations theory, which emerged partly from Freud and partly from debate raised about his structural model. Scharff uses the analogy of museum-exhibit cases arranged in parallel rows to examine elements of Freud's model as it evolved, and then to compare them to key elements of object relations theory as developed by Fairbairn, Klein, Balint, and others. The paths to the object relations theories of psychological development were opened by Freud. Each of the major object relations theorists chose starting places in Freud and used language that, in following Freud's vocabulary—or that of his English translators—was at once true to him and confusing when that same language actually began to mean something different from Freud's original intentions. By her comparison in this paper, Scharff makes it easier to see Freud's original contributions, and the extension of those paths that has resulted in the relational emphasis in so much current analytic theory.

Although the survey of Freud's theoretical contribution given in this section must remain far from complete, these four papers cover a large range, and demonstrate the dynamic quality of the evolution of psychoanalysis, which at the same time that it has changed and become more useful to a wider range of clinical situations, has thoughtfully conserved many elements of Freud's original model.

3

Freud Conserved and Revised: An Interview with David Scharff

Otto F. Kernberg

DES: Thank you for speaking with me, Dr. Kernberg. What we'd like to do this morning is talk about Freud at the millennium on the occasion of this exhibit and the conference that we have organized to talk about it, and the evolution of Freud's contribution. I thought we might start by talking about theory. What do you see as having happened with the various theories that he has proposed? How useful are they? For instance, topographical theory, theories of the unconscious, and so on.

OFK: Well, it's hard to put it all into a few words. When you say "theory," you refer to the theory of mind, the structure of the mind, the unconscious motivational forces that determine development, psychopathology, and treatment. The first thing that I would stress is the importance of unconscious forces at work. I think that the most important aspect of Freud's contribution is his discovery of the extent to which unconscious motivation is overshadowing our daily life, and determines what makes us happy, how we try to avoid anxieties, how we enter into intimate relations, love, and commitment to work. Of course, in the case of pathology, he showed how unconscious motivations may distort psychic structure and functioning, and this, of course, has enormous therapeutic implications.

I want to stress two aspects of Freud's theory. First, I think that Freud's theory of drives, which he gradually evolved, and finally consolidated in the theory of libido and the death drive, or libido and aggression, is fundamental. It's one of his most fundamental contributions, although it has remained controversial in psychoanalytic thinking. My own understanding is that this was a conceptualization of genius of the two basic forces that regulate psychological functioning in normality and pathology. I am convinced that the dual drive theory is as relevant today as when Freud formulated it, and although it has been hotly disputed and rejected by many psychoanalysts, I think that it still stands, but, in my view, with significant modifications. That unconscious libidinal and aggressive impulses are important in psychic functioning is obvious when you see patients, but Freud could not say anything about their origins, except that they were intermediate between the body and the mind.

When he formulated this theory, we were very far away in our understanding of affects from what we now know about them as primary motivational systems that operate from birth on. When Freud said that all we know about drives are representations and affects, he was remarkably close to a contemporary understanding of the structure of motivation, but formulated it in terms that did not do justice to its proper development. I believe that affects are the primary motivators, and that they can be grouped into rewarding, pleasurable, exciting, gratifying affects, and into aggressive, painful, threatening affects, and that these two series then determine, respectively, the integration of libido and aggression. I believe that the drives are hierarchically supraordinate integrations of the corresponding affect states, and that drives, therefore, are constituted by subordinate affects, and not an obscure, constitutionally predetermined entity about which we don't know anything else.

That affects are the primary motivators, operating from birth on, has been known since Piaget's work. They can be divided, as I mentioned, into rewarding, pleasurable, gratifying, exciting affects that motivate the individual to move towards the stimulus that is evoking that gratifying affect. On the other hand, affects that are aversive, painful, frightening, motivate the individual to move away from the situation that evokes that kind of affect, and, I repeat, it is the sum total of rewarding affects that are going to constitute libido as a drive, and the sum total of negative affects that will constitute aggression as a drive.

DES: What do you think about Freud's formulation of sex as the primary drive?

OFK: Sexual excitement is a central affect, I think, of libido as a drive. Sexual excitement is a primary affect, but not a very early one. It develops gradually in the first few years of life. It stems from the sensual excitability of skin, particularly body surface and mucous junctions, and combines with the diffuse sense of elation when basic instinctive needs are gratified, such as feeding, breathing, freedom from pain. I am using the term "instinctive" in contrast to "instinctual," in the sense that basic biological needs are gratified. The sense of elation is a primary, very early affect. That sense of elation gradually gets integrated with the sensual responsiveness of the skin, and in this way evolves into sexual pleasure that, of course, is maximum in the genital areas. So, gradually sexual excitement is developed as a sensual affect, but around which there evolve other gratifying aspects, related to the sense of fusion with a gratifying object. And, on the other hand, the affect of rage is an early, primary affect of aggression, but that becomes structured, in the context of internalized object relations: when rage becomes fixated, invested in a representation of self and other, it is transformed into hatred, which is the fundamental affect of the psychopathology of aggression.

Freud's dual drive theory points to the overall organization of affective systems as psychic motivators. This viewpoint cuts across, I believe, the contemporary controversy about whether or not to maintain Freud's theory of drives. Those who want to maintain it unchanged are often talking in general terms without any linkage of drive theory to new developments in neurobiology. I think that this is a great danger. At one point, psychoanalysis as a science has to relate to its surrounding fields. Those, on the other hand, who reject drive theory altogether, and are trying to replace it by affects as motivational systems, miss the complex integration of different affects into the same dominant object relations. We experience very different affects in our relations to the most important people in our childhood, and the replacement of drive theory by affect theory does not do justice to the organization of object relations in terms of major splitting processes, by which idealized "all good" and persecutory "all bad" relationships are split from each other. The multiplicity of affects does not do justice to this integration into an aggressive and a libidinal sector of psychic experience.

DES: Right, affects alone cannot provide the bridge.

OFK: The great advantage of a theory of drives linked to a theory of affects is that it establishes relationships with neurobiology, because we know about affects that there are genetic dispositions to them, that they are constitutionally determined, that there are neurochemical systems that activate and control them, about which we are learning more and more. We know that affects have a biological function, the protection of the infant in mammals, and that the more evolved the mammal—up to primates and human beings—the more evolved are affect systems. We can link the pathology of the neurochemical determinants of affects with the pathology of drive derived behavior. For example, we can now construe the determinants of clinical depression as a confluence of genetic predisposition and a particular organization of psychic structures derived from internalized object relations. The whole "mystery" of Freud's concept of drives, I believe, can be taken out, without doing injustice to the complex and unconscious nature of drives. Which brings me to a second aspect of Freud's theory, the structure of the mind.

DES: Before we get to that, I just want to take up the point that's of interest to me about the primacy of sexuality, which I know you have been very interested, as demonstrated in your book on love relations. I've written about sexuality, too. That seems to me to be somewhat controversial. Whether sex is the overarching or the acme of that developmental line, or whether it is one expression of the affiliative tendency as Fairbairn really put it.

OFK: It seems to me that, as you say, this is controversial, and there are two major positions in this regard. One, as you mentioned, concerning Fairbairn, is that he considered sexuality as one aspect of the wish for closeness, the relationship to objects.

DES: Closer to attachment theory.

OFK: Yes. That theory goes together with several other related theories. One, a tendency to divide developmental stages into pre-oedipal and oedipal stages, the preoedipal stages subdivided into Mahler's stages of symbiosis, separation-individuation, and object constancy. The central characteristic of these theories is a linear model of development: there is a sequence of developmental stages.

An opposite view is that represented by French psychoanalysis. Under the influence of Lacan, but without necessarily accepting his metapsychology—his insistence that the unconscious is structured like a language—French psychoanalysis rejects linear models of development. On the contrary, their focus on affects as basic psychic structures integrated with representations, gives a very different view of the unconscious than Lacan's. But, his stress on the fact that development is both synchronic and diachronic, and Lacan's putting emphasis on Freud's concept of *Nachträglichkeit*, in other words, the retrospective modification of experience, is relevant for the French view of sexuality. Something that is not traumatic originally, may retrospectively become traumatic under the influence of later history. That concept of *Nachträglichkeit*, or *aprés coup*, is linked in French psychoanalysis with the concept of an archaic Oedipus complex practically coinciding with the development of separation-individuation. It is symbolized by the "shadow of the father," which separates the infant from the symbiotic relation with mother, breaking up symbiosis, and bringing about the infant's separation, with a longing for reestablishing a symbiotic relation that can never be reestablished again, and that is at the origin of erotic desire. Sexual desire, therefore, becomes a structure of the mind from the beginning of life.

If we assume that there's no initial normal autistic stage of development, that object relations are established from the beginning of life; if we assume also that there are moments of intense fusion experiences under conditions of peak affect states of intense elation or rage, then the rupture of such fusional states under the impact of the father as a third, excluded object signals the early activation of oedipal triangulation. The satisfied baby at the breast, or the frightened baby experiencing pain and fear, experiencing itself at the height of such affects in a highly gratifying or a highly frightening, enraged situation in which self and object can no longer be differentiated, experiences fusional, symbiotic states. They are not stages, but *states*. When they are disrupted by the resolution of that intensity, and the establishment of more reasonable, logical relations between the infant and his parental images, one may say that these are the prototype of triangulation, of the disruption of the dyadic relationship, the origin of intense separation anxiety that evolves into castration anxiety, and of intense longing for refusion that evolves into erotic passion.

We can conceive an archaic oedipal situation as a basic condition of human existence, expressed in unconscious fantasies of fusion that acquire erotic qualities. Although initially the sexual element in the sense of genital excitement may be minimal, later experiences are retrospectively integrated into such a primitive, erotic desire, that establishes an oedipal situation years before the advanced oedipal situation originally described by Freud takes place. This consideration of the structure of the mind is a synchronic condensation of experiences from many ages that contain particular narratives—or diachronic elements—as part of the constituents of such synchronic experiences. The model of development thus becomes completely different, and then one can talk about the erotic and its oedipal implications, the search for sexual intimacy and fusion, the fear of castration as a basic developmental condition. All of this is eventually incorporated into a model of the primal scene, and what Jean Laplanche, one of the great French theoreticians, calls the "general theory of seduction." In other words, the mother, in relating to her infant, is already conveying unconscious erotic messages that the infant cannot yet understand, and that he will only retrospectively interpret erotically, which will then give rise to the deepest unconscious oedipal fantasies. So this viewpoint thinks of affiliation as erotic to begin with.

DES: Right, it's a much more sophisticated view that is, however, consistent with Freud's idea . . .

OFK: It's consistent with Freud's ideas. It's an alternative to the linear models to which we are accustomed both in the ego psychological tradition, as well as in the Kleinian tradition. It is a model that focuses on the centrality of the Oedipus complex and of erotic desire—in contrast to the assumption of early stages of development that predate genitality. In recent years I have come closer to this view. One can find support for both views in Freud. Freud had very little to say about the earliest stages of development. He assumed a primary autism, which went on as a tradition even to Margaret Mahler, who really did not observe children in the first few months of life, and followed Freud's theory.

DES: Picked up the theory and started with symbiosis . . .

OFK: But in the last few months of her life, Margaret Mahler agreed that there was no normal autism in children.

DES: Really?

OFK: She reached that conclusion. She didn't manage to write about this any more, but she was a close personal friend, and so I can assure you of that.

DES: Had she been informed by the infant research?

OFK: Yes, she was impressed by infant-research findings. In this connection, we have learned a great deal from infant research, but we need to keep in mind that most of the research on infants is done in relative optimal conditions, in that the infant is relatively at peace, and not in one of its most frightening, or aversive, moments under which very primitive, aggressive internalizations occur. Infant research thus naturally tends to underemphasize the aggressive segment of experience. In general, object relations theories that reject drive concepts tend to diminish the importance of aggression and sexuality, while object relations theories that affirm drive theory accentuate both aggression and eroticism. In this connection, Fairbairn occupies an intermediate position, in that, although theoretically he rejected the concept of aggression as a primary drive, for practical clinical purposes he described the fundamental function of aggression in determining the early split stages of the mind.

I should say one more thing about affects and the basic structures of drives: I think that I'm no longer alone in my view. Distinguished theoreticians, such as Joseph and Anna Marie Sandler in Great Britain, Serge Lebovici in France, and Rainer Krause in Germany, have reached similar conclusions. I really believe that this is a new development in psychoanalysis, and that it will focus more and more strongly on affect theory, and will reestablish a connection between the biological sciences and psychoanalytic thinking. I believe that neurobiology and psychoanalysis are really two basic sciences, that are not in competition with each other, but should complement each other.

DES: But you're seeing affect as a kind of link point, where the biology can be studied very effectively, which links with the drive concept as both a mental and a biological concept.

OFK: Yes, yes.

DES: In that sense, we're talking about coming full circle and reaffirming an idea of Freud's that has become more tangible as a kind of concept that can now be studied, which it couldn't be until . . .

OFK: Implicitly in what I have said so far, there is a concept of development that is relatively new, although it's commensurate with Freud. Lacan really highlighted one aspect of Freud's thinking, *Nachträglichkeit*. By the way, that concept of Freud's was badly translated in the *Standard Edition* as "retrospective action." That's a wrong translation from the German. It really should be called "retrospective modification."

DES: The rewriting of old history.

OFK: Yes, and the reinterpretation of old experience. For example, traumatic experiences really have two times: first, the moment when the trauma occurs, when the organism is flooded by the experience; and, second, when this experience is interpreted in a certain way that fits into the preexisting structure of the individual. The trauma is elaborated by interpreting it, and it then leaves definite traces. I think that's a concept that one finds in Laplanche, and in Sandler. In any case, that concept of development is a shift of emphasis from Freud, and represents a modern concept, I believe, of development, a replacement of linear models by hierarchical models that include synchronic and diachronic formulations.

DES: You had a second aspect of Freud's theorizing in mind to discuss.

OFK: The second aspect is his theory of mental structure. When it comes to psychic structure, I think there has been very little challenge of Freud's organization of the mind into superego, ego, and id, except that the emphasis has become more and more on the constituent structures of superego, ego, and id. Here, I think, the work of Fairbairn and Edith Jacobson, independently from each other, reached the same conclusions within totally different theoretical systems. Fairbairn described representations of self and representations of objects linked under the impact of a dominant affect, so that the basic unit of psychic structure is a self-representation and an object representation linked within a certain affective disposition. This was specified, following Fairbairn, by John Sutherland, who conceptualized these units even more clearly as the building blocks of ego, superego, and id. It's a revolutionary contribution.

Edith Jacobson applied a similar concept to the study of the superego, describing successive layers of internalized object relations out of which the superego develops. Joseph Sandler described how self-representations coalesce into an integrated concept of self, while representations of objects coalesce into integrated representations of objects. The conception of the id as the sum total of rejected, suppressed, dissociated, or projected internalized object relations reflecting peak affect states that cannot be tolerated in consciousness, transforms the id from a cauldron of impulses into a structure constituted by affective states organized into these dyadic, self-representation and object-representation units.

That is what we observe clinically in patients with severe psychopathology, where the conflicts don't seem to be interagency, interstructural between ego, superego, and id, but *intrastructural*, in the sense of a conflict between contradictory internalized object relations of an idealized and a persecutory nature. These object relations become mutually contradictory defense-impulse configurations in different moments. Thus a significant change regarding Freud has evolved—going back to your first question, in that we have come to think much more about the constituent structures of ego, superego, and id, as they become manifest in the activation of such primitive object relations in the transference, and are played out with reciprocal activation of self and object representations in the transference and countertransference, and in the dominant impact of an affect that now represents one of the two series of aggression or libido or their combination.

DES: This might lead—I don't know if you have more you want to say about structure—but it might lead us to talk about differences in the technical approach and the clinical approach to analysis since Freud.

I thought about this in regard to what we would now say about his case histories, and his published advice about technique.

OFK: I think that when it comes to psychoanalytic technique, there are relatively few new elements that have been included, no crucial change from Freud's recommendations. Techniques, however, have become more elaborated. We now have not only a standard classical psychoanalytic technique, but derived techniques of psychoanalytic psychotherapy. We know more about indications and contraindications, but the basic concepts really came from Freud.

First of all, the general discovery of transference as the unconscious repetition in the here and now of repressed or dissociated pathogenic experiences from the there and then: this is the central concept of psychoanalytic treatment. We are seeing in more sophisticated ways how the nature of the transference evolves in the clinical situation. At first, transferences reflect the activation of conflicts between ego, superego and id, and only gradually, the better functioning patients regress to the mutually contradictory activation of internalized object relations, the "building blocks" of the psychic structures. But basically, the unconscious conflicts from the past are still there to be activated in the transference, and haunt us in transference and countertransference developments. Now, Freud's technique of free association stands unchallenged, and is a basic instrument of our work. Thus, interpretation of unconscious meanings, transference analysis, and technical neutrality are still valid basic concepts, although they have been modified in clinically important ways, but still conceptually clearly traceable to Freud.

DES: Also, "abstinence" in the sense in which he seemed to mean it, rather than it's later . . .

OFK: Abstinence in the sense of not gratifying the transference. This brings us to the importance of countertransference analysis as part of psychoanalytic technique. Freud discovered countertransference in the context of the boundary violations of the psychoanalytic relationship on part of his leading disciples. Faced with erotic transferences, some of them couldn't control the temptations of getting sexually involved with their patients, and that was very frightening to Freud. Jung, Ferenczi, Steckel—all the great names had affairs with patients. This, I think, was frightening to Freud, who described the existence of countertransference, and stated that the analyst had to control it, to suppress it. I understand that he made the private recommendation that not too much should be written about it because he was afraid, with good reasons, that the prestige of psychoanalysis would suffer under the effect of what we now call boundary violations in psychoanalysis. There are some excellent books about this, in particular in the German literature. Anyhow, the taboo about countertransference analysis existed until the 1950s, when there appeared a spate of papers on this subject, and the psychoanalytic community became aware that countertransference was an important instrument for transference analysis. The contribution of Heinrich Racker—the description of concordant and complementary identification in the countertransference—meant a great step forward in our understanding, particularly of primitive transferences in which the countertransference may reflect the unconscious identification of the analyst with an internal object of the patient. At times the analyst becomes the patient's infantile self, while the patient enacts an early object, and ten minutes later the patient may enact his own infantile self while projecting the object of the relationship onto the analyst. An apparent chaos results that can be perfectly understood if one keeps in mind that the same object relation is enacted with reciprocally alternating distribution.

Technically, all this means that countertransference analysis has become extremely important. It becomes a source of empathy with the patient that transcends ordinary empathy, in the sense that in concordant identification one is empathic with the patient's central subjective experience, while in complementary identification one is empathic with what the patient cannot tolerate in himself, and has to project or dissociate. The accentuation of countertransference analysis now provides the psychoanalyst with three sources of information: communication of the patient's subjective experience by means of free association, the analysis of the nonverbal behavior, which becomes practically character analysis in the transference and countertransference analysis.

DES: That is a major evolution.

OFK: That is a major evolution since Freud, and it has led to the present-day controversy about "one-person psychology," "two-person psychology," and "three-person psychology," in which Freud is put in a position as if he had been proposing a one-person psychology, the problems to be analyzed being located exclusively inside the patient. The analyst only had to be a mirror, or participant observer—more of an observer than a participant. This one-person psychology then shifted because of the focus on the importance of transference and countertransference analysis, into the two-person psychology that culminated, I think, in Merton Gill's famous statement that the transference is a compromise formation between the unconscious problems of the patient from the past and the realistic or plausible reaction of the patient to the analyst's personality and countertransference, leading to a concept of intrinsic mutuality of transference and countertransference. This concept has been picked up in the theory of interpersonal psychoanalysis, intersubjective psychoanalysis, and self psychology, and has become, therefore, a very important contemporary trend.

Against this two-person psychology, you finally have the three-person psychology that has been proposed mostly by French psychoanalysis, but is also commensurate with contemporary Kleinian and ego psychological analysis. The three-person psychology implies that the analyst is split between one part that participates in the transference/countertransference bind, and another part, in which the analyst self-reflects on his or her experience in the countertransference, in combination with his or her knowledge and experience. This aspect of the analyst, therefore, remains outside the transference/countertransference bind, while he uses his experience of the transference/countertransference bind to interpret the transference. This position of the analyst as a "third-excluded other" for French psychoanalysis is analagous to the role of the oedipal father, who disrupts the symbiotic experience of the mother-infant relationship. It recreates symbolically a triangular oedipal situation in the analytic situation, and so activates oedipalization at both an archaic and an advanced developmental level. This coincides also with ego psychological and Kleinian emphasis on that function of the analyst. I personally like the three-person psychology approach, because I think that otherwise, there exists a danger of privileging the patient's experience as the basis for the analysis of transference and countertransference.

DES: Rather than a more balanced view where the analyst really is trying to hold both points of view in mind and stands for that experience. Actually, it also brings in the question of how it is that the analyst—maybe with the patient's cooperation—brings in the whole context of the wider group that the patient lives in—the society and cultural issues.

OFK: Yes. You are raising a valid issue, regarding that there has been some important development. I think we have become much more alert to the danger of the analyst's theories influencing the patient's free associations, his or her indoctrination by the analyst. The Kleinians, in particular, became aware of their tendency to indoctrinate the patient, and there has been a radical shift in Kleinian technique in the last twenty years that has made it come closer to the Independents and the ego psychologists, while on the other hand, the recognition of the prevalence of the transference from the beginning of the treatment that Merton Gill brought to ego psychology, made ego psychology come closer to the Kleinians. Nowadays, I think, very few people deny the reality of the primitive object relations and defensive operations described by Fairbairn and Klein. I think that this is generally accepted in most psychoanalytic approaches—except by the most isolated ego psychologists. The various psychoanalytic schools have come closer to each other in their technical approaches, the major contemporary controversy remaining that between the two-person and three-person psychology. On the other hand, there is, as I mentioned, still a significant criticism from French analysts regarding the Kleinians for their underemphasizing sexuality, and from ego psychologists to Kleinians in that they focus too much on the experience of the first few months or years of life. There is critique from the Kleinians to the ego psychologists that they still have a tendency to interpret too close to the surface, rather than going into most primitive experience.

DES: The Kleinians think ego psychologists stay too much on the surface, too much on resistance, and not enough on the very early months. The primitive object is a major Kleinian emphasis.

OFK: And a combined critique of ego psychologists, Kleinians, and French analysts of the intersubjective, interpersonal approach is that it tends to maintain interpretation also at a surface level, in the sense of the actual interaction between patient and analyst, instead of going into the deepest level of the patient's unconscious fantasies.

DES: That was the other thing I was going to ask about. We haven't said anything about self psychology and intersubjectivity as one of the most prominent recent developments, both theoretically and clinically.

OFK: Yes, well, I indirectly referred to them. Self psychology, intersubjective analysis, and interpersonal psychoanalysis are really American psychoanalytic tendencies that are much less significant in Latin America and Europe. They have a common focus on the actual experience between patient and analyst, and, how shall I put it, the nurturing quality of the actual object relation in the psychoanalytic treatment. That is, perhaps, another important controversy. The personality and the actual behavior of the analyst are considered by these approaches as important therapeutic elements, in contrast to the technique of interpretation per se. Freud implied that we modify the patient's abnormal and psychic structures through interpretation. These schools, in contrast, imply that we obtain significant change through interpretation carried out by an empathic analyst. I think self psychology puts it in the most dramatic terms: interpretation has to be carried out within a self-object/self-relationship, in contrast to technical neutrality. That is a major controversy. I stand clearly on the side of technical neutrality, and I am critical of this aspect of the self-psychological orientation. But this is a major controversy.

DES: It's a major controversy, as well as frequent criticism about their underemphasizing aggression because of the emphasizing nutrient factors.

OFK: Yes. In this regard, traditional self psychology—by now one can talk about traditional self psychology—denies the existence of negative introjects, of aggressively invested internalized object representations, while intersubjective analysis and interpersonal analysis accept such negative internalizations, and are therefore, closer to the British object relations theories. I think that sets another divide within American psychoanalysis.

DES: To shift ground again, I thought that I should take some time to ask you about your current interests. What is the current state of psychoanalysis as a field of science and as a clinical entity, and what do you see for its future? Are there areas of growth? What about its being under siege, in this country [the United States] at least? These kinds of questions.

OFK: I mentioned earlier that for me psychoanalysis is a basic science, together with neurobiology. I think that psychoanalysis has still major contributions to make, and has made some fundamental contributions that have not been fully explored. I believe that the attacks on psychoanalysis are really a reaction to the isolationist tendencies of psychoanalysis, and to the impression it conveys at times of being a complete science without relationship to neighboring fields, which has created, with good reasons, serious questions. Of course, there are other reasons for that attack as well. The general reluctance of academic psychology and biological psychiatry to acknowledge the importance of dynamic unconscious process, within the individual, and in society and the group, and the reluctance to recognize the enormous importance of primitive aggression in human existence, in spite of our sad experience of the twentieth century, are other sources of animosity toward psychoanalysis. Again, as before, the reluctance to accept infantile sexuality and its fundamental influence in later life is an old and not surprisingly recurring source of fear and hostility towards psychoanalysis. Just look at the sexual-harassment hysteria sweeping this country, and you'll see we're not so far away from 1900.

DES: Yes, that's true. Of course, sexual harassment really exists. But there are always puritanical efforts to stamp out sexuality throughout life.

OFK: A few more concrete areas of development. First of all, the area of personality disorders—the structure of normal and abnormal personality—what we call character pathology. I think that psychoanalysis is the only comprehensive theory that explains the entire field of personality disorders and character pathology; it has a conception of psychopathology, differential diagnosis, clinical description, and treatment. The proof of the pudding is that alternative theories have a kind of esoteric, superficial, clinically irrelevant quality that is quite impressive when you explore the literature in detail. The treatment of personality disorders, the transformation of a sick personality into a healthy personality is a major contribution of psychoanalysis and derived psychoanalytic techniques of psychotherapy.

A second major therapeutic area is the application of psychoanalysis to the understanding of intimate conflicts of individuals in close, long-term relationships: love, marriage, and family structure.

Third, the understanding of regression in groups, the influence of that regression on the work in organizations, on the relationship between members and management of institutions. I think this is a very important field, that I trust will be developed further, and hasn't been developed much because only few psychoanalysts have really specialized in this area, relatively little research has been carried out to explore this, and to the contrary, the tendency of psychoanalysis has been to "retrench behind the couch," so to speak, and so we are missing out on important applications of our field.

I think that the development of psychoanalytic psychotherapy for patients who are too sick to be analyzed and the development of supportive psychotherapies for patients who don't have the introspection or the capacity to work intensively through self-reflection, is another important application. In clinical psychiatry, there is nowadays much competition between cognitive-behavioral approaches and psychoanalytic modalities. It seems to me that in the long run, this is going to be resolved, because cognitive-behavioral psychology has only a limited personality theory behind it, while psychoanalysis, with its rich personality theory, is able to incorporate cognitive and behavioral techniques in supportive psychotherapeutic approaches. Psychoanalysis presents an enormous potential for a more scientific, precise, and broad theory for all kinds of psychotherapies, from standard psychoanalysis to consulting.

DES: As I hear you talking about it now, you are advocating a more active stance about reaching out to understand what these adjunctiive fields have to offer so that we can make use of them, rather than isolating analysis, claiming it's the only treatment in its unmodified form.

OFK: Yes, absolutely. I believe that psychoanalytic institutes should teach psychoanalytic psychotherapy to candidates, because it's still true that quite often when psychoanalysts—particularly those traditionally trained—don't do psychoanalysis, they do some sort of chaotic psychotherapy. Using all the instruments for a psychotherapeutic technique based on psychoanalytic principles that we have available now may significantly increase the therapeutic effectiveness of derivative psychoanalytic methods.

DES: Plus so many analysts are teachers of analytic therapists, but have not themselves necessarily developed a theory of analytic psychotherapy.

OFK: Right. Yes, yes. I think that the fact that the psychoanalytic community has become much more open to tolerate different theoretical developments, to tolerate that psychoanalysts have different views about central issues, and that they can be compared and tested, is a good development. We need to strengthen psychoanalytic research. I am talking about research in the broadest sense—empirical research, but also scholarly research, historical research, hermeneutic research, the research with small r that we do in our clinical practice.

DES: And this also includes in the United States nonmedical candidates?

OFK: Yes, in psychoanalytic education we have much to learn from other professionals, and I think this openness is important, but we also have to maintain a close linkage with medicine, with psychiatry, and psychology. Clinical psychology and psychiatry, it seems to me, are two fundamental fields that are closely related to the mainstream of our work.

DES: How about internationally? Areas of growth? Resistance?

OFK: Well, the International Psychoanalytic Association (IPA) has been growing significantly. Fifteen years ago North America had 40 percent of all the analysts in the world, and now this has been reduced to less than 30 percent. There is continuous growth in Europe, and particularly in Latin America. At the same time, I think psychoanalysis is under attack all over the world. There are similar problems: financial constraints; less money to pay for intensive long-term treatments; challenges from biological psychiatry and from cognitive-behavioral psychotherapies; and challenges from reimbursement agencies—insurance and government agencies. Also, the culture has become predominantly pragmatic, adaptational.

DES: Action-oriented!

OFK: Yes. Less interested in self-exploration and subjectivity. But these are historical fluctuations that I think won't be that important if psychoanalysis develops its scientific knowledge and scientific stance, relates to the sciences on its boundaries, and simultaneously psychoanalytic societies increase their relationship with the outside world, rather than rounding the wagons. In my role as President of the IPA, I have been trying to develop a number of initiatives in this regard. First, during my administration, we have created a committee on Psychoanalysis and Society, to help psychoanalytic societies deal with governments, governmental agencies, insurance, the media, the university, intellectual elites, and other professions. This committee is now working internationally. Second, we have appointed a committee on interregional conferences, to establish small conferences about selected subjects on theory and technique, developed by internationally leading psychoanalysts: three, five, eight leading psychoanalysts are brought together for the purpose for such state of the art conferences. Third, we are organizing trips of leading psychoanalysts to societies throughout the world, in order to contribute to the diffusion of psychoanalytic knowledge. Another initiative is a new committee on translations to help translate key psychoanalytic texts from other languages into English, because there are still significant language barriers between French, German, Italian, Spanish, and Portuguese psychoanalysis and the English-language psychoanalytic communities.

DES: Then a good deal of the strength would come from decreasing insularity and isolation from each other, as well as reaching out into the wider society.

OFK: Yes, yes. I have also taken the initiative of developing a fund for psychoanalytic research, which now invests $200,000 per year to foster research projects in psychoanalysis throughout the world on a competitive basis. We have had our first rounds of proposals submitted.

DES: I understand there were seventy-seven submissions.

OFK: Exactly. It has been a very successful initiative. Another important initiative involves psychoanalytic education. It seems to me that psychoanalytic institutes traditionally have taken the stance of transmitting knowledge, but not of developing new psychoanalytic knowledge. I think that psychoanalytic institutes need to develop new psychoanalytic knowledge and be centers that foster research. They may not have the resources to do this alone, but they may organize activities together with departments of clinical psychology and psychiatry as part of outreach.

DES: More like a university that is simultaneously developing knowledge and transmitting it, so that even the students have the sense of knowledge evolving.

OFK: I think we also have to study alternative models of psychoanalytic education. Most of the world follows the Eitingon model, developed in Berlin in 1923. It's our tripartite model with training analysis, four years of seminars, and individual supervision. There's an alternative model—the French psychoanalytic model, and there are still other modifications, both of the French model and of the Eitingon model. We should compare their effectiveness and experiment, rather than think that we have only one or two proven models for education. In all other scientific areas there's a lot of revolutionary education going on, and the IPA committee on education (COMPSED) has been given the mandate to carry out research on psychoanalytic education, and to help us develop in that area as well.

DES: Finally, I would like to ask if you can reflect on the significance of the Freud exhibit and the Freud collection—the Freud archives—for our field and for knowledge in general.

OFK: It's obvious that this is a very important public recognition of the fundamental importance of Freud's contribution to modern culture, to our knowledge in the broadest sense, and that psychoanalysis has a definite, firm, established role within the development of science as well as culture in the Western world. I think that the entire controversy around the exhibit has been artificially inflated by a few people with very private agendas, because is it not a matter of idealizing Freud and having a noncritical acceptance of everything he said, but utilizing his revolutionary thinking to develop the science further. From what I know, the spirit of that exhibition will be to get better acquainted with Freud's way of thinking, not with dogmatically accepting all his conclusions.

It is with a sense of great satisfaction that I am looking forward to that exhibition, and I hope that it will have an impact on our external environment. This is very important for our work in the next few years.

DES: Good. I appreciate your speaking with me and offering these comments. It's really been a pleasure. As always, I learn enormously from talking with you.

OFK: Thank you for inviting me to be interviewed. This is a challenge—to deal with all these issues without preparation. But then, most of the things I have talked about are close to my heart, and that helps.

DES: Yes, I noticed that you could discuss them easily. Thanks very much.

4

The Right Brain As the Neurobiological Substratum of Freud's Dynamic Unconscious

Allan N. Schore

Over the last two decades, Freud's seminal model of a dynamic, continuously active unconscious mind has undergone a major transformation. This reformulation has been driven by not only clinical advances, but also by modifications of the theoretical underpinnings of the theory, especially updated concepts of development and structure. A rapidly evolving trend within psychoanalysis, "the science of unconscious processes" (Brenner 1980), is an increasing appreciation of the centrality of affective phenomena. Freud first delineated his ideas about affect in the "Project for a Scientific Psychology" (1895), a work that appeared at the dawn of psychoanalysis, in which he attempted to create a systematic model of the functioning of the human mind in terms of its underlying neurobiological mechanisms. Although he subsequently contended that the work of psychotherapy is always concerned with affect (1915a), it is only recently that an increased emphasis on affect is impacting clinical models.

During this same time period, a host of other scientific disciplines, liberated from the narrow behavioral model that dominated psychology for much of the twentieth century, have begun to actively probe questions about the internal processes of mind that were for so long only addressed by psychoanalysis and deemed to be outside the realm of "scientific" analysis. In my ongoing work I document how a spectrum of sciences that border psychoanalysis are now researching the covert yet essential mechanisms that underlie overt behaviors, especially the role of emotional states. In a recent paper in the *Journal of the American Psychoanalytic Association*, "A Century after Freud's Project: Is a Rapprochement between Psychoanalysis and Neurobiology at Hand?," I have suggested that affect and its regulation are a potential point of convergence of psychoanalysis and neuroscience, and that the time is now right for the rapprochement Freud predicted (Schore 1997a).

Thus I, along with others who are calling for this integration, am quite pleased with the appearance of the new journal *Neuro-Psychoanalysis*. I am particularly honored to be part of an editorial board of distinguished psychoanalysts that includes Otto Kernberg and Arnold Modell, and neuroscientists such as Oliver Sacks, Eric Kandel, Karl Pribram, Joseph LeDoux, and Antonio Damasio. The first issue of the journal is devoted to Freud's theory of affect in the light of contemporary neuroscience, and in this chapter I want to offer some thoughts that are outlined in a paper I have contributed to the premier issue (Schore 1999).

In the journal I suggest that a common ground of both psychoanalysis and neuroscience lies in a more detailed charting of the unique structure-function relationships of the emotion-processing right brain, which Ornstein (1997) calls "the right mind." Psychoanalysis has been interested in the right hemisphere since the split-brain studies of the 1970s, when a number of psychoanalytic investigators began to map out its preeminent role in unconscious processes (Galin 1974, Hoppe 1977, McLaughlin 1978). I propose that Freud's affect theory describes a structural system, associated with unconscious primary process affect-laden cognition and regulated by the pleasure-unpleasure principle, which is organized in the right brain. Knowledge of this right brain system offers us a chance to more deeply understand not just the contents of the unconscious, but its origin, structure, and dynamics.

In the following I will briefly evaluate Freud's affect theory in light of contemporary neuroscience. Then I will offer a developmental perspective of affective phenomena, and finally outline a dynamic systems-theory perspective of emotional processes.

FREUD'S AFFECT THEORY IN LIGHT OF CONTEMPORARY NEUROSCIENCE

Basic Emotions

Freud's earliest ideas about affect were first presented in the "Project," a document that bridged his early career as a neurologist and later career as a psychologist. Throughout his subsequent writings he held that affects are "for the most part innately pre-wired, although some basic emotions are apparently forged during early development by momentous biological events of universal significance," and that in later life they represent "reproductions of very early experiences of vital importance" (Freud 1926). There is now an intense interest in "biologically primitive emotions," which are evolutionarily very old, appear early in development, and are facially expressed (Johnson and Multhaup 1992). The early maturing right hemisphere is dominant for the first three years of life (Chiron et al. 1997), and it contains a basic primitive affect system (Gazzaniga 1985) that is involved in the modulation of "primary emotions" (Ross et al. 1994).

The Perceptual Aspect of Affects

Although Freud repudiated the Project, its central ideas appear in the seventh chapter of *The Interpretation of Dreams*. Here Freud (1900) proposed that the psychical apparatus is "turned towards the external world with its sense-organ of the Pcpt. [perceptual] systems," and through the regulatory mechanism of the "pleasure principle" value is assigned to mental performance. Freud thus highlighted the importance of affective appraisals of the personal significance of external stimuli to the generation of value and meaning. Current emotion researchers are emphasizing the importance of the appraisal of facial expressions and the evaluative function of affects. The right hemisphere is dominant for the processing of facial information from infancy (Deruelle and de Schonen 1998) to adulthood (Kim et al. 1999), is faster than the left in performing valence-dependent, automatic, pre-attentive appraisals of emotional facial expressions (Pizzagalli et al. 1999) and is dominant for the recognition of the emotional prosody of language (Buchanan et al. 2000). Emotions involve rapid appraisals of events that are important to the individual (Frijda 1988) and represent reactions to fundamental relational meanings that have adaptive significance (Lazarus 1991).

From a neurobiological perspective LeDoux (1989) asserts that "the core of the emotional system" is a mechanism for computing the affective significance of stimuli. In a recent volume, I offer a chapter on the maturation of an evaluative system in the right cortex (Schore 1998). This lateralized system performs a "valence tagging" function (Watt 1998), in which perceptions receive a positive or negative affective charge, in accord with a calibration of degrees of pleasure-unpleasure. The essential roles of the right hemisphere in emotional perception (Adolphs et al. 1996, Anderson and Phelps 2000, Borod et al. 1998, Nakamura et al. 1999) and in the allocation of attention (Mesulam 1990, Sturm et al. 1999) are well documented.

The Expressive Aspect of Affects

In addition to a perceptual dimension, Freud (1915a) also intuited the "expressive" aspect of emotions, that the expression of emotions represented reflexive patterns of motor discharge. Current interdisciplinary research is demonstrating the dominance of the right hemisphere for facial displays of emotion (Borod et al. 1997, Dimberg and Petterson 2000) and spontaneous gestures (Blonder et al. 1995). In regard to Freud's ideas on the communication functions of affects, neuropsychological studies now report the preeminent role of the right hemisphere in emotional (Blonder et al. 1991), spontaneous (Buck 1994), and nonverbal (Benowitz et al. 1983) communication. And with respect to his speculations on the memorial aspects of affect, there is now evidence for a right cerebral representation of affect-laden autobiographical information (Fink et al. 1996).

The Adaptive Aspect of Affects

The editors of *Neuro-Psychoanalysis*, Mark Solms and Ed Nersessian (1999), emphasize Freud's characterization of the adaptive function of affects: "According to Freud, the mental apparatus as a whole serves the biological purpose of meeting the imperative internal needs of the subject in a changing . . . environment" (p. 5). This essential psychobiological function is echoed by Damasio (1994) who concludes, "The overall function of the brain is to be well informed about what goes on in the rest of the body, the body proper; about what goes on in itself; and about the environment surrounding the organism, so that suitable survivable accommodations can be achieved between the organism and the environment" (p. 90). But the two brain hemispheres have different patterns of cortical-subcortical connections, and therefore do not play an equal role in this function. The right hemisphere contains the most comprehensive and integrated map of the body state available to the brain (Damasio 1994) and is central to the control of vital functions supporting survival and enabling the organism to cope with stresses and challenges (Wittling and Schweiger 1993), and so its adaptive functions mediate the human stress response (Wittling 1997).

The characterization, in the neuroscience literature, of these adaptive right brain functions, performed at levels beneath awareness, is consonant with Winson's description, in current psychoanalytic writings, of revised models of the unconscious. Winson (1990) concludes, "Rather than being a cauldron of untamed passions and destructive wishes, I propose that the unconscious is a cohesive, continually active mental structure that takes note of life's experiences and reacts according to its scheme of interpretation" (p. 96).

Mind–Body Connections

From the beginning Freud posited that affective stimuli also arise "from within the organism and reaching the mind, as a measure of the demand made upon the mind in consequence of its connection with the body" (1915b, p. 122). In Freud's most widely used definition, "drive is a concept at the frontier between the psychic and the somatic, an endogenous source of stimulation which impinges on the mind by virtue of the mind's connection with the body" (Greenberg and Mitchell 1983, p. 21). Damasio (1994) argues that emotions are "a powerful manifestation of drives and instincts." Although some psychoanalysts are now becoming interested in the body, much of the field is still mired in "Descartes' Error"—the separation of the operations of the mind from the structure and operation of a biological organism, the body (Damasio 1994). Neuroscientists are now stressing that "the brain is but one component of the complex system that is the body. We take in information and interact with the world through our bodies, and our bodies change with—and in some cases change—cognitive and emotional processing" (Kutas and Federmeier 1998, p. 135).

Current "cognitive" neuroscience is less interested in the body that in the verbal and conscious capacities of the left hemisphere. But it is the right hemisphere that is more deeply connected into both the sympathetic and parasympathetic branches of the involuntary peripheral autonomic nervous system than the left (Spence et al. 1996), and thus dominant for "the metacontrol of fundamental physiological and endocrinological functions whose primary control centers are located in subcortical regions of the brain" (Wittling and Pfluger 1990, p. 260) and indeed for the corporeal and emotional self (Devinsky 2000). Solms (1996) notes that the right hemisphere encodes representations "on the basis of perception derived initially from the bodily ego" (p. 347), clearly implying its dominant role in drive-related functions. Recent psychobiological and neurobiological studies thus strongly indicate that the concept of drive, devalued over the last twenty years, must be reintroduced—though reformulated—as a central construct of psychoanalytic theory.

Affect Regulation

Freud's special interest in the problem of regulation also first appears in the Project, a document which suggests "a model whereby excitation from various sources arising both from within and from outside the individual might be *regulated* by processes essentially within the individual" (Sander 1977, p. 14). And in this same farsighted opus Freud goes on to say that there is a close connection between affect and primary process, and that memories capable of generating affect are "tamed" (regulated) until the affect provides only a "signal."

In my ongoing work, I have detailed the development and unique functional capacities of the orbital prefrontal area of the cortex that regulates emotional and motivational states (Schore 1994, 1998). Due to its extensive reciprocal connections with energy controlling bio-aminergic nuclei in the reticular formation and drive-inducing and drive-inhibiting systems in the hypothalamus, the orbitofrontal cortex is critical to the modulation of instinctual behavior (Starkstein and Robinson 1997), the experience of emotion (Baker et al. 1997), and the motivational control of goal-directed activities (Tremblay and Schultz 1999). Indeed, "the orbitofrontal cortex is involved in critical human functions, such as social adjustment and the control of mood, drive and responsibility, traits that are crucial in defining the 'personality' of an individual" (Cavada and Schultz 2000, p. 205). This prefrontal cortex, situated at the apogee of the "rostral limbic system," a hierarchical sequence of interconnected limbic areas in orbitofrontal cortex, insular cortex, anterior cingulate, and amygdala (Schore 1997b, 2000c, 2001a), is expanded in the right hemisphere (Falk et al. 1990). This hemisphere, more so than the left, is densely reciprocally interconnected with limbic regions (Tucker 1992), and therefore contains the major circuitry of emotion regulation (Porges et al. 1994). Furthermore, the orbitofrontal system matures at the end of a right hemisphere growth spurt in late infancy, and is centrally involved in attachment behavior (Schore 1994, 1996, 2000a,b, 2001a,c).

A DEVELOPMENTAL PERSPECTIVE OF AFFECTIVE PHENOMENA

In a continuation of Freud's principle of the primacy of early experience, recent developmental studies on the centrality of the attachment relationship have been a major contributor to the current emphasis on affect within psychoanalysis. Early attachment is the "momentous biological event of universal significance" that Freud alluded to, and although for much of his career he seemed ambivalent about the role of maternal influences in earliest development, in his very last work he stated, in a definitive fashion, that the mother–infant relationship "is unique, without parallel, established unalterably for a whole lifetime as the first and strongest love-object and the prototype of all later love-relations" (Freud 1940). This fundamental ontogenetic principle was subsequently explored by a number of developmental psychoanalysts, most importantly in John Bowlby's attachment theory, a point of convergence of psychoanalysis and behavioral biology. In a departure from the classical Freudian developmental model, contemporary psychoanalysis now views these "vital" attachment experiences of the first two years as more central to personality formation than the later occurring oedipal events of the third and fourth year.

My own work in this area (Schore 1994, 1996, 1997b, 1998, 2001a,b) has focused on the reciprocal affective transactions within the mother–infant dyadic system—in these face-to-face (Feldman et al. 1999) emotional communications the mother is essentially regulating the infant's psychobiological states. The attachment relationship is thus a regulator of arousal, and attachment is, in essence, the dyadic regulation of emotion (Sroufe 1996). But even more, these interactive affect regulating events act as a mechanism for the "social construction of the human brain" (Eisenberg 1995). Trevarthen (1993) concludes that "the affective regulations of brain growth" are embedded in the context of an intimate relationship, and that they promote the development of cerebral circuits. This interactive mechanism requires older brains to engage with mental states of awareness, emotion, and interest in younger brains, and involves a coordination between the motivations of the infant and the subjective feelings of adults. In this manner, "the intrinsic regulators of human brain growth in a child are specifically adapted to be coupled, by emotional communication, to the regulators of adult brains" (Trevarthen 1990, p. 357).

I have offered evidence which suggests that attachment transactions represent right hemisphere-to-right hemisphere affective transactions between mother and infant (Schore 1994, 1996, 1997b, 2000b). These affective communications of facial expressions, prosody, and gestures are thus central to the experience-dependent maturation of the infant's early maturing right brain. Confirming this model, Ryan et al. (1997), using EEG and neuroimaging data, now propose: "The positive emotional exchange resulting from autonomy-supportive parenting involves participation of right hemispheric cortical and subcortical systems that participate in global, tonic emotional modulation" (p. 719).

The emotional interactions of early life thus directly influence the organization of brain systems that process affect. In modeling the developmental neurobiology of attachment I have proposed that the attachment experiences of infancy are stored in the early maturing right hemisphere, and that for the rest of the lifespan unconscious working models of the attachment relationship encode, in implicit memory, strategies of affect regulation for coping with stress, especially interpersonal stress (Schore 1994, 2000b, 2001a,b,d). These internal representations are accessed as guides for future interactions, and the term "working" refers to the individual's unconscious use of them to interpret and act on new experiences.

This psychoneurobiological mechanism mediates the internalization of the attachment relationship and the mother's regulatory functions. A secure attachment relationship facilitates the emergence, at the end of the second year, of what Bowlby (1969) termed a control system in the cortex. I identify this as the orbitofrontal system which, via its control of the autonomic nervous system (Neafsey 1990), mediates the highest level of control of emotional behavior (Price et al. 1996), that is, affect regulation. This frontolimbic system comes to act in an executive function for the entire right brain, which is specialized for "inhibitory control" (Garavan et al. 1999).

As the "senior executive of the emotional brain" (Joseph 1996), its operations are essential to a number of adaptive intrapsychic and interpersonal functions: it appraises facial information (Scalaidhe et al. 1997), operates by implicit processing (Rolls 1996), generates nonconscious biases that guide behavior before conscious knowledge does (Bechara et al. 1997), functions to correct responses as conditions change (Derryberry and Tucker 1992), processes feedback information (Elliott et al. 1997), and thereby monitors, adjusts, and corrects emotional responses (Rolls 1986), and modulates the motivational control of goal-directed behavior (Tremblay and Schultz 1999).

So after a rapid evaluation of an environmental stimulus, the orbitofrontal system monitors feedback about the current internal state in order to make assessments of coping resources, and it updates appropriate response outputs in order to make adaptive adjustments to particular environmental perturbations (Schore 1998, 2000b). In this manner, "the integrity of the orbitofrontal cortex is necessary for acquiring very specific forms of knowledge for regulating interpersonal and social behavior" (Dolan 1999, p. 928).

The functioning of the "self-correcting" orbitofrontal system is central to self-regulation, the ability to flexibly regulate emotional states through interactions with other humans—interactive regulation in interconnected contexts via a two-person psychology, and without other humans, and autoregulation in autonomous contexts via a one-person psychology. The adaptive capacity to shift between these dual regulatory modes, depending upon the social context, emerges out of a history of secure attachment interactions of a maturing biological organism and an early attuned social environment.

THE RELEVANCE OF NEUROBIOLOGICAL AND PSYCHOBIOLOGICAL RESEARCH ON EMOTION FOR CLINICAL PSYCHOANALYSIS

These neurobiological data on affective structure-function relationships have implications for clinical psychoanalysis. In current treatment models, affects, including unconscious affects, are both "the center of empathic communication" and the "primary data," and "the regulation of conscious and unconscious feelings is placed in the center of the clinical stage" (Sandler and Sandler 1978). The direct relevance of studies of emotional development to the psychotherapeutic process derives from the commonality of interactive emotion-transacting mechanisms in the caregiver–infant relationship and in the therapist–patient relationship. In the current neurobiological literature, the right hemisphere is dominant for "subjective emotional experiences" (Wittling and Roschmann 1993). The interactive "transfer of affect" between the right brains of the members of the mother–infant and therapeutic dyads is thus best described as "intersubjectivity," a finding consonant with recent psychoanalytic "intersubjective" models of the mind (Stolorow and Atwood 1992). Emotions, by definition, involve subjective states, and studies of the right hemisphere are thus detailing the neurobiology of subjectivity.

Transference-countertransference interactions, occurring at levels beneath awareness in both patient and therapist, represent rapid right hemisphere-to-right hemisphere nonverbal affective transactions (Schore 1994, 1997c, 2001c, in press a). These rapid expressions of the emotional right brain suggest that the emotional tone of voice, small movements of facial muscles, spontaneous gestures, and gaze aversions may be a better reflection of a person's affective state than his or her verbalizations (Panksepp 1999, Schore 1994, 2001c, in press a). In contemporary clinical models, perhaps the most important advances in this realm have come from those working in the "nonverbal real of psychoanalysis" (i.e., Jacobs 1994, Schwaber 1995).

I suggest that just as the left brain communicates its states to other left brains via conscious linguistic behaviors, so the right nonverbally communicates its unconscious states to other right brains that are tuned to receive these communications (Schore, in press a, e). Marcus (1997) has recently written, "The analyst, by means of reverie and intuition, listens with the right brain directly to the analysand's right brain" (p. 238). This neurobiological perspective is consonant with Kantrowitz's (1999) emphasis of the centrality of "intense affective engagements" and conclusion that "it is in the realm of preconscious communication that the interwovenness of intrapsychic and interpersonal phenomena become most apparent" (p. 72).

Current psychobiological studies indicate that affects are not merely byproducts of cognition—they have unique temporal and physiological characteristics that, more than thoughts, define our internal experience of self. Although facial emotions can be appraised by the right brain within thirty milliseconds, spontaneously expressed within seconds, and continue to amplify within less than a half-minute, it can take hours, or days, or even weeks or longer for certain personalities experiencing extremely intense negative emotion to get back to a "normal" state again. Working with very rapid affective phenomena in real time involves attention to a different time dimension than usual, a focus on interpersonal attachment and separations on a microtemporal scale. This moment-to-moment tracking attends to the internal mechanism by which the patient regulates emotional distance. The emphasis is less on enduring traits and more on transient states, less on temporally distant and more on short-term, immediate motivational factors.

Furthermore, neurobiological studies now demonstrate the involvement of the right hemisphere in "implicit learning" (Hugdahl 1995) and "nonverbal processes" (Schore 1994). Such structure-function relationships may elucidate how alterations in what Stern and colleagues (1998) call nonverbal "implicit relational knowledge" are at the core of therapeutic change. In light of the central role of the limbic system in both attachment functions and in "the organization of new learning" (Mesulam 1998), the corrective emotional experience of psychotherapy, which can alter attachment patterns, must involve unconscious right brain limbic learning.

Integrated psychoanalytic-neurobiological conceptualizations of emotional development can thus generate clinically relevant, heuristic models of treatment. In recent writings Westen (1997) asserts that

"The attempt to regulate affect—to minimize unpleasant feelings and to maximize pleasant ones—is the driving force in human motivation" (p. 542). Affect dysregulation, a fundamental mechanism of the right hemispheric (Cutting 1992) dysfunctions of all psychiatric disorders (Schore 1997b, Taylor et al. 1997, Wasserstein and Stefanos 2000, Weinberg 2000), is now a primary focus of updated clinical psychoanalytic models. Very recent interdisciplinary models clearly suggest that an essential function of psychoanalytic treatment is to complete interrupted developmental processes (Gedo 1979), that all forms of psychotherapy promote affect regulation (Bradley 2000), and that a critical role of the psychotherapist is to act as an affect regulator of the patient's dysregulated states and to provide a growth-facilitating environment for the patient's immature affect-regulating structures (see Schore 1994, 1997c, in press a).

In other words, dyadic affective transactions within the working alliance co-create an intersubjective context that allows for the structural expansion of the patient's orbitofrontal system and its cortical and subcortical connections. Orbitofrontal function is essential to not only affect regulation but also to the processing of cognitive-emotional interactions (Barbas 1995) and affect-related meanings (Teasdale et al. 1999). This "thinking part of the emotional brain" (Goleman 1995) functions as an "internal reflecting and organizing agency" (Kaplan-Solms and Solms 1996), is involved in "emotion-relating learning" (Rolls 1994), and acts to "integrate and assign emotional-motivational significance to cognitive impressions; the association of emotion with ideas and thoughts" (Joseph 1996), a characterization of the psychoanalytic therapeutic process.

A recently published functional magnetic resonance imaging (fMRI) study (Hariri et al. 2000) provides evidence that higher regions of specifically the right prefrontal cortex attenuate emotional responses at the most basic levels in the brain, that such modulating processes are "fundamental to most modern psychotherapeutic methods" (p. 43), that this lateralized neocortical network is active in "modulating emotional experience through interpreting and labeling emotional expressions" (p. 47), and that "this form of modulation may be impaired in various emotional disorders and may provide the basis for therapies of these same disorders" (p. 48).

According to Emde (1990), the therapeutic context mobilizes in the patient a biologically prepared positive development thrust. The findings that the prefrontal limbic cortex, more than any other part of the cerebral cortex, retains the plastic capacities of early development (Barbas 1995) and that the right hemisphere cycles into growth phases throughout the lifespan (Thatcher 1994) allows for the possibility of changes in "mind and brain" (Gabbard 1994) in psychotherapy. Updated, psychobiologically oriented psychoanalytic treatment models may potentiate what Kandel (1998), in a clarion call for a paradigm shift in psychiatry, describes as "biology and the possibility of a renaissance of psychoanalytic thought."

A DYNAMIC SYSTEMS-THEORY PERSPECTIVE OF EMOTIONAL PROCESSES

I would also like to suggest that the psychobiological realm of affective phenomena represents not only a convergence point of psychoanalysis with neuroscience, but also with the trans-scientific perspective of nonlinear dynamic systems theory (e.g., Prigogine and Stengers 1984, Gleik 1987, Kaufmann 1993). The causal variables involved in affect and its regulation are notoriously dynamic; they may change rapidly over time in intensity and frequency in a nonlinear pattern. In a recent work Taylor and colleagues (1997) assert that ". . . linear models may be inappropriate for the study of affect regulation and state transitions. . . . [T]he study of affect regulation may be improved by utilizing concepts and ideas from chaos theory and non-linear dynamical modelling" (p. 270).

Nonlinear dynamic systems theory, which the Scharffs (1998) and others are now delivering into psychoanalysis, models the mechanism of self-organization, of how complex systems that undergo discontinuous changes come to produce both emergent new forms yet retain continuity. A central assumption of this theory is that energy flows are required for self-organizing processes. In a recent article on the self-organization of developmental paths, Lewis (1995) asks, "What is the best analogy for energy in psychological systems?" He points out that the energy flowthrough for self-organization has been conceived of as "information," an idea that fits well with Harold's (1986) formulation that information is a special kind of energy required for the work of establishing biological order. He then goes on to argue that information can be defined subjectively as that which is relevant to an individual's goals or needs, an idea which echoes recent concepts of emotion as adaptive functions that guide attention to the most relevant aspects of the environment, and of emotional appraisals that monitor and interpret events in order to determine their significance to the self. Lewis concludes that there is no better marker of such information than the emotion that accompanies it, that emotions amplify fluctuations to act in self-organization, and that the processing of relevant information in the presence of emotion may be analogous to the flowthrough of energy in a state of disequilibrium. Stability is a property of interpersonal attractors that maintain their organization by perpetuating equilibrium as well as resolving emotional disequilibrium.

A central tenet of dynamic systems theory holds that at particular critical moments, a flow of energy allows the components of a self-organizing system to become increasingly interconnected, and in this manner organismic form is constructed in developmental processes. As the patterns of relations among the components of a self-organizing system become increasingly interconnected and well ordered, it is more capable of maintaining a coherence of organization in relation to variations in the environment. In previous work I have proposed that emotional transactions involving synchronized ordered patterns of energy transmissions (directed flows of energy) represent the fundamental core of the attachment dynamic (Schore 1994, 2000c).

More specifically, in right brain-to-right brain emotion-transacting attachment communications, patterns of information emanating from the caregiver's face, especially of low visual and auditory frequencies (Ornstein 1997), trigger metabolic energy shifts in the infant. The caregiver is thus modulating changes in the child's energetic state, since arousal levels are known to be associated with changes in metabolic energy. A recent article in *Science* indicates that "mothers invest extra energy in their young to promote larger brains" (Gibbons 1998, p. 1347). Furthermore, these regulated emotional exchanges trigger synchronized energy shifts in the infant's developing right brain, and these allow for a coherence of activity within its cortical and subcortical levels and the organization of the emotion-processing right brain into a self-regulating "integrated whole." In this manner, "the self-organization of the developing brain occurs in the context of a relationship with another self, another brain" (Schore 1997b, 2000c).

This description of how early affective experience creates energy that, in turn, facilitates the organization of developing internal structure directly applies to psychoanalytic energetic metapsychological constructs, a body of knowledge that has been ignored or devalued over the last forty years. In very recent psychoanalytic writings, Schulman (1999) argues that energic "binding" is viewed as energy tied up in structures, and is therefore needed for "the transformation and structuralization of the ego" [and superego]. Energic concepts, he states, become the means for "new psychological developments" such as "ordered thoughts, goal-directed behavior, and controlled affect" (p. 480). Freud's energy models, long considered obsolete, need to be modernized and reintegrated into psychoanalysis (Schore 1994, 1997a, Solms 1996, Shevrin 1997).

Indeed, throughout the lifespan, energy shifts are the most basic and fundamental features of emotion, discontinuous states are experienced as affect responses, and nonlinear psychic bifurcations are manifest as rapid affective shifts. Such state transitions result from the activation of synchronized bioenergetic processes in central nervous system limbic circuits that are associated with concomitant homeostatic adjustments in the autonomic nervous system's energy-expending sympathetic and energy-conserving parasympathetic branches. Emotional mind–body states thus reflect the nonlinear pulsing of energy flows between the components of a self-organizing, dynamic, right-lateralized mind-body system. Furthermore, the fact that affectively-charged psychobiological states are known to be a product of the balance between energy-expending and energy-conserving components of the autonomic nervous system may be specifically relevant to Freud's emphasis on a *dynamic conception* of forces in the mind that work together or against one another in order to strive toward a goal.

A cardinal tenet of dynamic theory is that the nonlinear self acts iteratively, so that minor changes, occurring at the right moment, can be amplified in the system, launching it into a qualitatively different state. An example of this principle is found within the intersubjective field co-constructed by the patient and therapist. According to Kohut (1971) the empathically immersed clinician is attuned to the continuous flow and shifts in the patient's feelings and experiences.

The empathic clinician's right orbitofrontal cortex, a preconscious (Frank 1950) intrapsychic system activated by affective shifts and responsive to fluctuations in the emotional significance of stimuli (Dias et al. 1996), is responsible for his or her "oscillating attentiveness" (Schwaber 1995) to "barely perceptible cues that signal a change in state" in both patient and therapist (Sander 1992), and to "nonverbal behaviors and shifts in affects" (McLaughlin 1996). In line with the principle that affect acts as an "analog amplifier" that extends the duration of whatever activates it (Tomkins 1984), the clinician's resonance with the patient's psychobiological states allows for an amplification of affect within the intersubjective field.

This interactive regulation of the patient's state enables him or her to now begin to verbally label the affective experience. In a "genuine dialogue" with the therapist, the patient raises to an inner word and then into a spoken word what he needs to say at a particular moment but does not yet possess as speech. But the patient must experience this verbal description of how an internal state is heard and felt by an empathic other. This, in turn, facilitates the "evolution of affects from their early form, in which they are experienced as bodily sensations, into subjective states that can gradually be verbally articulated" (Stolorow and Atwood 1992, p. 42).

The patient's affectively charged but now regulated right brain experience can then be communicated to the left brain for further processing. This effect, which must follow a right-brain-then-left-brain temporal sequence, allows for the development of linguistic symbols to represent the meaning of an experience, *while one is feeling and perceiving the emotion generated by the experience*. The objective left hemisphere can now co-process subjective right brain communications, and this allows for a linkage of the nonverbal and verbal representational domains.

In addition, I have recently argued that as opposed to the verbal left hemisphere's "linear" consecutive analysis of information, the processing style of the visuospatial right hemisphere is best described as "nonlinear," based on multiple converging determinants rather than on a single causal chain (Schore 1997b, 2000c). According to Ramachandran and colleagues (1996), the cognitive style of the right hemisphere shows a highly sensitive dependence to initial conditions and perturbations, a fundamental property of chaotic systems. This minor hemisphere utilizes image thinking, a holistic, synthetic strategy that is adaptive when information is "complex, internally contradictory and basically irreducible to an unambiguous context" (Rotenberg 1994, p. 489). These characterizations also apply to primary process cognition, a right hemispheric function (Galin 1974, Joseph 1996) of the unconscious mind.

Current neurobiological studies are revealing greater right hemispheric involvement in the unconscious processing of emotion-evoking stimuli (Wexler et al. 1992) and conditioned autonomic responses after subliminal presentations of faces to the right and not left cortex (Johnsen and Hugdahl 1991). Most intriguingly, a very recent positron emission tomographic (PET) study demonstrates that unconscious processing of emotional stimuli is specifically associated with activation of the right and not left hemisphere (Morris et al., 1998), supporting the idea that "the left side is involved with conscious response and the right with the unconscious mind" (Mlot 1998, p. 1006). These, and the aforementioned studies, strongly suggest that the emotion-processing right mind (Ornstein 1997) is the neurobiological substrate of Freud's unconscious.

Freud's concept of the dynamic unconscious is usually interpreted to refer to the self-regulatory capacities of an unconscious system, which operates via the process of repression in order to bar access of sexual and aggressive wishes into consciousness. This characterization describes the left hemispheric horizontal inhibition of right hemispheric cognitive-emotional representations. The current expanding body of knowledge of the right hemisphere suggests a major alteration in the conceptualization of the Freudian unconscious, the internal structural system that processes information at nonconscious levels.

It is now established that "operation of the right prefrontal cortex is integral to autonomous regulation" (Ryan et al. 1997, p. 718), that the right hemisphere is dominant for the processing of "self-related material" (Keenan et al. 1999, 2001), and that the self concept is represented in right frontal areas (Craik et al. 1999). Freud's seminal model of a dynamic, continuously active unconscious mind thus describes the moment-to-moment operations of a hierarchical, self-organizing regulatory system that is located in the right brain. The center of psychic life thus shifts from Freud's *ego*, which he located in the "speech-area on the left-hand side" (1923) and the posterior areas of the verbal left hemisphere, to the highest levels of the nonverbal right hemisphere, the locus of the bodily-based *self* system (Craik et al.

1999, Devinsky 2000, Mesulam and Geschwind 1978, Schore 1994) and the unconscious mind (Joseph 1992).

Twenty-five years after the Project, Freud (1920) described the unconscious as "a special realm, with its own desires and modes of expression and peculiar mental mechanisms not elsewhere operative." In this same work he proclaimed "*the unconscious is the infantile mental life*" [italics in original]. Further studies of this early-developing right brain, unconscious, affectively charged, dynamic mind–body system are now called for.

REFERENCES

Adolphs, R., Damasio, H., Tranel, D., and Damasio, A. R. (1996). Cortical systems for the recognition of emotion in facial expressions. *Journal of Neuroscience* 23:7678–7687.

Anderson, A. K., and Phelps, E. A. (2000). Perceiving emotion: there's more than meets the eye. *Current Biology* 10:R551–R554.

Baker, S. C., Frith, C. D., and Dolan, R. J. (1997). The interaction between mood and cognitive function studied with PET. *Psychological Medicine* 27:565–578.

Barbas, H. (1995). Anatomic basis of cognitive-emotional interactions in the primate prefrontal cortex. *Neuroscience and Biobehavioral Reviews* 19:499–510.

Bechara, A., Damasio, A. R., Damasio, H., and Anderson, S. W. (1994). Insensitivity to future consequences following damage to human prefrontal cortex. *Cognition* 50:7–15.

Bechara, A., Damasio, H., Tranel, D., and Damasio, A. R. (1997). Deciding advantageously before knowing the advantageous strategy. *Science* 275:1293–1295.

Benowitz, L. I., Bear, D. M., Rosenthal, R., et al. (1983). Hemispheric specialization in nonverbal communication *Cortex* 19:5–11.

Blonder, L. X., Bowers, D., and Heilman, K. M. (1991). The role of the right hemisphere in emotional communication. *Brain* 114:1115–1127.

Blonder, L. X., Burns, A. F., Bowers, D., et al. (1995). Spontaneous gestures following right hemisphere infarct. *Neuropsychologia* 33:203–213.

Borod, J., Cicero, B. A., Obler, L. K., et al. (1998). Right hemisphere emotional perception: evidence across multiple channels. *Neuropsychology* 12:446–458.
Borod, J., Haywood, C. S., and Koff, E. (1997). Neuropsychological aspects of facial asymmetry during emotional expression: a review of the adult literature. *Neuropsychology Review* 7:41–60.
Bowlby, J. (1969). *Attachment*. London: Penguin.
Bradley, S. (2000). *Affect Regulation and the Development of Psychopathology*. New York: Guilford.
Brenner, C. (1980). A psychoanalytic theory of affects. In *Emotion: Theory, Research, and Experience, Vol. 1*, ed. R. Plutchik and H. Kellerman. New York: Academic Press.
Buchanan, T. W., Lutz, K., Mirzazade, S., et al. (2000). Recognition of emotional prosody and verbal components of spoken language: an fMRI study. *Cognitive Brain Research* 9:227–238.
Buck, R. (1994). The neuropsychology of communication: spontaneous and symbolic aspects. *Journal of Pragmatics* 22:265–278.
Cavada, C., and Schultz, W. (2000). The mysterious orbitofrontal cortex. Foreword. *Cerebral Cortex* 10:205.
Chiron, C., Jambaque, I., Nabbout, R., et al. The right brain hemisphere is dominant in human infants. *Brain* 120:1057–1065.
Craik, F. I. M., Moroz, T. M., Moscovitch, M., et al. (1999). In search of self: a positron emission tomography study. *Psychological Science* 10:26–34.
Cutting, J. (1992). The role of right hemisphere dysfunction in psychiatric disorders. *British Journal of Psychiatry* 160:583–588.
Damasio, A. R. (1994). *Descartes' Error*. New York: Grosset/Putnam.
Dimberg, U., and Petterson, M. (2000). Facial reactions to happy and angry facial expressions: evidence for right hemisphere dominance. *Psychophysiology* 37:693–696.
Derryberry, D., and Tucker, D. M. (1992). Neural mechanisms of emotion. *Journal of Clinical and Consulting Psychology* 60:329–338.
Deruelle, C., and de Schonen, S. (1998). Do the right and left hemispheres attend to the same visuospatial information within a face in infancy? *Developmental Neuropsychology* 14:535–554.
Devinsky, O. (2000). Right cerebral hemisphere dominance for a sense of corporeal and emotional self. *Epilepsy & Behavior* 1:60–73.

Dias, R., Robbins, T. W., and Roberts, A. C. (1996). Dissociation in prefrontal cortex of affective and attentional shifts. *Nature* 380:69–72.

Dolan, R. J. (1999). On the neurology of morals. *Nature Neuroscience* 2:927–929.

Eisenberg, L. (1995). The social construction of the human brain. *American Journal of Psychiatry* 152:1563–1575.

Elliott, R., Frith, C. D., and Dolan, R. J. (1997). Differential neural response to positive and negative feedback in planning and guessing tasks. *Neuropsychologia* 35:1395–1404.

Emde, R. N. (1990). Mobilizing fundamental modes of development: empathic availability and therapeutic action. *Journal of the American Psychoanalytic Association* 38:881–913.

Falk, D., Hildebolt, C., Cheverud, J., et al. (1990). Cortical asymmetries in frontal lobes of Rhesus monkeys (Macaca mulatta). *Brain Research* 512:40–45.

Feldman, R., Greenbaum, C. W., and Yirimiya, N. (1999). Mother–infant affect synchrony as an antecedent of the emergence of self-control. *Developmental Psychology* 35:223–231.

Fink, G. R., Markowitsch, H. J., Reinkemeier, M., et al. (1996). Cerebral representation of one's own past: neural networks involved in autobiographical memory. *Journal of Neuroscience* 16:4275–4282.

Frank, J. (1950). Some aspects of lobotomy (prefrontal leucotomy) under psycho-analytic scrutiny. *Psychiatry* 13:35–42.

Freud, S. (1895). Project for a scientific psychology. *Standard Edition* 1. London: Hogarth.

——— (1900). The interpretation of dreams. *Standard Edition* 4/5. London: Hogarth.

——— (1915a). The unconscious. *Standard Edition* 14. London: Hogarth. 1957.

——— (1915b). Instincts and their vicissitudes. *Standard Edition* 14. London: Hogarth.

——— (1920). A general introduction to psycho-analysis. *Standard Edition* 16. London: Hogarth.

——— (1923). The ego and the id. *Standard Edition* 19. London: Hogarth.

——— (1926). Inhibitions, symptoms and anxiety. *Standard Edition* 20. London: Hogarth.

——— (1940). An outline of psychoanalysis. *Standard Edition* 23. London: Hogarth.
Frijda, N. H. (1988). The laws of emotion. *Amerian Psychologist* 43:349–358.
Gabbard, G. O. (1994). Mind and brain in psychiatric treatment. *Bulletin of the Menninger Clinic* 58:427–446.
Galin, D. (1974). Implications for psychiatry of left and right cerebral specialization: A neurophysiological context for unconscious processes. *Archives of General Psychiatry* 31:572–583.
Garavan, H., Ross, T. J., and Stein, E. A. (1999). Right hemisphere dominance of inhibitory control: an event-related functional MRI study. *Proceedings of the National Academy of Sciences of the United States of America* 96:8301–8306.
Gazzaniga, M. S. (1985). *The Social Brain*. New York: Basic Books.
Gedo, J. E. (1979). *Beyond Interpretation*. New York: International Universities Press.
Gibbons, A. (1998). Solving the brain's energy crisis. *Science* 280:1345–1347.
Gleik, J. (1987). *Chaos: Making a New Science*. New York: Viking Penguin.
Goleman, D. (1995). *Emotional Intelligence*. New York: Bantam.
Greenberg, J. R., and Mitchell, S. A. (1983). *Object Relations in Psychoanalytic Theory*. Cambridge, MA: Harvard University Press.
Hariri, A. R., Bookheimer, S. Y., and Mazziotta, J. C. (2000). Modulating emotional responses: effects of a neocortical network on the limbic system. *NeuroReport* 11:43–48.
Harold, F. M. (1986). *The Vital Force: A Study of Bioenergetics*. New York: W.H. Freeman.
Hoppe, K. D. (1977). Split brains and psychoanalysis. *Psychoanalytic Quarterly* 46:220–244.
Hugdahl, K. (1995). Classical conditioning and implicit learning: the right hemisphere hypothesis. In *Brain Asymmetry*, ed. R. J. Davidson and K. Hugdahl, pp. 235–267. Cambridge, MA: MIT Press.
Jacobs, T. J. (1994). Nonverbal communications: some reflections on their role in the psychoanalytic process and psychoanalytic education. *Journal of the American Psychoanalytic Association* 42:741–762.

Johnsen, B. H., and Hugdahl, K. (1991). Hemispheric asymmetry in conditioning to facial emotional expressions. *Psychophysiology* 28:154–162.

Johnson, M. K., and Multhaup, K. S. (1992). Emotion and MEM. In *The Handbook of Emotion and Memory: Research and Theory*, ed. S-A. Christianson, pp. 33–66. Mahwah, NJ: Erlbaum.

Joseph, R. (1992). *The Right Brain and the Unconscious: Discovering the Stranger Within.* New York: Plenum.

——— (1996). *Neuropsychiatry, Neuropsychology, and Clinical Neuroscience, Second Ed.* Baltimore, MD: Williams & Wilkins.

Kandel, E. R. (1998). A new intellectual framework for psychiatry. *American Journal of Psychiatry* 155:457-469.

Kantrowitz, J. L. (1999). The role of the preconscious in psychoanalysis. *Journal of the American Psychoanalytic Association* 47:65–89.

Kaplan-Solms, K., and Solms, M. (1996). Psychoanalytic observations on a case of frontal-limbic disease. *Journal of Clinical Psychoanalysis* 5:405–438.

Kaufmann, S. A. (1993). *The Origins of Order: Self-organization and Selection in Evolution.* New York: Oxford University Press.

Keenan, J. P., McCutcheon, B., Freund, S., et al. (1999). Left hand advantage in a self-face recognition task. *Neuropsychologica* 37:1421–1425.

Keenan, J. P., Nelson, A., O'Connor, M., and Pascual-Leone, A. (2001). Self-recognition and the right hemisphere. *Nature* 409:305.

Kim, J. J., Andreasen, N. C., O'Leary, D. S., et al. (1999). Direct comparison of the neural substrates of recognition memory for words and faces. *Brain* 122:1069–1083.

Kohut, H. (1971). *The Analysis of the Self.* New York: International Universities Press.

Kutas, M., and Federmeier, K. D. (1998). Minding the body. *Psychophysiology* 35:135–150.

Lazarus, R. S. (1991). Progress on a cognitive-motivational-relational theory of emotion. *American Psychologist* 46:819–834.

Ledoux, J. E. (1989). Cognitive-emotional interactions in the brain. *Cognition and Emotion* 3:267–289.

Lewis, M. D. (1995). Cognition-emotion feedback and the self-organization of developmental paths. *Human Development* 38:71–102.

Marcus, D. M. (1997). On knowing what one knows. *Psychoanalytic Quarterly* 66:219–241.

McLaughlin, J. T. (1978). Primary and secondary processes in the context of cerebral hemispheric specialization. *Psychoanalytic Quarterly* 47:237–266.

——— (1996). Power, authority, and influence in the analytic dyad. *Psychoanalytic Quarterly* 63:201–235.

Mesulam, M.-M. (1990). Large-scale neurocognitive networks and distributed processing for attention, language, and memory. [Review]. *Annals of Neurology* 28:597–613.

——— (1998). From sensation to cognition. *Brain* 121:1013–1052.

Mesulam, M.-M., and Geschwind, N. (1978). On the possible role of neocortex and its limbic connections in the process of attention in schizophrenia: clinical cases of inattention in man and experimental anatomy in monkey. *Journal of Psychiatric Research* 14:249–259.

Mlot, C. (1998). Probing the biology of emotion. *Science* 280:1005–1007.

Morris, J. S., Ohman, A., and Dolan, R. J. (1998). Conscious and unconscious emotional learning in the human amygdala. *Nature* 393:467–470.

Nakamura, K., Kawashima, R., Ito, K., et al. (1999). Activation of the right inferior frontal cortex during assessment of facial emotion. *Journal of Neurophysiology* 82:1610–1614.

Neafsey, E. J. (1990). Prefrontal cortical control of the autonomic nervous system: anatomical and physiological observations. *Progress in Brain Research* 85:147–166.

Ornstein, R. (1997). *The Right Mind: Making Sense of the Hemispheres.* New York: Harcourt Brace.

Panksepp, J. (1999). Emotions as viewed by psychoanalysis and neuroscience: an exercise in consilience. *Neuro-Psychoanalysis* 1:15–38.

Pizzagalli, D., Regard, M., and Lehmann, D. (1999). Rapid emotional face processing in the human right and left brain hemispheres: an ERP study. *NeuroReport* 10:2691–2698.

Porges, S. W., Doussard-Roosevelt, J. A., and Maiti, A. K. (1994). Vagal tone and the physiological regulation of emotion. *Monographs of the Society for Research in Child Development* 59:167–186.

Price, J. L., Carmichael, S. T., and Drevets, W. C. (1996). Networks related to the orbital and medial prefrontal cortex: a substrate for emotional behavior? *Progress in Brain Research* 107:523–536.

Prigogine, I., and Stengers, I. (1984). *Order out of Chaos*. New York: Bantam

Ramachandran, V. S., Levi, L., Stone, L., et al. (1996). Illusions of body image: what they reveal about human nature. In *The Mind-Brain Continuum: Sensory Processes*, ed. R. Llinas and P. S. Churchland, pp. 29–60. Cambridge, MA: MIT Press.

Rolls, E. T. (1986). Neural systems involved in emotion in primates. In *Emotion: Theory, Research, and Practice*, Vol. 3, ed. R. Plutchik and H. Kellerman, pp. 125–143. Orlando, FL: Academic Press.

—— (1996). The orbitofrontal cortex. *Philosophical Transactions of the Royal Society of London Bulletin* 351:1433–1444.

Rolls, E. T., Hornak, J., Wade D., and McGrath, J. (1994). Emotion-related learning in patients with social and emotional changes associated with frontal lobe damage. *Journal of Neurology, Neurosurgery, and Psychiatry* 57:1518–1524.

Ross, E. D., Homan, R. W., and Buck, R. (1994). Differential hemispheric lateralization of primary and social emotions: Implications for developing a comprehensive neurology for emotions, repression, and the subconscious. *Neuropsychiatry, Neuropsychology, and Behavioral Neurology* 7:1–19.

Rotenberg, V. S. (1994). An integrative psychobiological approach to brain hemisphere functions in schizophrenia. *Neuroscience and Biobehavioral Reviews* 18:487–495.

Ryan, R. M., Kuhl, J., and Deci, E. L. (1997). Nature and autonomy: an organizational view of social and neurobiological aspects of self-regulation in behavior and development. *Development and Psychopathology* 9:701–728.

Sander, L. W. (1977). Regulation of exchange in the infant caretaker system: a viewpoint on the ontogeny of structures. In *Communicative Structures and Psychic Structures*, ed. N. Freedman and S. Grand, pp. 13–34. New York: Plenum.

—— (1992). Letter to the editor. *International Journal of Psycho-Analysis* 73:582–584.

Sandler, J., and Sandler, A.-M. (1978). On the development of object relationships and affects. *International Journal of Psycho-Analysis* 59:285–296.

Scalaidhe, S. P., Wilson, F.A.W., and Goldman-Rakic, P. S. (1997). Areal segregation of face-processing neurons in prefrontal cortex. *Science* 278:1135–1138.

Scharff, J. S., and Scharff, D. E. (1998). *Object Relations Individual Therapy*. Northvale, NJ: Jason Aronson.

Schore, A. N. (1994). *Affect Regulation and the Origin of the Self: The Neurobiology of Emotional Development*. Mahwah, NJ: Erlbaum.

―――― (1996). The experience-dependent maturation of a regulatory system in the orbital prefrontal cortex and the origin of developmental psychopathology. *Development and Psychopathology* 8:59–87.

―――― (1997a). A century after Freud's Project: is a rapprochement between psychoanalysis and neurobiology at hand? *Journal of the American Psychoanalytic Association* 45:841–867.

―――― (1997b). Early organization of the nonlinear right brain and development of a predisposition to psychiatric disorders. *Development and Psychopathology* 9:595–631.

―――― (1997c). Interdisciplinary developmental research as a source of clinical models. In *The Neurobiological and Developmental Basis for Psychotherapeutic Intervention*, ed. M. Moskowitz, C. Monk, C. Kaye, and S. Ellman, pp. 1–71. Northvale, NJ: Jason Aronson.

―――― (1998). The experience-dependent maturation of an evaluative system in the cortex. In *Brain and Values: Is a Biological Science of Values Possible?*, ed. K. Pribram, pp. 337–358. Mahwah, NJ: Erlbaum.

―――― (1999). Commentary on emotions: neuro-psychoanalytic views. *Neuro-Psychoanalysis* 1:49–55.

―――― (2000a). Foreword to the reissue of *Attachment and Loss, Vol. 1: Attachment* by John Bowlby. New York: Basic Books.

―――― (2000b). Attachment and the regulation of the right brain. *Attachment & Human Development* 2:22–41.

―――― (2000c). The self-organization of the right brain and the neurobiology of emotional development. In *Emotion, Development, and Self-Organization*, ed. M. D. Lewis and I. Granic, pp. 155–185. New York: Cambridge University Press.

―――― (2001a). The effects of a secure attachment relationship on right brain development, affect regulation, and infant mental health. *Infant Mental Health Journal* 22:7–66.

―――― (2001b). The effects of relational trauma on right brain development, affect regulation, and infant mental health. *Infant Mental Health Journal* 22:201–269.

——— (2001c). The Seventh Annual John Bowlby Memorial Lecture: Attachment, the developing brain, and psychotherapy. *British Journal of Psychotherapy* 17:299–328.

——— (2001d). Plenary address: Parent–infant communications and the neurobiology of emotional development. In *Proceedings of Head Start's Fifth National Research Conference, Developmental and Contextual Transitions of Children and Families, Implications for Research, Policy, and Practice*, pp. 49–73.

——— (in press a). Clinical implications of a psychoneurobiological model of projective identification. In *Primitive Mental States, Vol. II: Pre- and Peri-natal Influences on Personality Development*, ed. S. Alhanati. New York: Other Press.

Schulman, M. A. (1999). Book review of *Freud's Model of the Mind*, by J. Sandler, A. Holder, C. Dare, and A. U. Dreher. *Psychoanalytic Psychology* 16:477–480.

Schwaber, E. A. (1995). A particular perspective on impasses in the clinical situation: further reflections on psychoanalytic listening. *International Journal of Psycho-Analysis* 76:711–722.

Shevrin, H. (1997). Psychoanalysis as the patient: high in feeling, low in energy. *Journal of the American Psychoanalytic Association* 45:841–867.

Solms, M. (1996). Towards an anatomy of the unconscious. *Journal of Clinical Psychoanalysis* 5:331–367.

Solms, M., and Nersessian, E. (1999). Freud's theory of affect: questions for neuroscience. *Neuro-Psychoanalysis* 1:5–14.

Spence, S., Shapiro, D., and Zaidel, E. (1996). The role of the right hemisphere in the physiological and cognitive components of emotional processing. *Psychophysiology* 33:112–122.

Sroufe, L. A. (1996). *Emotional Development: The Organization of Emotional Life in the Early Years*. New York: Cambridge University Press.

Starkstein, S. E., and Robinson, R. G. (1997). Mechanism of disinhibition after brain lesions. *Journal of Nervous and Mental Disease* 185:108–114.

Stern, D. N., Nahum, J. P., Sander, L., and Tronick, E. Z. (1998). The process of therapeutic change involving implicit knowledge:

some implications of developmental observations for adult psychotherapy. *Infant Mental Health Journal* 19:300–308.

Stolorow, R. D., and Atwood, G. E. (1992). *Contexts of Being: The Intersubjective Foundations of Psychological Life*. Hillsdale, NJ: Analytic Press.

Sturm, W., de Simone, A., Krause, B. J., et al. (1999). Functional anatomy of intrinsic alertness: evidence for a fronto-parietal-thalamic-brainstem network in the right hemisphere. *Neuropsychologia* 37:797–805.

Taylor, G. J., Bagby, R. M., and Parker, J.D.A. (1997). *Disorders of Affect Regulation: Alexithymia in Medical and Psychiatric Illness*. Cambridge, UK: Cambridge University Press.

Teasdale, J. D., Howard, R. J., Cox, S. G., et al. (1999). Functional MRI study of the cognitive generation of affect. *American Journal of Psychiatry* 156:209–215.

Thatcher, R. W. (1994). Cyclical cortical reorganization: origins of human cognitive development. In *Human Behavior and the Developing Brain*, ed. G. Dawson and K. W. Fischer, pp. 232–266. New York: Guilford.

Tomkins, S. (1984). Affect theory. In *Approaches to Emotion*, ed. P. Ekman. Mahwah, NJ: Erlbaum.

Tremblay, L., and Schultz, W. (1999). Relative reward preference in primate orbitofrontal cortex. *Nature* 398:704–708.

Trevarthen, C. (1990). Growth and education of the hemispheres. In *Brain Circuits and Functions of the Mind*, ed. C. Trevarthen, pp. 334–363. Cambridge, UK: Cambridge University Press.

——— (1993). The self born in intersubjectivity: the psychology of an infant communicating. In *The Perceived Self: Ecological and Interpersonal Sources of Self-knowledge*, ed. U. Neisser, pp. 121–173. New York: Cambridge University Press.

Tucker, D. M. (1992). Developing emotions and cortical networks. In *Minnesota Symposium on Child Psychology, Vol. 24: Developmental Behavioral Neuroscience*, ed. M. R. Gunnar and C. A. Nelson, pp. 75–128. Mahwah, NJ: Erlbaum.

Wasserstein, J., and Stefanos, G. A. (2000). The right hemisphere and psychopathology. *Journal of the American Academy of Psychoanalysis* 28:371–394.

Watt, D. F. (1998). Affect and the limbic system: some hard problems. *Journal of Neuropsychiatry* 10:113–116.

Weinberg, I. (2000). The prisoners of despair: right hemisphere deficiency and suicide. *Neuroscience and Biobehavioral Reviews* 24:799–815.

Westen, D. (1997). Towards a clinically and empirically sound theory of motivation. *International Journal of Psycho-Analysis* 78:521–548.

Wexler, B. E., Warrenburg, S., Schwartz, G. E., and Janer, L. D. (1992). EEG and EMG responses to emotion-evoking stimuli processed without conscious awareness. *Neuropsychologia* 30:1065–1079.

Winson, J. (1990). The meaning of dreams. *Scientific American*, November, pp. 86–96.

Wittling, W. (1997). The right hemisphere and the human stress response. *Acta Psysiologica Scandinavica*, Supplement 640:55–59.

Wittling, W., and Pfluger, M. (1990). Neuroendocrine hemisphere asymmetries: salivary cortisol secretion during lateralized viewing of emotion-related and neutral films. *Brain and Cognition* 14:243–265.

Wittling, W., and Roschmann, R. (1993). Emotion-related hemisphere asymmetry: subjective emotional responses to laterally presented films. *Cortex* 29:431–448.

Wittling, W., and Schweiger, E. (1993). Neuroendocrine brain asymmetry and physical complaints. *Neuropsychologia* 31:591–608.

5

Modern Revisions of Freud's Concept of Transference

Steven Ellman

It is my reading of Freud that up to a certain point in his career we might see his development as prototypic of many elements in psychoanalytic theory and practice (Ellman 1991). In addition his clinical concepts are a good reflection of the struggles he endured while creating both a theory of mind and a theory of treatment. Given these assumptions, it may be that the understanding of the development of his clinical concepts may shed some light on current controversies in contemporary psychoanalysis. Today I will look at the fate of two of Freud's ideas on transference and try to show their relevance to contemporary analysts. The two concepts are transference as memory or action, and the "unobjectionable positive transference." It is my view that the recent literature on enactments is in part a growing realization that it is a difficult task for the analyst to maintain what I have called narcissistic equilibrium in the face of intense transference-countertransference sequences. I believe that each current theoretical perspective has characteristic ways of deflecting transference reactions while allowing enactments to continue outside of the analytic process. Freud's struggles with transference manifestations were not unique to him, but were rather prototypic struggles of an analyst attempting to survive situations beyond his comprehension.

FREUD'S VISION[1]

Freud was at the height of his career as an analyst during the period of 1905 through 1914. Before that time (1890–1905) his efforts were devoted almost solely to the uncovering of pathogenic memories. Transference (up to the postscript to the Dora case (1905)) was considered to be an obstacle in his hypnotic or psychotherapeutic procedure (1895). Later, in the 1920s and 30s, he no longer practiced as an analyst. It is a sign of the religious devotion of psychoanalysts that Kanzer (1980) could say that at the end of his career Freud was evolving into a contemporary psychoanalyst. At the end of his career Freud's practice consisted largely of intellectual discussions and quasi training analyses. In these analyses he was frequently blatantly disregarding some of the strictures that he thought were necessary for an analytic process to unfold (Ellman 1991).

My use of the term "unfold" is anachronistic, since Freud had only a glimpse of analysis as an unfolding process. This was in *Repetition, Recollection and Working Through* (1914a). There he sounds almost Winnicottian, he is inviting, even facilitating in his tone, he seems at home with the clinical manifestations of transference. But I am getting ahead of myself, for I wish to go back in Freud's career and try to look at some of the difficulties in Freud's conceiving of the importance of transference. We know there was a point in his career when he distinguished between psychogenic and actual neuroses. From 1894 to 1896 he was in the midst of conceiving both forms of neurosis in terms of accumulated libido (Stewart 1969). In the psychogenic neurosis the accumulation could be conceived of as a vulnerability caused by the patient being sexually overstimulated or traumatized as a child. This stimulation (usually by a parent) excited

---

1. In the historical review I provide documentation for my contentions in *Freud's Technique Papers: A Contemporary Perspective* (1991). London: Allen & Unwin.

the child, but owing to sexual immaturity there was excitement without the possibility of discharge. This made children vulnerable as adults to stimulation and the accumulation of excess (undischarged) libido. The actual neurosis, on the other hand, was caused by sexual practices of adult patients. "Coitus reservatus," for example, could lead to anxiety neurosis, excessive masturbation led to neurasthenia, and so forth. How did Freud arrive at conclusions that today seem so foreign to our ears. I want to offer a partial explanation of how a theorist with such literary sensibilities could be so blatantly mechanistic.[2]

We must remember this is before Freud had fully developed his concepts of the importance of unconscious motivation and universal childhood sexuality. But at this point in time Freud relies heavily on the idea of undischarged excitation (Stewart 1969). Freud will leave these concepts, but it will take him a surprisingly long time to leave the idea of the actual neuroses.[3] In fact, when he develops the concept of narcissism (1914b), he purposes another category of actual disorders, an actual narcissistic state, that is hypochondria. Freud maintains that:

> I am inclined to class hypochondria with neurasthenia and anxiety-neurosis as a third "actual" neurosis. It would probably not be going too far to suppose that in the case of the other neuroses a small amount of hypochondria was regularly formed at the same time as well. [p. 83]

That Freud has even posited the category of actual neurosis is an issue that still is not completely explained, but it may be that we get important clues to Freud's difficulties[4] if we consider the concept of an actual hypochondriacal state. I posit that he sees the hypochondriacal patient as an actual disorder (there is an increase of libido in a particular part of the body) because he is unable to understand his experience of the transference while interacting with hypochondriacal

---

2. See Stewart's *The First Ten Years: 1888–1898* (1969) for what I consider to be the most definitive account of this era of Freud's career.

3. Not until *Inhibitions, Symptoms and Anxiety* (1926) does Freud renounce the idea of actual disorders in writing.

4. I am anachronistically considering the concept of actual disorders a difficulty. It can be considered a difficulty in the sense that Freud eventually disavowed the concept (1926) and that most modern analysts no longer find the concept useful in their clinical conceptualizations.

patients. They come to him and talk about their pains or somatic concerns, and he feels left out of their object world. Freud virtually tells us that without the beginnings of a positive transference relationship, he is not able to experience a connection with a patient (1912b). Without this experience, he casts them out of the analytic world; by labeling them an actual disorder, he maintains that they are untreatable in terms of psychological methods. He attempts to perform a similar excision with psychogenic narcissists or patients who have intense negative transference states; he maintains that they are not analyzable. He postulates that narcissistic patients have little object libido, cannot form transference relationships, and are thus unanalyzable (1916). They are analytic exiles bound to wander the byways and offices of the psychotherapist. My hypothesis is that patients diagnosed as actual neurotics (in the 1890s) were primarily types of narcissistic or borderline disorder. These patients did not provide Freud with a transference love relationship, and were thus relegated to the position of receiving advice about their sexual life.[5] We see that Freud is not unlike a number of present-day analysts; it is difficult in general to tolerate the patient who does not include us in their object world, particularly if the patient is noncompliant. He had particular difficulty if the patients were skeptical about psychoanalysis.

Earlier, I maintained that Freud for a period of time began to understand the centrality of transference. I cited *Repetition, Recollection and Working Through*, but in his paper "On Transference Love" he also shows his insights into the emergence of transference. Here he provides warnings to analysts about some of the dangers of acting out (enacting) transference-countertransference sequences. This warning demonstrates he has experienced and recognized the intensity of transference (and countertransference) reactions. He has seen that transference can have a compelling impact on the analyst and at times stimulate the analyst to act in a manner that is out of control—and perhaps irreversible—in an analytic treatment.

---

5. This clearly is only one aspect of Freud's response to these patients. We know that Freud treated severely disturbed patients such as the Wolf Man, and that if a patient could engage intellectually (the Rat Man), then he underdiagnosed such a patient. It is also my view that Kohut is correct in some of his corrections of Freud's views on narcissism. Freud, in some instances, is not consistent in his ideas on technique with his own view of narcissism (Ellman 1991).

Modern Revisions of Freud's Concept of Transference / 93

One main way of understanding the competing schools of analysis is to see how they have transformed, extended, or at times truncated the idea of transference. Before I go to that I will summarize what I believe to be Freud's most complete vision of how to utilize the transference in the analytic situation.

Freud (1914) tells us that:

> The main instrument . . . for curbing the patient's compulsion to repeat . . . is the transference. We render the compulsion harmless, and indeed useful, by giving it the right to assert itself in a definite field. We admit it into the transference as a playground in which it is allowed to expand in almost complete freedom and in which it is expected to display to us everything . . . that is hidden in the patient's mind. [Cited in Ellman 1991, pp. 60–61]

How do we facilitate a definite field in which this can occur? Here Freud says that "We must allow the patient to become attached to the analyst (physician) before we can interpret the transference." Then when "We have made it clear to ourselves that the patient's state of being ill cannot cease with the beginning of his analysis," than we must wait until the transference develops and treat the person's conflicts, "not as an event of the past, but as a present-day conflict." Transference thus "creates an intermediate region between illness and real life through which the transition from one to the other is made." Let me add some additional quotes of Freud: "The negative transference deserves a detailed examination, which it cannot be given within the limits of the present paper." As we know, this detailed examination never took place. If we summarize these quotes (1912–1915), we can say that Freud did not believe that transference could be interpreted before an attachment was made to the person of the analyst (physician). He did not believe that the patient could accept an interpretation before a transference love relationship was initiated. He came to accept (for a short time) the transference as not simply a resistance, but rather as the thing itself, in fact the only thing where "a patient arrives at a sense of conviction of the validity of the connections which have been constructed during the analysis." He does tell us, prophetically, that dealing with the transference "happens, however, to be by far the hardest part of the whole analytic task." Here I would agree with Freud. A good part of the analytic world has been struggling with the practice and concept of transference since he wrote these words in his postscript to the Dora case. However, I would disagree with Freud when he says, "Practical experience, at all events shows conclusively that there is no means of avoiding it (transference)" (1905, p. 116). He, as well as contemporary analysts, have shown that there are a variety of means of avoiding, suppressing, and overlooking the transference. Let me give some examples.

CONTEMPORARY ANALYSTS[6]

Gill

Gill, in his conceptualization of the here-and-now transference, starts with the idea that analysts have underestimated the extent to which there are transference manifestations in the treatment situation. Gill conceives of transference as ubiquitously present from the beginning to the end of a treatment. In his view transference should be interpreted from the beginning, and throughout the course of the treatment. To my mind, here is an example of an analyst who correctly criticizes an aspect of practice, and then truncates Freud's vision. For once he recognizes the ubiquitous nature of transference he does not allow the patient to develop consistent repeated reactions to the analyst without immediately intervening and offering interpretations.

I will cite a brief clinical illustration taken from Gill's taped sessions:

> A woman patient is dressed in a T-shirt. Gill begins the session by asking the patient "What is the writing on your T-shirt?" [Coney Island or Bust.] This is done before the patient has sat down or said anything. The rest of the session is spent detailing and interpreting the patient's seductive, provocative transference state. Let us assume that Gill is correct in his understanding of the patient's behavior. Can the patient gain a sense of conviction in the treatment if the analyst is so consis-

---

6. These sections on Gill, Brenner, and Kohut are taken from Ellman 1991.

tently providing interpretations?[7] Does the patient feel invited into the playground of transference given Gill's stance? In this example and in others, Gill does not tolerate the unfolding of the transference; instead he stimulates and at times provokes the patient to respond to him. He correctly states that transference is a ubiquitous experience, but he can't allow it to develop. He creates a relationship in analysis where he proves that all of analysis is an interaction between analyst and patient. He correctly criticizes Freud for not persisting in his insights about transference but he rejects Freud's depiction of the playful (in Winnicott's sense) and illusory quality of transference experience of psychoanalysis.

Brenner

There are interesting parallels between Gill and Brenner. They are in agreement in some ways in their handling of the transference. Both interpret transference early in the treatment. Neither analyst distinguishes between the transference and the transference neurosis. Brenner advocates interpreting whenever an unconscious derivative appears, regardless of how often this element may emerge. Brenner seems to imply that the repeating of an interpretation will have a cumulative effect.

Although Brenner and Gill address transference in a systematic manner, they do so in a way that in my view is highly dependent on the patient accepting the analyst as the authority (the interpreter). It is difficult to see how the analysand will gain conviction through the transference if the analyst is interjecting and penetrating with interpretative efforts. It may be that neither analyst sees phenomena like the transference neurosis because of iatrogenic factors in their treatment approach. Early and frequent interpretations may not allow for the type of intense, cohesive transference reactions that are described in continuous states that have been labeled "transference neurosis."

---

7. Perhaps the patient was attempting to be seductive but felt deeply ashamed of the fact that this was her only mode of relating and was focusing more on her sense of shame and emptiness than on the seductive behavior. Perhaps the last session had induced some change, and so forth.

Kohut

Kohut is perhaps the only analyst I will mention (I have not included B. Bird) [1972], who allows the transference to unfold and be experienced over a period of time without interpretation. Kohut (1968, 1977), on the other hand, allows either mirroring or idealizing (or bipolar self) transference states to continue until there is a perceived (on the patient's part) break in empathy. One might say it is as if all transference is unobjectionable (I am referring to Freud's concept), according to Kohut. The implications of handling transference in this manner are two-fold: defensive tendencies are reinforced, and the patient is not helped to explore active fantasies, particularly active fantasies that have aggressive content. Kohut has provided an invitation to the playground but he is only willing to watch, not interact in, the illusory play. At crucial points in the manifestation of transference Kohut turns a two-person back into a one-person field. In his terminology it is as if the only developmental processes have to do with mirroring and lending oneself to idealization.

RELATIONAL ANALYSIS

Up to this point in the paper I have tried to show how aspects of Freudian thought have been clarified, transformed, and truncated by contemporary analysts. Nowhere do these tendencies seem to be more pronounced than with authors who derive their inspiration from a relational orientation. To demonstrate this I will look at a distinction that Greenberg (1993) has recently introduced and relate this distinction to the other parts of the present paper.

In highlighting these distinctions Greenberg relates: "In his highly technical language Freud is telling us that we can become conscious of something when we can name it." Greenberg emphasizes that for Freud "the cure awaits the word."

Greenberg continues:

> It will help us to look at this view of therapeutic action from a contemporary perspective if we realize that, for Freud, actions are things. The work of analysis is to move the patient beyond the act or repetition (in the transference), which is a thing, to the memory, which is a

word. . . . The development of mind itself depends upon restraining drive discharge. The reality principle gets established when thinking (which depends upon the ability to use the word) replaces impulsive discharge (the action, which is a thing that cannot be delayed because it has not been symbolized). [pp. 5–6]

Greenberg takes the distinction he has derived from Freud and then characterizes Freud's ideas on technique as requiring restraint on the part of the analyst and patient. "The patient is pledged to try to follow the fundamental rule, which requires saying rather than doing." The patient pledges restraint by promising not to make decisions during the analysis and Freud is in favor of "avoiding action in favor of the word." However, "Our broader experience with the psychoanalytic process allows us to see clearly what Freud initially overlooked: words do not restrain or substitute for action; they *are* actions." This applies equally to patient and analyst. Free association is an action and is not necessarily "a phylogenetically fixed higher way of being." Freud therefore fails to see that there are continuous interactions between analyst and analysand.

Greenberg concludes that "Freud's early model of the mind has stifled discussion about what actually goes on in analysis. . . . Neutrality or the blank screen or reflecting mirror" are all myths that attempt to camouflage the fact that all that the analyst does involves action.

Let me start with a relatively small point and yet to me it seems glaring. Dr. Greenberg writes as if affect didn't exist in Freud's ideas on technique. He takes one dichotomy—the thing and the word representation—and from this derives that for Freud the cure awaits the appropriate words. But Freud's treatment method always involved not just in the word, but in the affect and the representation being brought together. From *Studies on Hysteria* (1895) onward, Freud continuously intoned against memories, fantasies, and experiences that were only intellectual. This was true when he used the cathartic, and later, the psychotherapeutic or the analytic method. What Freud discovered in the transference was that the feeling or the desire is conveyed most directly via the transference. It is no wonder that his interest in the topic fluctuated throughout his career. But while he was interested in the topic between 1905 and 1915, he assumed that transference is the vehicle that fuels the analysis. It is the vehicle through which the language of desire and emotion is communicated. Thus the transference is not simply a recapturing of words, but the vehicle through which affect is expressed and united with representations.

By leaving out affect, Greenberg can more easily dichotomize Freud's ideas. He can see Freud's technique as a translation into words while attempting to restrict or limit actions. Although Freud at times undoubtedly attempted to restrict the activity of his patients, it is only the classical tradition in the United States that made this a matter of technique. Greenberg can make his statements about Freud since for many relational analysts there is so much interaction via disclosure and other means that manifestations of the transference are frequently lost. It is the interaction that becomes the focus rather then the transference. This position is more extreme if one actualizes an "intersubjective" position, which I will not detail here.

ANALYTIC TRUST

If we go back to Freud's original requirements for interpretation, he says that the patient must first become attached to the person of the analyst before he/she is in a position to interpret. Freud's conceptualization of this attachment had two components; what he called the unobjectionable transference from the patient, and the natural generally kindly behavior of the analyst towards his patients. I will not discuss his behavior at this point. But the "unobjectionable transference" was a component of Freud's method of attempting to influence patients based on the authority of the analyst. The concept of the unobjectionable transference was attacked from all sides. Classical analysts maintained that it affected neutrality and that all transference should be analyzed. Critics included the unobjectionable transference as part of the Freudian authoritarian stance towards patients. I maintain that both groups were correct in their criticisms. They however did not address the question that Freud raised: Why should a patient trust the analyst and continue in treatment particularly when difficult material arises? Freud's answer was that the unobjectionable transference allows patients to continue because of their respect for, fear of, or general compliance with the implicit voice of authority. Later analysts (Greenson 1965, Zetzel 1966, Stone 1967) answered this question with the concept of the therapeutic or working alliance. Greenson says:

> The reliable core of the working alliance is formed by the patient's motivation to overcome his illness, his conscious and rational willingness to cooperate, and his ability to follow the instructions and insights of his analyst. The actual alliance is formed essentially between the patient's reasonable ego and the analyst's analyzing ego. The patient is willing to cooperate with the analyst's instructions and maintain an effective working relationship with the analyst. [p. 162]

Brenner has criticized the therapeutic, or working alliance, on the same basis as the unobjectionable transference. That is the working alliance is the use of transference to attempt to influence the patient's behavior rather than analyzing the patient's transference reactions. Even as benign a concept as the alliance can be seen as using the analyst's authority to influence the patient (Hoffman 1996). Nevertheless, Greenson, Stone, and Zetzel were striving to answer the question that Freud posed. I have tried to answer this question and my answer is based on writings over the last thirty years that in my mind—not necessarily in agreement with the authors I cite—has led to specifying the conditions under which transference becomes interpretable. To be more specific, it is a way of looking at the conditions under which a patient can come to trust an analyst, based not on the analyst's instructions or identifying with the analyst, but rather on the patient's experience of the analytic situation which obviously includes the analyst's behavior.

I am positing that what I have labeled as "analytic trust" is the necessary condition during which transference becomes interpretable in the analytic situation. I define analytic trust as the continuing sense between analyst and patient that the analyst is able to feel and process the patient's experiences in a meaningful manner. At the beginning of treatment this may mean reflecting back and providing new syntheses of the patient's conscious but often suppressed experiences. It also entails being able to contain and not necessarily interpret frustrating and destructive fantasies that the patients provide and perhaps fill the room with. That fills both analyst and analysand. As the analysis continues and the patient is able to develop more continuous transference experiences, analytic trust is renewed by the patients being able to see their internal worlds in a deepened and new light. The analyst's interpretive efforts are only one way to achieve insight. In an optimal therapeutic relationship, interpretations by both analysand and analyst are joined. A crucial aspect of this trust is the analyst as container. The analyst is able to receive the patient's actions without malevolently returning the patient's conscious and unconscious messages. Although I doubt that any analyst would deny that enactments by both patient and analyst are continuous and necessary occurrences, I would maintain that if the patient does not trust in the analyst's ability to contain, control, and eventually observe their enactments, then the analytic process can be irreversibly damaged. An important aspect of both the issue of containment and enactment are the limits and boundaries of these experiences.

To come back to shifts in transference states: I have seen, for example, analyst's reacting in a surprised manner when a patient who has come to meet the analyst, once again views them with suspicion or distrust. From my perspective this is not always—or perhaps even usually—the other side of a split. Rather it is frequently a sign of different transference material arising in a new phase of the treatment. If it is recognized as such (or at least if the possibility is recognized) then some aspects of the beginning phase of treatment may have to be repeated briefly. To be sure this happens more dramatically with patients who utilize splitting and projective identification as significant defensive structures, but to some extent I believe that this occurs in all treatments. In some treatments it may happen to such a minor extent that it will go largely unnoticed or be seen as a bad day for one or another reason. This it seems to me is the relatively rare case in today's analytic world. Most times, if the transition is missed, either the patient is disrupted or has to present an aspect of his false self in other parts of the analysis.

Let me conclude by stating that analytic trust is an answer to Freud's question, "Why should a patient trust the analyst?" It is an attempt to take in the criticisms of contemporary analysts while not truncating Freud's concepts. Trust develops when there is a shared experience of understanding, first in the conscious but often suppressed aspects of the mind, and later through understanding how the unconscious world has influenced patients' lives more thoroughly than one could have imagined before Freud offered us his revolutionary vision.

REFERENCES

Bird, B. (1972). Notes on transference: universal phenomenon and hardest part of analysis. *Journal of the American Psychoanalytic Association* 20:267–301.

——— (1973). *Talking with Patients*. 2nd Ed. Philadelphia: J. B. Lippincott.

Brenner, C. (1976). *Psychoanalytic Technique and Psychic Conflict*. New York: International Universities Press.

——— (1979). Working alliance, therapeutic alliance, and transference. *Journal of the American Psychoanalytic Association* 27:137–158.

——— (1981). Defense and defense mechanisms. *Psychoanalytic Quarterly* 50:557–569.

——— (1982). *The Mind in Conflict*. New York: International Universities Press.

Breuer, J. and Freud, S. (1895). Studies on hysteria. *Standard Edition* 2.

Ellman, S. J. (1991). *Freud's Technique Papers: A Contemporary Perspective*. Northvale, NJ and London: Jason Aronson.

Freud, S. (1905). Fragment of an analysis of a case of hysteria. *Standard Edition* 7.

——— (1912a). The employment of dream-interpretation in psychoanalysis. *Collected Papers, Volume 2*. New York: Basic Books, 1959.

——— (1912b). Recommendations to physicians on the psychoanalytic method of treatment. *Collected Papers, Volume 2*. New York: Basic Books, 1959.

——— (1913). Further recommendations in the technique of psychoanalysis—on beginning the treatment. In *Collected Papers, Volume 2*. New York: Basic Books, 1959.

——— (1914a). Further recommendations in the technique of psychoanalysis—recollection, repetition and working through. *Collected Papers, Volume 2*. New York: Basic Books, 1959.

——— (1914b). On narcissism: an introduction. *Standard Edition* 14.

——— (1916). Introductory lectures on psycho-analysis. *Standard Edition* 15/16.

——— (1923). Remarks upon the theory and practice of dream-interpretation. In *Collected Papers, Volume 5*. New York: Basic Books, 1959.

―――― (1925). Some additional notes upon dream-interpretation as a whole. In *Collected Papers, Volume 5*. New York: Basic Books, 1959.

―――― (1937a). Analysis terminable and interminable. In *Collected Papers, Volume 5*. New York: Basic Books, 1957.

―――― (1937b). Constructions in analysis. In *Collected Papers, Volume 5*. New York: Basic Books, 1959.

Greenberg, J. (1993). *Discussion of Freud's Technique Papers*. Symposium at Division 39 meetings, Spring.

Greenson, R. R. (1965). The working alliance and the transference neurosis. *Psychoanalytic Quarterly* 34:155–181.

Hoffman, I. Z. (1996). The intimate and ironic authority of the psychoanalyst's presence. *Psychoanalytic Quarterly* 65:102–136.

Kanzer, M. (1980). Freud's "Human Influence" on the Rat Man. In *Freud and His Patients*, ed. M. Kanzer and J. Glenn. New York and London: Jason Aronson.

Kohut, H. (1968). The psychoanalytic treatment of the narcissistic personality disorders: outline of a systematic approach. *Psychoanalytic Study of the Child* 23:86–113.

―――― (1977). *The Restoration of the Self*. New York: International Universities Press.

Stewart, W. A. (1969). *Psychoanalysis: The First Ten Years, 1888–1898*. New York: Macmillan, London: Allen & Unwin.

Stone, L. (1967). The psychoanalytic situation and transference: postscript to an earlier communication. *Journal of the American Psychoanalytic Association* 15(1):3–58.

Zetzel, E. R. (1996). The analytic situation. In *Psychoanalysis in the Americas*, ed. R. E. Litman, pp. 86–106. New York: International Universities Press.

6

Freud and Object Relations Theory

Jill Savege Scharff

INTRODUCTION

The 1998 Freud Exhibit at the Library of Congress presented an opportunity to acknowledge and celebrate Freud's genius and his impact on twentieth-century culture. Moving into the twenty-first century, we recognize the multifaceted potential of his invention to generate a cascade of new theories of human development, each differing from the other and from Freud's classical theory. All of them spring from the Freudian platform, even those that reject Freud's views on the instinctual basis of human development.

From the classical Freudian emphasis on the instinctual basis of development, contemporary psychoanalysis is diverging into self psychology, intersubjectivity, relational psychology, Kleinian, and object relations theories (Greenberg and Mitchell 1983, Mitchell and Black 1995). These new developments reflect the sociocultural diversity, philosophical influences, and scientific advances of the twentieth century. They challenge the original psychoanalytic findings and theories discussed by Freud, and some of them appear to depart radically from his views. Here my discussion focuses on British object relations theory, and my argument is that it builds upon and elaborates aspects that Freud identified but did not take further, possibly because of the inevitable constraint on the outer limits of his thinking due largely to his gender, his ethnicity, and his historical period (J. S. Scharff and D. E. Scharff 1998). I will focus on object relations theory, as an example of one of these new theories, so as to catalogue the ways in which, though radically different, it nevertheless derives from Freudian theory.

Imagine an exhibit in which Freudian theory is presented in a series of showcases along one side of an aisle, and object relations theory in cases across the aisle. Imagine yourself as a visitor to this exhibit. You can examine classical concepts in the showcase on one side and then look across the aisle to see elements of object relations theory that bear a relationship to them, whether of similarity or difference. Continuing, I proceed along the object relations aisle to describe the formation of the self as a system of internal object relationships and along the Freudian aisle to review the pre- and post-structural stages of Freudian theory from which I isolate some concepts. From time to time I crisscross between the aisles to compare and contrast Freudian concepts with elements of object relations theory in the neighbouring showcases. I speculate as to why Freud's theory did not develop in the direction of object relations theory. In some elements of Freudian theory I find the seeds of object relations theory which thrived in the intellectual environment of the twentieth century after Freud's time. Following the exhibit metaphor to its conclusion, I must leave empty some display cases at the end of the aisles to accommodate other concepts in Freud, object relations, and self psychology that readers might consider relevant to this discussion (Ellman 1998).

OBJECT RELATIONS THEORY

Our tour begins with an introductory section on object relations. For the purpose of this chapter, I use the term *object relations theory*, a title coined by Fairbairn, to refer to the body of work contributed by British analysts Fairbairn, Balint, Winnicott, Guntrip, and Sutherland,

and more recently Bollas, Ogden, and D. and J. Scharff (Bollas 1987, 1989, 1992, 1995, Balint 1952, 1968, Birtles and Scharff, ed. 1994, Fairbairn 1952, Guntrip 1961, 1969, 1986, Ogden 1982, 1986, 1989, 1994, D. E. Scharff 1992, 1996, J. S. Scharff 1992, J. S. and D. E. Scharff 1992, 1998, D. E. Scharff and Birtles 1994, Sutherland 1980, Winnicott 1958, 1965, 1971). I have not included those theories that present object relations as representations complementing Freud's existing drive/structure models (Jacobson 1964, Mahler et al. 1974, Kernberg 1976, 1979, 1980), or as functions of unconscious phantasy driven by the death and life instincts (Klein 1955), because, in retaining a primarily instinctual basis for development, they clearly derive from Freud, and therefore I find no need to argue the point. So, I refer only to the kind of object relations theory that radically eschews instinct as the central organizer of development, and in particular to Fairbairn's theory.

Stated briefly, British object relations theory holds that the infant is motivated by the need to relate to another person, not by the wish for instinctual gratification. How the infant manages the early years, helped or hindered by the mothering person's capacity for environmental holding and eye-to-eye relating at the center of her being, is thought to be as crucial as the resolution of the Oedipus complex in determining personality development. There is only a pristine ego at birth, not an id out of which the ego will arise. This whole ego then experiences the vicissitudes of infantile dependency after birth when needs are no longer met automatically by uterine conditions. The infant ego grows by taking in experience with the infant's caregivers and storing it inside the self as internal object structures. Good experience infuses the ego and is retained in consciousness as an accepted object associated with feelings of satisfaction in relation to the central ego. The ego deals with experience that has been overwhelmingly frustrating, by splitting it off from what has felt good, and repressing it as an unsatisfactory object associated with feelings of frustration. The object is further divided and sorted into two main categories according to whether the frustration is associated with rage and rejection, or with longing and clinging. The ego also splits off parts of itself in relation to these objects and represses them too along with the associated affects.

In object relations theory, the unconscious is not preexisting and filled with instinctual energy. Instead, it is thought of as being formed from the ego's experience with relationships, the drives being given meaning by experience with objects. It is peopled by repressed parts of the ego, its objects, and associated affects. Objects that were experienced as being rejecting or exciting of need, are related to by a repressed antilibidinal ego and a libidinal ego respectively. The quality of the repressed ego and object is colored by the affects of rage or of longing that connects them. Ego, object, and affect together form an internal object relationship. The self consists of a central ego in relation to an accepted objected connected by feelings of satisfaction, all in consciousness, while in unconsciousness there are need-rejecting and need-exciting internal object relationships connected by feelings of rage and longing. The self is a system of conscious and unconscious inter-related internal object relationships all in dynamic relation.

Object relations theory is a radical revision of Freud's theory, yet one that builds on his concepts of object, libido, narcissism, group psychology, repetition compulsion, identification, splitting of the ego, and structural conflict.

FREUDIAN INSTINCT THEORY AND THE PLEASURE PRINCIPLE

Our tour of the Freudian aisle begins at instinct theory with reference to Freud's *Five Lectures on Psychoanalysis* (1910) and *Instincts and Their Vicissitudes* (1915). Freudian instinct theory derives from biological, scientific, neuroanatomical, and philosophical concepts of energy, hierarchy, and dualism. It holds that instincts (also referred to as drives) are biological givens that consist of impulses of energy that seek expression and gratification of erogenous zones, but are opposed by countervailing instinctual forces. For instance, the libidinal (sex) instinct may be opposed by the self-preservative instinct (later the death instinct) so that the organism can return to the resting, nonexcited state in keeping with the principle of entropy.

When unsuitable instincts are successfully opposed they do not invade consciousness in which rational thinking takes place. They are given acceptable expression by the pre-conscious, or remain in the unconscious, a seething mass of instinctual energy where thinking is not rational but is governed by the primary process. Conceptualizing the mind in layers from surface to depth, Freud's theory at this stage has also been called the *topographic theory*.

In Freud's theory of early development, the infant is not looking for a mother, for a relationship, or for food. The infant is driven by the libido (the sexual instinct) to seek satisfaction through stimulation of the oral orifice that happens to occur during feeding. In object relations theory, the infant's need to be in a relationship is primary. The infant finds security and meaning in the loving arms and eyes of the mother and other family members, and in the predictable rhythm of stimulation and rest, togetherness and tolerable separation.

Freud's instinct theory depends upon the *pleasure principle*. The libido seeks expression by being gratified at the site of the pleasure zone that predominates at the different psychosexual stages—oral, anal, phallic, and genital. In emphasizing the source, expression, and control of the pleasure-seeking libido as it meets an environment experienced as hostile to its aims, instinct theory minimizes the human reality of people and their families, even though in practice Freud was well aware of the importance of family relationships as his case histories show. Unconscious sexual instincts give rise to impulses for pleasure without regard for the destruction of the object. They are opposed by the self-preservative instincts that safeguard the self. These impulses are in conflict as they compete for expression along the reflex arc to consciousness and their associated affects compete for release. This conflict is experienced as anxiety, a *discharge affect*.

Freud developed the hypothesis that this anxiety is a fear of the consequences of not being able to tame the instinct, these consequences being loss of the object, loss of the love of the object, or loss of the love of the self. Here the theory begins to require an object relational focus to explain why the instincts have to be opposed. And indeed, as Freud moved on to develop his ideas on the Oedipus complex and explore mourning reactions to lost objects, the objects of the drives acquired an increasingly personal significance for personality development. Nevertheless, Freud did not give up the instinctual basis for the organization of development in favor of an object relational motivating drive.

FREUD ON THE OBJECT

The next item on display in the imaginary museum is Freud's concept of the object and its implications for identification. Freud

(1895) first used the term *object* in *Project for a Scientific Psychology*. After a helpful person responds specifically to the cry of the helpless infant, the infant has an experience of satisfaction from which follows "a cathexis of one (or several) of the neurones which correspond to the perception of an object" (p. 318). Freud's argument concerns the released reflex movement between the endogenous excitation (the scream), the extraneous excitation (the helpful action), the removal of the endogenous excitation, and the facilitation of cathexis. He does not define object. It could refer to any perception of the person, but in context, it can be read as a term used to refer to the perception of the person as the agent of the satisfaction. Of most interest to the object relations theorist, Freud describes this total event as constituting "an *experience of satisfaction*, which has the most radical results on the development of the individual's functions" (p. 318).

The Infantile Narcissistic Object

In *Three Essays on Sexuality* (1905) Freud used the term *object* to refer to the *object of the drives, the source of gratification that the sexual drives are aimed at*. The object is the infant's own dominant erogenous zone. In the beginning, he thought, there is no external object in the environment, human or non-human. The libido is directed internally and finds its primary object in itself. Infants look to their own bodies for stimulation, gratification, and soothing, and expect sources outside the self to be ungratifying or even traumatizing if the barrier around the self is broken. This is the stage of *primary autoerotism*.

In "On Narcissism," Freud (1914) developed these ideas. He said that the internal object of the auterotic stage is infused with narcissistic libido, and he called this stage *primary narcissism*.

Gradually the libido develops *object cathexis*, that is to say, energy is aimed outside the self: Infants reach out when their mothers seem to promise gratification of the libidinal aims. When the mother proves disappointing, hurtful, rejecting, or traumatic in response to the baby's needs for pleasure, the baby stops looking to her as the source of gratification. In Freud's words, the infant retreats to using the self as the primary object after the external object fails to gratify the libido. Freud called this the stage of *secondary narcissism*.

After persistent nonoccurrence of satisfaction, the disappointed infant abandons the attempt at satisfaction through hallucination.

Then under the influence of the self-preservative ego instincts, the infant ego accepts the state of unpleasure as real and looks for useful ways to change its reality (Freud 1911). When the mother gratifies the libido, the infant finds pleasure, and then refinds it in fantasy. When the source of this pleasure is found and refound, the infant recognizes the source of pleasure in the object outside the self. Narcissism gives way to a capacity for *object love*.

In a relational tone, Freud holds that "persons who are concerned with a child's feeding, care, and protection become his earliest sexual objects" (1914, p. 87), unless the child makes an object-choice based on himself as the model. But Freud's energy goes into showing how this observation proves that the sexual instincts were originally tied to the ego-instincts and later become independent of them. He also shows that the individual has two types of object choices open to him: the *narcissistic* (based on himself, or a part of himself as he is or was or wishes to be, as the model) or the *anaclitic* (leaning on the early caregiver as the model), also called the *attachment type* of object choice. In an even more relationally inclined tone, Freud subdivided the attachment type of object choice into two basic models: the woman who fed him and the man who protected him.

Object relations theory—which holds that the infant is not motivated by sexual and self-preservative instincts, therefore has no id, and has a pristine whole ego at birth—views narcissism as always secondary to frustration due to lack of fit between the infant's constitutional ego capacities for expressing need and tolerating organismic distress and the quality of maternal response. Object relations theory follows Freud in observing withdrawn ego states (Guntrip 1969), but regards them as a secondary phenomena, not as a retreat to an original condition.

In Freudian theory the mother is the *object of the drives, the object that the drive attaches to, and eventually the object of love*. In object relations theory the mother's self is *the object of attachment, the object that her infant attaches to from the beginning, and the object of love and hate*.

The Anaclitic Object

The ego may look to the external object not just for gratification but for support. When the ego seems weak and the object is viewed as strong, the ego's relation to the object is of an exaggeratedly anaclitic type. Freud (1917) drew upon the concept of the anaclitic object in his paper "Mourning and Melancholia" to explain the depression of bereaved adults who have relied so heavily on the presence of their loved ones that they are devastated by their departures. But dependency was a pathological condition in Freudian theory, not a natural condition for development, as it is in object relations theory. Freud recognized the importance of the parents as objects of the drives, but he did not focus on the child's ego in relation to its objects until the oedipal stage. Even then, when he took the family dynamics into account, he retained a drive-oriented approach. Although he said that "it is inevitable and perfectly normal that a child should take his parents as the first objects of his love," he nevertheless revealed his commitment to an instinct-based view of the object, when he continued "but his libido should not remain fixated to these first objects; later on, it should merely take them as a model" (Freud 1910, p. 48).

The Lost Object

Freud (1917) studied the effect of the loss of the object on development. He saw the *lost object* as an important stimulus to thinking. In its absence, the person learned to hallucinate the missing object to secure wish fulfillment. In this way *the person has the object*. When the person identifies with the lost object that is being hallucinated, the *person becomes the object*. Then the ego is divided into two pieces, one of which rages against the other piece that is identified with the lost object. In this way, *the ego is split by its relation to the lost object*.

From studies of the narcissistic, anaclitic, and lost objects, Freud filled out his concept of *identification*, which he acknowledged as the original form of emotional tie to the object. He thought that identification could operate regressively so that the object was introjected into the ego as a substitute for a libidinal object tie, or could operate healthily to enrich the personality when it occurred in relation to any person with whom one shared a quality in common and who was not an object of the libido. This line of thinking elaborated on Freud's earlier conception of *splitting of the mind* (Breuer and Freud 1893).

Turning briefly to the object relations exhibit, we note that the concept of *splitting of the ego* was further developed by Fairbairn and Klein. Fairbairn saw it along a continuum as a response to the temporarily or chronically unresponsive external object, and Klein saw it as a response to perceptions of the object colored good or bad by projective identification under the force of the life or death instincts.

INTRAPSYCHIC VERSUS RELATIONAL PERSPECTIVES IN FREUD

The State of Being in Love

At this point in our journey through the imagined museum space, we dart back and forth between the Freudian and object relations displays, comparing and contrasting Freudian and object relations perspectives. Freud (1914) noted that adults in love do not see each other's characteristics objectively. Instead, they overvalue each other because each of them needs the other as a wonderful object to be gratifying to the libido. The object is used to aggrandize the ego rather than the object being loved and appreciated for its unique characteristics, its otherness. In Freud's way of putting it, the new love object is overvalued by being infused with narcissistic libido. The new object has to be glorified so that it can serve as a successful substitute for the unattainable oedipal object. Only this level of achievement can satisfy the narcissistic aims of the libido.

In the state of falling in love, as Freud saw it, the lover may become so preoccupied with the loved one that he or she may lose the sense of being a separate person, or the lover's idealization may obstruct the individuality of the loved one. In that case, to use Freud's language, the loved object may consume the lover's ego, or the ego may consume the object, because the choice is dominated by the narcissistic aims of the libido.

The object relations view of marriage derives from Henry Dicks. Dicks (1967) used Fairbairn's theory of the individual personality composed of parts of ego, object, and affect connected in internal object relationships and looked at how these interact with the personality of the marital partner. He applied the Kleinian mechanism of projective identification to explain how the internal object relationships communicate with the spouse's internal set in a reciprocal process to create a marital joint personality. In the healthy marriage, this has a modifying effect on each spouse's internal world, but in the marriages that come to treatment, it cements faulty internal constellations (Dicks 1967).

In Freud's theory of mating, the adult is driven by the sexual instinct to find a partner with whom to gratify the libido in fully genital sexual intercourse, whereas foreplay simply gratifies the component pregenital instincts by stimulation of the relevant erogenous zones. In object relations theory, the adult is seen as finding a partner with whom, through projective identification, to refind, reexperience, and reintegrate lost parts of the self in a mutual psychosomatic process of growth and enrichment, supported by the fully expressive, bodily and genitally interactive, psychologically interpenetrating, intensely pleasurable sexual relationship (D. Scharff 1981).

Group Psychology

Freud (1921) again seems to be moving toward a relational approach in *Group Psychology and the Analysis of the Ego*. He noted that, "in the individual's mental life someone else is invariably involved, as a model, as an object, as a helper, as an opponent; and so from the very first individual psychology is at the same time a social psychology as well" (Freud 1921, p. 69). He observed that human beings tend to want to live and work in groups and establish emotional ties to others in the group even if only to avoid the conflict between following the leader or doing for oneself. Freud found that the human is a social animal. This was quite a move beyond his intensely intrapsychic, drive-motivated view of development, but not surprisingly, Freud had to find an instinct to explain it. He named it *the social instinct*. But instead of giving it a solely biological basis, he looked for its origin in social terms. He said "that the social instinct may not be a primitive one and insusceptible of dissection, and that it may be possible to discover the beginnings of its development in a narrower circle, such as that of the family" (p. 70). Freud acknowledged the family as the possible source of the human tendency to want to live and work in groups.

This tentative move toward an object relational approach based on the psychology of family, social, and individual development was not maintained, perhaps because Freud was horrified when the social instinct, augmented by the death instinct, led to group efforts at mass destruction in the First World War. Freud also turned against his early seduction hypothesis regarding the pathology resulting from the actualities of traumatic relationships in early childhood and adolescence, perhaps because it was unacceptable to a society that felt accused and might then be more inclined to reject his theories of psychosexual development. From his study of primary and secondary narcissism, identification in loss and mourning, and his watershed discovery of oedipal fantasy, Freud moved toward producing the concept of parts of ego and object in a structural relationship. By 1920, he had prepared the way for an object relations theory to study the dynamic, intrapsychic relation between these parts of the self and also their continuing development in interaction with significant others through the life cycle. Perhaps Freud could have moved more solidly in this direction himself, but his concept of identification received too little attention from his colleagues and from himself. In any case, he could not pursue every theory at once. He made his choices according to personal inclination, scientific credibility, and political implications.

FREUD ON PSYCHIC STRUCTURE

Returning to concentrate on the development of Freud's thought, we will look in on the decade before the 1923 publication of the *The Ego and the Id*. We will trace some of the developments that paved the way for Freud's new structural theory of the mind: in chronological order, the discovery of the reality principle, the repetition compulsion, identification in mourning, mental structure, and oedipal development.

The Reality Principle and the Capacity for Delay

In *Formulations on the Two Principles of Mental Functioning*, Freud (1911) added to the pleasure principle (to safeguard it, not to depose it) another principle of mental functioning, called the *reality principle*. The reality principle comes into play when maturing cognitive functions enable the object to be held in mind as a reality whether it is agreeable or not. It is held there long enough to hold off the frustrated instinctual impulse until a moment convenient for the object. The reality principle governs the *capacity for delay*. The reality principle also infers the need for consideration of the object as having a separate reality to which adjustment must be made. This element might have sparked a substantially relational theory at that time, but it did not because there was still more interest in drive than object. Instead, the reality principle became a crucial building block for Freud's later monumental leap to structural theory.

The Repetition Compulsion and the Death Instinct

In his 1920 paper *Beyond the Pleasure Principle*, Freud continued his emphasis on the reality principle, in contrast to the pleasure principle. He pointed to the recurrence of the same unsatisfying behaviors and unwelcome incidents in a person's life, unpleasant dreams in a traumatized person's sleep, and repetitive themes in a child's play. He called this phenomenon "the compulsion to repeat" (p. 36) and noted that it reflected a peculiar pleasurable investment in unpleasure, and must therefore be due to a force that overrode the pleasure principle. Freud continued to refer to the pleasure principle-driven conflict between the sexual and the self-preservative instincts, and made a long and tortuous argument redefining the nature of the duality of the instincts. He proposed that the concept of the sexual instinct be broadened to include all tendencies aimed at unity and life directed toward objects, and that it be called the life instinct (and sometimes the object instinct). Instinctual trends not related to and opposing this life instinct had earlier been called the ego instincts (because they were not directed toward an object but tended instead to return the organism to the resting state). In 1920, Freud argued that they did in fact also have libidinal tendencies. Therefore he lumped together the ego instincts and object instincts, called them the life instincts, and then found a fresh opposition to them in destructive impulses residing in the ego. Those instincts formerly known as self-preservative were then seen not just as securing survival, but as permitting the organism to follow its own inherent path toward death, undisturbed by external forces or object-oriented impulses. From this argument, Freud arrived at his concept of the *death instinct* as the opposition to the life instinct (1920).

Let us for a moment glance over at the display on object relations for a contrasting view. Maintaining that the death instinct was superfluous, Fairbairn (1943) thought that there was no need for a repetition compulsion to explain the persistence of traumatic scenes in a person's dreams and relationships. Instead, Fairbairn thought of the person as being haunted by internal bad objects to which his ego is attached, a result of spontaneous release of repressed objects activated by trauma similar enough to rekindle awareness of the originally repressed constellation. He thought that the destructive traumatic repetition Freud described in terms of the death instinct is better explained by an internalized object relationship with a bad object of a sadomasochistic type, an object relationship that needs to be recovered from through its emergence and reworking within the therapeutic relationship.

Identification, Mental Structure, and Oedipal Development

Moving back to the Freud side of the exhibit, we note another contribution toward structural theory that emerged from Freud's study *Mourning and Melancholia* (1917). Freud noted that it was as if the lost object was being held inside the self to deal with the libido remaining cathected to the lost object and not released through the grieving process. So Freud was led to think of the mind as having different parts, constructed by identification with lost objects in order to exercise power over the drives. This gave him the idea that the drives are to be controlled by mental structure rather than by other drives.

Applying his findings in melancholia to normal development, Freud became aware that, at each stage, the child has to give up the object of the earlier stage. He proposed that the child does so by incorporating the redundant versions of the object that related to the earlier component instincts. It is out of these introjections of lost developmental objects that the ego is formed.

This concept acquired special developmental significance when applied to the lost object of the oedipal phase. The libido that seeks to express itself in relation to the loved parent of either sex is blocked from receiving gratification because the object is not available: the one parent is already the object of the other parent's libido. Ultimately the child must transfer the libido to the opposite-sex parent and then renounce this sexual aim as inappropriate. The child's libido has to be repressed or sublimated until it finds a new, nonincestuous object. At the point of renunciation, the child's ego usefully identifies with parts of the parents upon which it models itself. Depending on the force of the instincts and the strength of the opposition to them, the oedipal-stage identifications might be either with the parental traits or in reaction formation against them.

The most admired and respected parts of the other lead to the development of the *ego ideal* toward which the personality aspires and from which it derives its sense of self-esteem when it comes close to the ideal. The *superego* forms from selective identification with some of these highly valued aspects and reaction formation against other aspects of the parents associated with their prohibition of the child's libidinal longings.

Identification was the last major building block Freud needed for arriving at his structural theory.

Structural Theory

As the infant matures and mental functioning comes under the force of the reality principle, the instincts undergo delay, detour, binding, and neutralization of their energy. The drives that are constantly pressing for gratification can be persuaded to hold off until a later date when their eventual satisfaction can be expected with confidence and greater personal pleasure (Rapaport 1960). The absence of the object and the resulting delay in instinctual expression leads to mental structure formation that is then capable of securing further delays. Then conflict is experienced between the id, where the drives are located, and the reality-oriented ego, formed from identification with the lost objects.

This line of development in his thinking culminated in Freud's *The Ego and the Id* (1923). Freud now viewed *conflict as structural*, occurring between parts of the self, not between instincts. The conflict is experienced as anxiety, now in the form of *signal affect*, not discharge affect. To account for this capacity for managing delay, Freud postulated the existence of the ego as an executive agency in the conscioius and preconscious parts of the mind, in which lost objects are represented, and which can respond to the signal affect by alerting the mind's defences against the threat of instinctual energy release.

Freud did not give up the old topographic theory of the

broadly-based realms of conciousness and unconsciousness. He still held that the infant progresses along a predetermined timeline, relating to its objects because they satisfy instinctual demands specific to each psychosexual stage, and experiencing them progressively through the oral, anal, and phallic routes, with oedipal-level renunciation of the object as the ultimate. Freud superimposed the new structural theory on the old topographic theory, much as the ego sat upon the id (Mitchell and Black 1995, J. S. and D. E. Scharff 1998).

The *Three Essays on the Theory of Sexuality* (Freud 1905) and the *Case Histories* (Breuer and Freud 1893–1895) had demonstrated Freud's understanding of the infant's need for holding and handling, and then the older child's need for family support and validation. His emphasis on family influence was clear when he claimed that neurosis was caused when actual seduction by a family member overwhelmed a young person's capacity to oppose the demands of the libido to seek such gratification. But in his most developed structural theory, Freud gave less attention to the influence of the actualities of family relationships on the child's developing personality structure than to the impact of the child's inherent constitutionally and phylogenetically predetermined characteristics. Although he outlined the way in which the child selectively identifies with or creates reaction formations against the character traits of the parents in the oedipal phase, and although he said that the ego is filled with the lost objects, he mainly claimed that the ego formed out of the id, the cauldron of instinctual energy. Nevertheless, the structural theory did take account of childhood misperceptions of parent figures and by extension it includes the role of the family as the carrier of culture and shaper of human ideals and behaviors.

A last look along the object relations aisle shows that Fairbairn followed Freud in being interested in internal conflict, but he did not agree that it occurs between the agencies of id, ego and superego. In his theory there is no id. For Fairbairn, the ideal object, the nucleus of the superego function is an internalized accepted object shorn of its troublesome libidinal and anti-libidinal features more like Freud's ego ideal, and the central ego is subdivided into parts that relate to the accepted, libidinal, and anti-libidinal objects. Conflict may be experienced between parts of self at any point in the dynamic system of partly conscious, and (depending on the degree of the trauma and the strength of the constitution) partly repressed, and partly dissociated, ego, parts of object, and affect.

CONCLUSION

To the object relations theorist looking back, Freud's structural theory seems to hold within it the potential for an object relations view of the mind. But it remained a biologically centered, intrapsychic, individually oriented theory of linear and deterministic type, in keeping with the scientific influences of the time, and in distinction to the diverging ideas and methodologies of Ferenczi (1933) that later influenced his analyzands Balint and Klein toward the object relations perspective that flourished later in the twentieth century (Falzeder 1994). In addition, the English translators' choice of Latin terminology—id, ego, superego—had the unfortunate effect of reifying Freud's structural concept of the mind. Bettleheim (1982) made the point that in the original German, Freud had used the highly personal term "I" (translated as *ego*) and the impersonal "it" (translated as *id*). "Ego" seems to suggest a rather mechanistic, reflexively operant management function, as opposed to what I think Freud intended—a proactive, personal, executive structure for receiving affect signals and managing affect states, integrating experience with the objects, selecting object qualities to identify with or defend against, and in general, dealing with internal and external reality. Perhaps Freud's concern for the person's self—as opposed to his ego structures—expressed in his German theory-building was not evident to his English-language followers, and may have contributed to delaying the emergence of an object relations perspective.

For various historical, personal, and professional reasons, the radical, redefining potential of this aspect of Freud's ideas remained undeveloped, for he continued to subscribe to his model of the mind as one that generated its own form and did so under pressure from the instincts as the driving force that governed development. It was not until new information infused the culture that disparate and overlooked elements in Freudian theory led to a radical revision according to the object relations perspective. The crucial new influences from the realm of science that were not available to push Freud in this direction stemmed from advances in models of science influenced by the theory of relativity (D. E. Scharff and Birtles 1994), cybernetic systems (Bertalannfy 1950), and most recently chaos theory (J. S. Scharff and D. E. Scharff 1998). Other developments in psychiatry—studies of attachment and separation (Bowlby 1958, 1969, 1973, 1980), infant attachment style (Ainsworth et al. 1978), neurological development (Schore 1994), group dependency, fight/flight, and pairing subgroup responses to task and leader (Bion 1959, 1962), and war neuroses resulting from unresolved infantile dependence (Fairbairn 1943)—pushed toward object relations theory. As we move further into the twenty-first century, the cultural effects of feminist theory, the scientific advances in chaos theory, the communication explosion, and whatever the future may bring, will move Freud's invention of psychoanalysis in yet new directions.

REFERENCES

Ainsworth, M.D.S., Blehar, M. C., Waters, E., and Wall, S. (1978). *Patterns of Attachment: A Psychological Study of the Strange Situation.* Mahwah, NJ: Erlbaum.

Balint, M. (1952). *Primary Love and Psychoanalytic Technique.* London: Tavistock.

——— (1968). *The Basic Fault: Therapeutic Aspects of Regression.* London: Tavistock.

Bertalanffy, L. von. (1950). The theory of open systems in physics and biology. *Science* 111:23–29.

Bettleheim, B. (1982). Reflections: Freud and the soul. *The New Yorker*, March 1, pp. 59–93.

Bion, W. (1959). *Experiences in Groups.* New York: Basic Books.

——— (1962). *Learning from Experience.* New York: Basic Books.

Birtles, E. F., and Scharff, D. E., eds. (1994). *From Instinct to Self: Selected Papers of W.R.D. Fairbairn vol. 2.* Northvale, NJ: Jason Aronson.

Bollas, C. (1987). *The Shadow of the Object.* New York: Columbia University Press.

——— (1989). *Forces of Destiny: Psychoanalysis and Human Idiom.* London: Free Association Books.

——— (1992). *Being a Character: Psychoanalysis and Self Experience.* New York: Hill and Wang.

——— (1995). *Cracking Up.* New York: Hill and Wang.
Bowlby, J. (1958). The nature of the child's tie to his mother. *International Journal of Psycho-Analysis* 39:1–24.
——— (1969). *Attachment and Loss: Volume I.* New York: Basic Books.
——— (1973). *Attachment and Loss: Volume II.* "Separation: Anxiety and Anger." New York: Basic Books.
——— (1980). *Attachment and Loss: Volume III.* "Loss: Sadness and Depression." New York: Basic Books.
Breuer, J., and Freud, S. (1893). On the psychical mechanism of hysterical phenomena: preliminary communication. *Standard Edition* 2:1–17.
——— (1893–1895). Case histories. *Standard Edition* 2:21–181.
Dicks, H. (1967). *Marital Tensions: Clinical Studies Towards a Psychoanalytic Theory of Interaction.* London: Routledge and Kegan Paul.
Ellman, S. (1998). *Psychoanalytic Theory Reconstructed.* Manuscript in preparation.
Fairbairn, W.R.D. (1943). The repression and return of bad objects (with special reference to the "war neuroses"). In *Psychoanalytic Studies of the Personality*, pp. 59–81. London: Routledge.
——— (1952). *Psychoanalytic Studies of the Personality.* London: Routledge.
Falzeder, E. (1994). The threads of psychoanalytic filiations or psychoanalysis taking effect. *Cahiers Psychiatriques Genevois*, Special Issue, pp. 169–194.
Ferenczi, S. (1933). Confusion of tongues between the adult and the child. In *Final Contributions to the Problems and Methods of Psychoanalysis*, pp. 156–167. London: Hogarth Press.
Freud, S. (1895). Project for a scientific psychology. *Standard Edition* 1:295–357.
——— (1905). Three essays on sexuality. *Standard Edition* 7:135–243.
——— (1910). Five lectures on psycho-analysis. *Standard Edition* 11:9–55.
——— (1911). Formulations on the two principles of mental functioning. *Standard Edition* 12:218–226.
——— (1914). On narcissism: an introduction. *Standard Edition* 14:67–102.
——— (1915). Instincts and their vicissitudes. In *Standard Edition* 14:109–140.

―――― (1917). Mourning and melancholia. *Standard Edition* 14:243–258.
―――― (1920). Beyond the pleasure principle. *Standard Edition* 28:7–64.
―――― (1921). Group psychology and the analysis of the ego. *Standard Edition* 18:69–143.
―――― (1923). The ego and the id. *Standard Edition* 19:12–66.
Greenberg, J. R., and Mitchell, S. A. (1983). *Object Relations in Psychoanalytic Theory*. Cambridge, MA: Harvard University Press.
Guntrip, H. S. (1961). *Personality and Human Interaction*. London: Hogarth.
―――― (1969). *Schizoid Phenomena, Object Relations, and the Self*. New York: International Universities Press.
―――― (1986). My experience of analysis with Fairbairn and Winnicott. In *Essential Papers on Object Relations*, ed. P. Buckley, pp. 447–468. New York: New York University Press.
Jacobson, E. (1964). *The Self and the Object World*. New York: International Universities Press.
Jones, E. (1955a). *The Life and Work of Sigmund Freud 1856–1900: The Formative Years and the Great Discoveries*. New York: Basic Books.
―――― (1955b). *The Life and Work of Sigmund Freud 1901–1919: The Years of Maturity*. New York: Basic Books.
―――― (1955c). *The Life and Work of Sigmund Freud 1919–1939: The Last Phase*. New York: Basic Books.
Kernberg, O. (1976). *Object Relations Theory and Clinical Psychoanalysis*. New York: Jason Aronson.
―――― (1979). An overview of Edith Jacobson's contributions. *Journal of the American Psychoanalytic Association* 30:793–819.
―――― (1980). *Internal World and External Reality*. New York: Jason Aronson.
Klein, M. (1955). *New Directions in Psycho-Analysis*. London: Tavistock.
Mahler, M., Pine, F., and Bergman, A. (1974). *The Psychological Birth of the Human Infant*. New York: Basic Books.
Mitchell, S., and Black, M. (1995). *Freud and Beyond*. New York: Basic Books.
Ogden, T. (1982). *Projective Identification and Psychotherapeutic Technique*. New York: Jason Aronson.

——— (1986). *The Matrix of the Mind: Object Relations and the Psychoanalytic Dialogue*. Northvale, NJ: Jason Aronson.

——— (1989). *The Primitive Edge of Experience*. Northvale, NJ: Jason Aronson.

——— (1994). *Subjects of Analysis*. Northvale, NJ: Jason Aronson.

Rapaport, D. (1960). The structure of psychoanalytic theory. *Psychological Issues Vol. 2, No. 2, Monograph 6*. New York: International Universities Press.

Scharff, D. E. (1981). *The Sexual Relationship*. New York: Jason Aronson, 1998.

——— (1992). *Refinding the Object and Reclaiming the Self*. Northvale, NJ: Jason Aronson.

——— (1996). *Object Relations Theory and Practice*. Northvale, NJ: Jason Aronson.

Scharff, D. E., and Birtles, E. F., eds. (1994). *From Instinct to Self: Selected Papers of W.R.D. Fairbairn. Vol.1*. Northvale, NJ: Jason Aronson.

Scharff, J. S. (1992). *Projective and Introjective Identification and the Use of the Therapist's Self*. Northvale, NJ: Jason Aronson.

———, ed. (1994). *The Autonomous Self: The Work of John D. Sutherland*. Northvale, NJ: Jason Aronson.

Scharff, J. S., and Scharff, D. E. (1992). *A Primer of Object Relations Therapy*. (formerly *Scharff Notes*). Northvale, NJ: Jason Aronson.

——— (1998). *Object Relations Individual Therapy*. Northvale, NJ: Jason Aronson.

Schore, A. (1994). *Affect Regulation and the Origin of the Self: The Neurobiology of Emotional Development*. Mahwah, NJ: Erlbaum.

Sutherland, J. D. (1980). The British object relations theorists: Balint, Winnicott, Fairbairn, Guntrip. *Journal of the American Psychoanalytic Association* 28(4):829–60. In *The Autonomous Self: The Work of John D. Sutherland*, ed. J. S. Scharff, pp. 25–44. New York: Jason Aronson.

Winnicott, D. W. (1958). *Collected Papers: Through Peadiatrics to Psycho-Analysis*. London: Tavistock. (Reprinted by Hogarth Press 1975.)

——— (1965). *The Maturational Processes and the Facilitating Environment*. London: Hogarth Press.

——— (1971). *Playing and Reality*. London: Tavistock.

PART III

LEARNING FROM HYSTERIA

Imre Szecsödy's and **Iréne Matthis's** papers on Freud's histories of Dora and Katherina continue our examination of how his patients taught Freud. These cases still enable us to return to the data, to study and enlarge our understanding as we review and revise history, as we learn more about ourselves in the present in order to be able to live with our collective psychoanalytic past.

Psychoanalysis still rests on what we learn from patients. They can teach us, if we can listen. Freud documented this process from the beginning. In *Studies on Hysteria*, he listened to Emmy and conceived a method in that the patient was free to tell him all she could, and Freud, in turn, was free to listen with free-floating attention, using all his modalities of conscious and unconscious receptiveness.

Imre Szecsödy's "Dora: Freud's Pygmalion?" reexamines one of Freud's most famous case histories. He looks at the effect of the analyst on the form and outcome of the treatment, and on the patient herself. Szecsödy's theme deepens the argument of our opening two papers on history and psychoanalysis by showing specifically how Freud's desire to establish analytic truth at any cost constituted a violence perpetrated on Dora's development and on her search for validation.

Szecsödy's argument helps us see an aspect of Freud's history at an intersection with—and in conflict with—the needs of an actual patient. Because Freud is self-revealing in his writing, he offers us the chance to understand the Dora case history in the wider context of his development of analytic theory, and also in the context of the prevailing society. In this way, Szecsödy offers an investigation of Freud's discoveries—the psychodynamics of hysteria, the role of seduction, the interpretation of dreams, transference—and at the same time gives a wide perspective on early psychoanalytic history.

Iréne Matthis's "Finger-Twisting and Cracked Voices: The Hysterical Symptom Revisited" continues the reexamination of hysteria begun in this book by Michael Roth and by Szecsödy. Where they emphasized issues of social and personal history, Matthis steers us in a line begun by Freud's passion for theory. She moves Freud's early theory that he presented in *Studies on Hysteria*—"hysterics suffer mainly from reminiscences"—to a modern theory of semiotics. In this way she adds to Freud's discovery of the symbolic meaning of bodily symptoms by drawing on the field of semiotics, the study of language and symbols. The result is an advance of our understanding in a kind of bodily grammar, applicable to an integrated view of bodily expression in health and disease.

The final contribution in this section is **Harold Blum's** marvelous discussion of the preceding two papers. In a few words he sets the historical and cultural context for medicine's interest in hysteria in 1900, and the prominence of interest in bodily conversion symptoms. He is especially interested in the disturbances of voice, which he describes as symbolizing the difficulty women had in "finding a voice" in Western culture a century ago. The irony that Freud was also struggling to make his scientific voice heard is part of what makes the Dora case so pivotal in the history of psychoanalysis.

7

Dora: Freud's Pygmalion?[1]

Imre Szecsödy

BACKGROUND

Dora started her psychoanalytic treatment with Sigmund Freud in the beginning of October and broke it off after three months, on December 31, 1900. At the turn of the century, there was in Vienna a "distinctive, creative ambiance in the split between old and new, between an apocalyptic sense of doom as the century drew to a close and the bright transitional optimism which was also a hallmark of the times—*la belle époque.*" It was in this field of high tension between the authority and rhetoric of the old Hapsburg Empire on the one hand and subversive, revolutionary movements and ideas on the other that Freud's work evolved. The emperor was no longer the master in his own

---

1. To a great extent these reflections are identical with those presented in Chapter 3 of *On Freud's Couch: Seven New Interpretations of Freud's Case Histories* (eds: I. Matthis and I. Szecsödy) published 1998 by Jason Aronson.

house but was compulsively, neurotically occupied with taking personal charge of inspecting his kingdom and its finances; the empress, neurotic, visibly anorexic with narcissistic traits, traveled continually; the son Rudolf, the crown prince, committed suicide, staged as the conclusion of intercourse where the consenting partner was put to death. The emperor was informed of their death by Katharina Schratt, the friend who by her calm, discreet affection consoled him for Empress Elizabeth's emotional unease" (Hallerstedt 1990, p. 9). Freud's consulting room and residence on Berggasse was close to the University and the imposing Ring, a magnificent street lined with palaces, museums, operas, theaters, castles, and the Parliament building. Seven minutes by streetcar from Ringen, there was an apartment house, called the Beehive, with 216 apartments and a total of more than 1,000 inhabitants, as every tenant had only one room for his or her family.

PRESENTATION OF DORA[2]

Dora, or Ida Bauer as she was really called, was born in Vienna on November 1, 1881. Like Freud, her emancipated Jewish family could be traced back to Bohemia. The father, Philip Bauer, was a wealthy textile manufacturer, "a man of rather unusual activity and talents," (Freud 1905 p. 18) in comfortable circumstances, the owner of a large factory. "His daughter was most tenderly attached to him, and for that reason her critical powers, which developed early, took all the more offense at many of his actions and peculiarities. Her affection for him was still further increased by the many severe illnesses he had been through since her sixth year" (Freud 1905, p. 18). At that time Dora's father had fallen ill with tuberculosis, and when she was about 10 years old he was treated for a detached retina. Two years later, he consulted with Freud concerning symptoms of paralysis

---

2. With the hope of letting Freud—at least partly—own his history, I have chosen to use long quotations from his own text: "Fragment of an analysis of a case of hysteria," in *The Standard Edition of the Complete Psychological Works of Sigmund Freud* (1905) 7:1–122.

and slight mental disturbances; Freud prescribed an energetic course of antiluetic treatments. Her mother, Käthe Gerber Bauer, was "an uncultivated woman and above all a foolish one, who had concentrated all her interests upon domestic affairs, especially since her husband's illness and the estrangement to which it led. She presented a picture, in fact, of what might be called 'housewife's psychosis.'" (1905, p. 20). Dora's only brother, Otto, who was fourteen months older than she, was one of the leaders of the Austrian Social Democratic Party (from 1918 to 1934) and the Austrian foreign minister from 1918 to 1920. Dora had neurotic symptoms since the age of 8, and was brought to Freud for a consultation when she was 16. At 18, when the analysis started, she

> had grown into a girl in the first bloom of youth with intelligent and engaging looks. But she was a source of heavy trials for her parents. Low spirits and an alteration in her character had now become the main features of her illness. She was clearly satisfied neither with herself nor with her family; her attitude toward her father was unfriendly and she was on very bad terms with her mother, who was bent upon drawing her into taking a share in the work of the house. She tried to avoid social intercourse and employed herself—so far as she was allowed to by the fatigue and lack of concentration of which she complained—with attending lectures for women and with carrying on more or less serious studies. One day her parents were thrown into a state of great alarm by finding on the girl's writing-desk, or inside it, a letter in which she took leave of them because, as she said she could no longer endure her life. Her father, indeed, being a man of some perspicacity, guessed that the girl had no serious suicidal intentions. But he was nonetheless very much shaken and when one day, after a slight passage of words between him and his daughter, she had a first attack of loss of consciousness—an event which was subsequently covered by an amnesia—it was determined, in spite of her reluctance, that she should come to me for treatment. [p. 23]

BEYOND THE SEDUCTION THEORY— INTRODUCING A NEW TECHNIQUE

Several years earlier, Freud had abandoned the theory of actual sexual abuse as a prerequisite for neurotic symptoms and had made new enemies instead by accentuating the role of infantile sexuality in these symptoms. Studying his own dreams he did find that "a recurring theme was love and jealousy, a triangle where the parent of the opposite sex was the desired one, following the structure in the antique drama of fate, *Oedipus Rex*." Publishing his article on Dora 1905 he wrote:

> In my *Interpretation of Dreams*, published in 1900, I showed that dreams in general can be interpreted, and that after the work of interpretation has been completed they can be replaced by perfectly correctly constructed thoughts which can be assigned a recognizable position in the chain of mental events. The following fragment from the history of the treatment of a hysterical girl is intended to show the way in which the interpretation of dreams plays a part in the work of analysis. [p. 15]

He also emphasized that he did introduce a new technique: "I now let the patient himself choose the subject of the day's work, and in that way I start out from whatever surface his unconscious happens to be presenting to his notice at the moment" (p. 12). The practical goal of treatment was to cure all the damage to the patient's memory and that when a successful conclusion has been reached it will be possible for him to *own his history*.

WHO OWNED DORA'S HISTORY?

When Erikson asks this question in *Insight and Responsibility* (1964), he makes a distinction between reality and actuality. He says that reality is a phenomenonic experience whereas actuality is what is current, present, immediate, and active; it includes a participation in the world in the company of others, preferably with a minimum of defensive attitudes and a maximum of mutual activation.

Ida Bauer, an 18-year-old young woman—in a sense still a girl—was seriously involved in a complicated relation between her father and his mistress, Frau K.—a tangled web of relations between adult men and women. The situation both frightened and fascinated

Dora, as Freud was to call her in his case history. She is brought to Freud by her father, who appeals to Freud to try and bring her to reason. With this as a starting point, what stance is she to take in the consulting room? How can the daughter's observations be of use? What can she make of her experiences? How can her history be told? Who will be able to tell it? Can she do it without help from adults? How is one to get at the truth? What is the truth? Whose truth is the truth? Will Freud be able to search for it with her? Can we do that? Can anyone?

When Dora confronted her environment, hoping to get it to divulge its secrets and reveal its lies, she did this out of a young person's need and right to test the correctness, the durability, and the truth of the attitudes, methods, ideas, and ideals of her environment. Loyalty, constancy, and fidelity are the strengths and crises of adolescence. According to Erikson, Dora was concerned with the immediate, historic truth while Freud wanted to get at the genetic truth behind the symptoms, for Freud considered it the patient's duty and responsibility to come to a realization of these genetic connections and not be inhibited by environment, as was the case with Dora.

Many have accused Freud of having used Dora as his "Pygmalion"—on the one hand to serve as a demonstration to the world of the central place occupied in therapy by the interpretation of dreams, and on the other hand to be used as proof of the unique place of sexuality in the understanding of the origin of neurosis. Many others, especially feminist research workers, have asserted that Freud exploited Dora, and that he lost his head over her and it was out of his own need and preconceived ideas that he constructed her "story."[3] In a postscript Freud writes:

> On a date which is not a matter of complete indifference, on the first of April (times and dates, as we know, were never without significance for her), Dora came to see me again: to finish her story and to ask for help once more. One glance at her face, however, was enough to tell me that she was not in earnest over her request . . . she had come for help on account of a right-sided facial neuralgia, from which she was now suffering day and night. I do not know what kind of help she wanted

---

3. In Bernheimer and Kahane, eds. (1985); Thompson (1990).

from me, but I promised to forgive her for having deprived me of the satisfaction of affording her a far more radical cure for her troubles. [p. 122]

What can have happened to Dora and between her and Freud? Freud himself asked that question, just as many analysts after him have returned to the Dora case history to state, clarify, interpret, explain, and go through the problems and difficulties Freud and Dora had when they met each other. Freud wrote:

> Her father and his family had formed an intimate friendship with a married couple, Herr and Frau K. Frau K. had nursed him during his long illness, and had in that way, he said, earned a title to his undying gratitude. Herr K. had always been most kind to Dora. He had gone for walks with her when he was there, and had made her small presents; but no one had thought any harm of that. Dora had taken the greatest care of the K.'s two little children, and been almost a mother to them. [p. 25]

When Dora was 16, Herr K. "had the audacity to make her a proposition while they were on a walk." Herr K. accused Dora of being overexcited by reading certain books, and had merely "fancied" the whole scene. Even if her father did not doubt that this incident was responsible for Dora's depression, he could not do what Dora demanded, which was to break off relations with the K. family. His friendship with Frau K. was honorable; nothing unseemly had been kept secret; they were just two poor wretches who gave each other comfort and he wanted Freud's help to bring her to her senses. Freud assumed that the experience, the insult to her honor, could have provided her with a psychical trauma, but he also learned to go beyond his earlier theory and to look for the effects in his patient's earliest years.

When the first difficulties of the treatment had been overcome, Dora told him of an earlier episode that occurred when she was 14: Herr K. arranged things so that he was alone with her at his place of business, where:

> He suddenly clasped the girl to him and pressed a kiss upon her lips. This was surely just the situation to call up a distinct feeling of sexual excitement in a girl of fourteen who had never before

been approached. But Dora had at that moment a violent feeling of disgust, tore herself free from the man, and hurried past him to the staircase and from there to the street door. [p. 25]

Freud considered Dora's reaction hysterical, as he considered it to be in anyone in whom an occasion for sexual excitement elicits feelings that are predominantly or exclusively unpleasurable, and interprets the reaction as a reversal of affect and a displacement of genital sensations. Freud makes the point that it was difficult to get Dora to concentrate her attention on Herr K. She declared that she was finished with him but she could not forgive her father for continuing his relations with the K. family. She was also completely convinced that her father's relation to Frau K. was a common love affair.

> [Freud] could not in general dispute Dora's characterization of her father; and there was one particular respect in which it was easy to see that her reproaches were justified. When she was feeling embittered she used to be overcome by the idea that she had been handed over to Herr K. as the price of his tolerating the relations between her father and his wife; and her rage at her father's making such a use of her was visible behind her affection for him. At other times she was quite well aware that she had been guilty of exaggeration in talking like this. . . . But as a matter of fact things were in a position in which each of the two men avoided drawing any conclusions from the other's behavior which would have been awkward for his own plans. [p. 34]

Freud saw how vulnerable Dora's position was in respect to men and how men and women close to her behaved, but for a number of reasons it is probable that he put up defenses against unconditionally investigating Dora's question: "What do you want to change?" He may have unconsciously shared the blindness of the patriarchal society around him with its focus on exploitation, or he lacked our present knowledge and insight into the particularly fragile identity and self-esteem of adolescence. We have learned that there may be fateful consequences if adults close to young persons, on whom they are still dependent, exploit them to satisfy their own needs. To be a failure, to be humiliated in dealing with those who are near and dear, may shake to the foundations their faith in their own powers and put their self-esteem completely out of balance. Rage against the adults who have so betrayed the child by failing to support the development of the adolescents' ego and superego releases primitive aggression that may be turned against their own bodies, intensifying the symptoms or be turned against the analyst, putting the treatment at risk.

Altogether too busy proving his own theories, Freud directed all his attention to Dora's inner reality, her own contribution to the events, going "back to the speaker's own person." The truth was to be found within the ailing Dora and not in her environment. For that reason Freud was not willing to follow his own instructions, presented a decade later, to "listen with evenly suspended attention, allowing yourself to taken by surprise by every new turn in the process, and always with an open mind" (Freud 1912). He insisted on getting Dora to confess her love and longing for Herr K., and in spite of the fact that he saw the connection between himself and Herr K., he did not seem capable of seeing how Dora might interpret his own commitment, which was his own desire to discover the truth of his own theories. His technique was suggestive, persuasive, and convincing; he constantly pressed Dora to confirm his impressions and interpretations, giving Dora little room to follow up her associations herself. He worked brilliantly from details, aiming at the reconstruction of the original oedipal situation, and he thought his most important duty was to discover the hidden meaning, rooted in childhood, in every symptom.

TAKING OVER

There are many interpretations, explanations, excuses, defenses, and rebukes in the extensive literature about Dora derived from Freud's case histories. Everyone knows that it is easy to be wise after the fact and advance ingenious theories for others; quite simply, there is more freedom in observing from a distance. But we also know that outsiders only possess a "normative" competence—that is, a general understanding—while the involved participants, the patient and the analyst, have a "privileged" competence. With a certain amount of hesitation, one can put the question, How would you consult or supervise Freud if he applied for it? Would you point out the complication that he knew the family? That her father brought Dora to him with the order: Get her to listen to reason? That he had advance information about Dora and had already anticipated a great deal about her that might interfere with the need to listen with freely shifting attention. Freud might be warned that Dora would interpret his inquisitive, argumentative attitude as evidence that his motive was not to analyze her in order to help her understand herself, her predicament, and help her deal with it, but that he was analyzing the material from the perspective of his own aims, where he only wanted to confirm what he already knew. It may be possible to prove how his premature interpretations and active interrogation were bound to increase Dora's defensiveness and resistance. He might then defend himself by saying that "Everything I call Dora's attention to is present in what she says!" One could well ask Freud, "What do you want to do? What is your goal?" Freud might answer, "I want to create and validate the psychoanalytical theory, I want to confirm my theories about hysteria and use the patient for this end—and there I must often use all my brilliance and my power of persuasion to gather all the details into an argument so I will not to be silenced as I was after I published my book *The Interpretation of Dreams*. But let me tell you her dream:

> Just at the moment when there was a prospect that the material that was coming up for analysis would throw light on an obscure point in Dora's childhood, she reported that a few nights earlier she had once again had a dream which she had already dreamt in exactly the same way on many previous occasions. A periodically recurrent dream was by its very nature calculated to rouse my curiosity; and in any case it was justifiable in the interests of the treatment to consider the way in which the dream worked into the analysis as a whole. I therefore determined to make an especially careful investigation of it. And here is the dream related by Dora: 'A house was on fire. My father was standing beside my bed and woke me up. I dressed quickly. Mother wanted to stop and save her jewel case; but Father said: I refuse to let myself and my two children be burnt for the sake of your jewel-case. We hurried downstairs, and as soon as I was outside I woke up.' [p. 64]

I posed, as usual, questions about every detail. One could point out that it is risky to seek the clearing up of the dream before Freud made sure that he could understand what Dora wants to say about the relationship between the two of them. In the dream, one could hear that she says that we (Dora, the children) are in danger; Father (that is, the analyst holding the frame) is going to save us. Mother is too occupied with her jewel case and there is a risk that the analyst will be too, if his main wish is to validate the psychoanalytical theory and confirm his theories about hysteria using her, the patient, to that end. Freud can now react in various ways. He may be able to accommodate the supervisor's perspective on the interactive significance of the dreams. He may already be open to following up in the here and now his impressions and experiences of the communicative importance of transference. He is, however, likely to be conditioned to too great an extent by his duty to bring out the hidden truth (*per via di levare*), and as a result he will probably turn defensive at every effort to get him to pay attention to the importance and the consequences of his own interventions and his motives for them. Freud could end the supervision by summarizing the synthesis of the dream:

> The wish which the dream wants to come true always springs from the period of childhood. The dream expresses this wish anew, and it tries to correct the present day by the measure of childhood. And what Dora is trying to express in her dream is: "Dear Father, protect me again as you used to in my childhood, and prevent my bed from being wetted!" The day after, Dora brought me an addendum: each time after waking up she had smelt smoke. I reminded her that I would often say, "There can be no smoke without fire!" She answered that everyone smokes. Add to this that dreams usually contain the most obscure thought, which here was the longing for a kiss, linked both to the episode when she was fourteen years old and to childhood thumb-sucking. I realized that there was also a link to me in the transference, that she would like to have a kiss from me. I told her this and added in addition that from the re-emergence of the dream during the last few days I had to conclude that she was saying that the same situation had returned and that she had decided to stop the treatment, which, of course, she had only been induced to start through the agency of her father. [p. 69]

Here the supervisor is left with many unanswered questions and suppositions. Who has put Freud in the seducer's position? Is it he himself, a middle-aged man tempted by the young girl's secrets and jewel box? Is it Dora who has chosen this role for him in accordance with what Freud writes about the importance of transference in his postscript to the case history? To Freud, transfers are new editions or facsimiles of the impulses and fantasies which are aroused and made conscious during the progress of the analysis; but they have this peculiarity, which is characteristic for their species, that they replace some earlier person by the person of the physician. To put it another way: a whole series of psychological experiences are revived, not as belonging to the past, but as applying to the person of the physician at the present moment. . . . Some of these . . . are merely new impressions or reprints. Others are more ingeniously constructed. [p. 116]

What part does Freud play in establishing his position as seducer, the one who arouses Dora's desire, fear, and defenses? Of what importance in this process is the circumstance that Freud works with the metaphor "a regularly formed dream stands upon two legs," placing the dream at the point of intersection between the legs, at the genitals? The dream may then be seen as a sexual organ to be inspected, penetrated. Freud insisted that Dora confess her love and longing for Herr K., and although he recognized the connection between himself and Herr K., he was blinded by his own strong involvement, his desire and eagerness to reveal "the secret." Dora may very well have interpreted this as Freud's desire to penetrate her, as his own desire to play with fire.

REVENGE: "DO YOU KNOW, DOCTOR, THAT I AM HERE FOR THE LAST TIME TODAY?"

Many have reacted to Freud's tone with Dora, that blooming young girl with intelligent, attractive features, that pathetic teenager brought by her father to him, a 44-year-old neurologist and paterfamilias. She told him a sad story of being exploited, molested, and betrayed by the adults around her. But instead of showing her compassion and sympathy, Freud treated her as a dangerous adversary. He wrestled with her, set traps, pressed her against the wall with confrontations and interpretations.

Several weeks after the first dream, Dora related her second dream. When work with this had been concluded, the analysis was broken off.

The labor of elucidating the second dream had so far occupied two hours. At the end of the second session, when I expressed my satisfaction at the result, Dora replied in a deprecatory tone: "Why, has anything so very remarkable come out?" These words prepared me for the advent of fresh revelations. She opened the third session with these words: "Do you know that I am here for the last time today?"—"How can I know, as you have said nothing to me about it?"—"Yes, I made up my mind to put up with it till the New Year (12/31/1900). But I shall wait no longer than that to be cured."—"You know that you are free to stop the treatment at any time. But for today we will go on with our work. When did you come to this decision?"—"A fortnight ago, I think."—"That sounds just like a maidservant or a governess—a fortnight's notice."—"There was a governess who gave notice with the K.s, when I was on my visit to them that time by the lake."—"Really? You have never told me about her. Tell me." [p. 105]

The following was then interpreted by Freud as Dora's rage against Herr K and her wish to take revenge for being betrayed by him, as she "did fancy that Herr K's proposals were serious, and that he would not leave off until you had married him. She had listened, without any of her usual contradictions. She seemed to be moved; she said good-bye to me very warmly, with the heartiest wishes for the New Year, and—came no more" (p. 108).

Freud contributed to the making the grammar of the unconscious, which had always been open to poets and artists, accessible to those engaged in health care and in science of the mind. Speech begins with the original dialogue between child and mother (or "the attentive other"). The infant's cry calls forth the accessible mother, and in this first dialogue the concepts are created, phase-specific and via the paternal order, which are then integrated into inner endeavors that give meaning to the child's experiences. At the same time the relation between the internal and the external reality is being organized. The original dialogue was revived in Dora's dream; out of her painful, distressing situation she calls out for her father to save her and this is repeated in the analytical situation. She sought shelter with the analyst at the same time as she was setting up precisely the danger from which she was trying to be saved. The aim of the relation and the analytical situation is just this: to facilitate the creation of mutual concepts through which the participants can communicate about such experiences. The patient expresses himself or herself, like Dora, both verbally and nonverbally. For both parties, they create a comprehensible language, assuming that the analyst is able to listen and understand what the patient is trying to say about him, the analyst. The image the patient creates of the analyst may also provide important guidance leading to a better understanding of his own person, technique, and countertransference, presenting material for self-analysis and supervision. Freud was much too preoccupied with his own desire to force the secret out of Dora's dream, and this prevented him from seeing anything other than what he wanted to see.

What we have also learned from Freud's experiences with Dora is that we must understand and deal with transference within an established working relationship. The patient's tendency to repeat and, in the situation with the analyst, recognize previous experiences, has its roots in old expectations and infantile wishes. The fear of being caught by life, of being drawn in, violated by it in pain and desire—just this commits Dora and many others to the repetition of wishes and fantasies linked to figures from their childhood. In analysis these patterns can be discovered and surveyed—if the analyst does not abandon the patient by being too bound up in his own expectations and theories. Then the risk is, as in the case of Dora, that the analysis will be broken off. Otherwise new experiences which the analysand will have within the analytical situation may offer fresh strategies and solutions to problems. By his interpretations the analyst can help the patient to gain increased self-knowledge. In this process the patient can make surprising discoveries, reaching an insight into himself and his relations. It is important to remember that the analyst's interpretations are always only made up from "ideas" expressing his own interpretations and opinions. They can have a permanent effect only if they stand up against the patient's critical study and dovetail with his or her own inner reality. Only on this basis can the patient change his or her own life.

REFERENCES

Bernheimer, C., and Kahane, C., eds. (1985). *Dora's Case: Freud—Hysteria—Feminism*. New York: Columbia University Press.

Erikson, E. H. (1964). *Insight and Responsibility*. New York: Norton.
Freud, S. (1905). Fragment of an analysis of a case of hysteria. *Standard Edition* 7:1–122.
―――― (1912). Recommendations to physicians practicing psychoanalysis. *Standard Edition* 12:109–120.
Hallesretdt, G. (1990). *Introduction and Postscript to the Swedish Translation of Freud, S. (1905): Dora: Brottstycke av en hysterianalys*. Göteborg: Alster Förlag.
Szecsödy, I. (1998). Dora: Freud's Pygmalion or the unrecovered patient of a famous analyst? In *On Freud's Couch: Seven New Interpretations of Freud's Case Histories*, ed. I. Matthis and I. Szecsödy, pp. 57–93. Northvale, NJ and London: Jason Aronson.
Thomson, A. (1990). The ending of Dora's story: Deutsch's footnote as a narrative. *Psychoanalysis and Contemporary Thought* 13:509–534.

8

Finger-Twisting and Cracked Voices: The Hysterical Symptom Revisited

Iréne Matthis

> [. . .] it still strikes me [. . .] as strange that the case histories I write should read like short stories [. . .]. I must console myself with the reflection that the nature of the subject is evidently responsible for this, rather than any preference of my own. The fact is that [. . .] a detailed description of mental processes such as we are accustomed to find in the works of imaginative writers enables me [. . .] to obtain at least some kind of insight into the course of [hysteria]. Case histories of this kind [. . .] have [. . .] an intimate connection between the story of the patient's sufferings and the symptoms of his illness.
>
> —Freud 1893–1895, *Standard Edition* 2:136

The importance of Freud's early insight into the role of narrative in the patient's history of sickness cannot be overestimated. Several times, in *Studies on Hysteria*, he mentions aspects of a narrative perspective, and he uses metaphors borrowed from literature and drama. However, he does so only in passing, as if he was just noticing something of interest that was a bit perplexing. Freud had not yet fully realized the importance of his discovery.

In the case of Emmy von N., whose treatment he began in the spring of 1888, he remarks on the fact that incidents in her history that were widely separated in time were told to him "in a single sentence and in such a rapid succession that they might have been a single episode in four acts" (*Standard Edition* 2:57). He points out that "the accounts she gave of traumas arranged like these in groups began with a 'how,' the component traumas being separated by an 'and'" (ibid.). "How," "and"! Actually, he initiates a linguistic analysis of the patient's "text" rather than a medical examination of her bodily symptoms.

Later, in the case of Rosalie, he describes how incidents, collected into groups like this, form "mnemic symbols." The recollected occasions often seem to be of a very ordinary, and even trivial, character, and Freud writes that he "should have been prepared to deny that they could play a part in the etiology of a hysterical symptom." (*Standard Edition* 2:172) But as drops of water, hitting the same spot, slowly will make an impact that each drop by itself cannot, so the collected impetus of all the small incidents, having some element in common, will finally attain a force that, given the right circumstances, will make itself felt. The affects connected with the "mnemic symbol" will again be aroused when a freshly experienced affect—by way of association—will stir anew the dormant forces. "[A] process of this kind is the rule rather than the exception in the genesis of hysterical symptoms. Almost invariably when I have investigated the determinants of such conditions what I have come upon has not been a *single* traumatic cause but a group of similar ones" (ibid.).

DISPLACEMENT AND CONDENSATION

As is well known, Freud worked out the mechanisms of "a process of this kind" in *The Interpretation of Dreams*, published five years later (1900). Through the processes of displacement and condensation a connection is created between otherwise disparate events. In this way meaning is established, where hitherto none could be divined, and an understanding is accomplished, which it seems the patient benefits from—even to the point of getting well.

We generally think of displacement and condensation as linguistic terms applicable to textual material and, in a figurative sense, to matters of body and behavior—as when the concepts are applied to a hysterical bodily symptom or an obsessional conduct in order to make them intelligible. Freud's writings, from the *Studies* onwards, as well as modern psychoanalytical publications, abound with examples of these uses. It is perhaps less well known, or taken into account, that the linguistic terms thus transferred to bodily and behavior spheres in this transposition are actually only returning back to the fields from which they originated.

After Darwin (1872) it can hardly be argued that man's expressions were given from the beginning as they now appear to us (for some as God-given capacities). They originated in specific contexts and were reinforced and slowly developed for specific purposes (for instance, survival). This is applicable even to those capabilities particular to *Homo Sapiens*—as Carl von Linné christened humans in his system of nature: "the sensible and intelligent man." This judiciousness resides in man's highly developed symbolic functions, which are a prerequisite for spoken and written language, and for using symbols on a theoretical level.

Theoretical concepts like displacement and condensation, so indispensable in all psychoanalytical work, are fruits of this symbolic capacity, but the thought processes to which they generally refer have a deep bodily anchorage: in motor behavior (movements and rhythms) and finally, of course, in the processes of the nervous and humorous systems of the body. This, however, does not reduce thought processes, nor conscious human feelings, to impulses and energies of nervous and muscular tissues. So many other things are involved, that we cannot here venture into.[1] Freud, however, was already wrestling with these problems at the end of last century, and they found an outlet in his

---

1. For a discussion on some of the issues related to this interface between neuroscience and psychoanalysis, see, for example, Mark Solms' article "What Is Consciousness" in *Journal of the American Psychoanalytic Association* (1997) 45:3, and the discussion that followed, in the journal as well as on the Internet. For an excellent survey of the field, see Pally (1997, 1998a,b), and for further information, see Damasio (1994), Edelman (1992), Freeman (1995), Johnson (1987), Lakoff (1987), Penrose

Project for a Scientific Psychology, written in 1895 (Freud 1950). In this venture he was, I believe, on the right track, but neuroscience during his lifetime had not yet evolved sufficiently to give to his arguments an organic foundation. Therefore, Freud never published the *Project* in his own lifetime.

Today, neuroscience has made great advances and, to my mind, modern neuroscientists have convincingly substantiated psychoanalytical knowledge, even if many of the scientists themselves do not yet like to acknowledge the fact, as they do not want to be connected to Freud. Freud's own thinking in these matters have timely been revitalized, for example, by Mark Solms in London and the New York Psychoanalytical Institute Neuroscience Study Group.

Luckily, despite the miscarriage of the *Project*, Freud did not desert the subject. Instead he developed its implications in an area which was more easily accessible at the time: man's dream life. In *The Interpretation of Dreams* (1900) he explores the dark continents of the unconscious by way of textual analysis of narrative structures. Free association was to become the route to the shadowy quarters where latent and repressed meanings were hidden. Displacement and condensation were the mechanisms unconsciously employed in the process.

FREE ASSOCIATION

Free association is a paradoxical designation of what is going on, as the whole idea with the method is that the thoughts that will appear are not, as a matter of fact, free in the sense that they are under no other influence but chance. Actually, they are determined to the same degree as our conscious thoughts. However, the forces at work are different from those deciding the course of conscious deliberations. Conscious communication with other people is marked by choices and omissions determined mainly by demands and expectations from the environment as well as from one self. It is exactly this influence that free association is supposed to free us from. But instead, other,

---

(1994), Schachter (1996), Searle (1997), and Shevrin (1996). For a metapsychological model of the role of affect in this interaction, see Mathis (2000).

unconscious, influences will make themselves felt, as for example the bodily dispositions that constitute the matrix of the unconscious processes of our psyche. It is because of this bodily anchorage that the method of free association is effective in exploring unconscious psychic life.

When analysts talk or write about free association it is usually done in terms of the many difficulties encountered in our efforts to make the patient oblige to the rule of free association; or the opposite is emphasized: the astounding connections revealed in the material by the method and the impact of these moments of "mutative change." But for Freud, free association signified more than a pure method of treatment. It was a step toward a theoretical psychological system:

> With the help of the method of free association and of the related art of interpretation, psycho-analysis succeeded in achieving one thing which appeared to be of no practical importance but which in fact necessarily led to a totally fresh attitude and *a fresh scale of values in scientific thought*. [Standard Edition 20:43; emphasis added]

Thus there are, at least, two aspects of "free association," as Freud formulated it. One having to do with clinical work and the practice of psychoanalysis, the other with its paradigmatic theoretical impact, which will effect the theories of conscious and unconscious processes, and the issues of body and mind.

In the scientific world at large the theoretical implications of free association is hardly acknowledged at all. But something of the same ignorance in this matter will, I suspect, be found even among psychoanalysts—with a few exceptions. I might be wrong in this and then I hope someone will enlighten me, but if I am correct it is not difficult to understand why this should be. So far, there has been no reliable scientific methods to substantiate the findings of psychoanalysis from a different perspective. Today, advances in the methods of neuroscientific examinations have made Freud's words all the more meaningful, as it is now possible to verify, in the field of neuropsychology, the importance of the psychoanalytical method of free association—as has been shown for example by Mark Solms in his recent work *The Neuropsychology of Dreams* (1997a).

The importance of free association as a step forward in understanding the human psyche can also be illustrated with the result it showed when transferred to the field of the interpretation of dreams. If dreams are formed through influences from those layers of our mental structure to which consciousness does not have access, they will compare to material produced in free association. In "On the History of the Psycho-Analytical Movement" Freud writes: "I need say little about the interpretation of dreams. It came as the first-fruits of the technical innovation I had adopted when, following a dim presentiment, I decided to replace hypnosis by free association" (*Standard Edition* 14:19).

It would be tempting to probe more deeply into this subject, but the clinical material that I am soon going to present (a Freud case) is not adequate to such an endeavor and therefore I will content myself with trying to point to a way in which the two aspects of free association here mentioned could be related.

For this purpose we will start with the concrete clinical situation, in which the method of free association is applied. If free association is the means of getting to the unconscious wishes and fears that lie behind a patient's symptom, then it must be important for the analyst to know what factors could obstruct and what circumstances could facilitate the process.

In his work with Frau Emmy, Freud had discovered early on that his suggestions to the patient did not give the expected result if the patient had not first been permitted to tell her whole story without being interrupted. Even when under hypnosis, Frau Emmy kept a watching eye on Freud's proceedings, and he writes: "I now saw that I had gained nothing by this interruption and that I cannot evade listening to her stories in every detail to the very end" (*Standard Edition* 2:61).

In the psychoanalytical method of free association it is, however, not only important to listen to the story told spontaneously, but equally, or even more significantly, the stories forgotten or actively withheld by the patient. Through the associative pattern slowly established by way of mechanisms like displacement and condensation, the analyst will eventually discern forms and contents that reveal the conflictual basis for the symptoms in question. This constitutes the material which the analysand and the analyst together elaborate in the day-to-day process of analysis.

I have found a semiotic model helpful in illustrating these processes.

A SEMIOTIC MODEL

A basic assumption in a semiotic model is that we know every object in the world by way of some sort of sign.[2] The sign stands as a symbol for the object to which it refers. This means that all our experiences and all our knowledge of the world are mediated: we know what we know only by way of something else, which has a referring function. This is apparent, for example, in the case when a patient comes to the hospital with a symptom, let's say a breathing difficulty. The physician on duty might easily decide on the cause behind the dyspnœa: heart failure with pulmonary edema. He acts accordingly, not on the presented symptom, but on the cause; acts not on the sign, but on that to which the sign refers: the pulmonary edema. The physician reads the sign and remedies the cause:

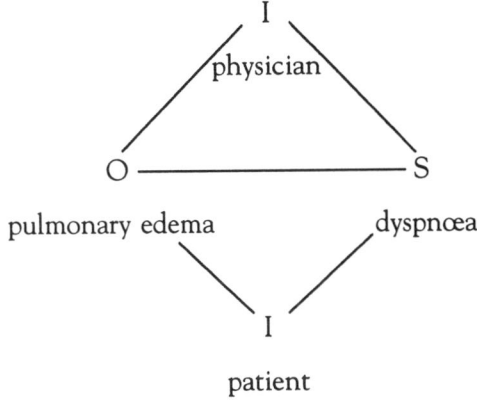

---

2. I have used the semiotic model of C. S. Peirce, but adopted it for my special purposes. C. S. Peirce (1839–1914)—a physicist, mathematician, and philosopher—created a model for human interaction which he labeled semiotic. He is regarded as the founding father of pragmatism in the United States, and he played an important role for William James and his work. I also think his influence on Lacan's writings (not only thinking but style) was great.

The semiotic model here presented goes beyond the Saussurian dual-sign theory. It introduces a triadic conception which, to my mind, makes a much better fit with our experience in the psychoanalytic situation. It can also be extended—as I do here—to a model of intersubjective interaction which takes place by way of some kind of sign (neurotic, psychotic or somatic symptoms, dreams, parapraxis, acting-out behavior, yes, even the lack of a "sign"—that ought to be there—is a sign). Space does not

Everybody is satisfied.

But often enough the object to which the sign refers is not easily detected. So was, for example, the case with the hysterical patients Freud treated a hundred years ago, and so is the case with the new psychosomatic disorders confronting the medical-care system of today; chronic fatigue syndrome, environmental illness, fibromyalgia, and other pain syndromes. The bodily symptoms in these cases can often not be related to any known organic cause. Thus the sign is invalidated, and the question of what the symptom signifies remains unanswered:

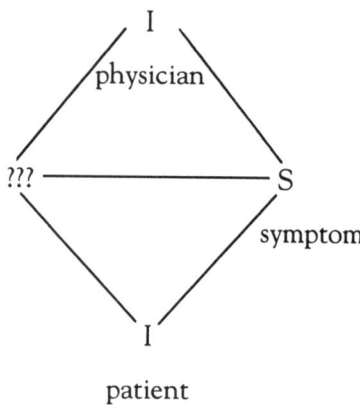

In the hysterical patients Freud met and worked with at the end of the last century, this question was central. Trying to solve the enigma of the hysterical symptom, Freud—together with his patients—invented the genial method of free association. When "the object" cannot be found, the sign will instead give rise to a series of questions, such as: When? Where? Why? and How? In turn, these questions will initiate a process of storytelling: the talking cure. Katharina, for example, a young girl Freud treated in 1893 for breathing difficulties,

---

allow me to present a full semiotic model in this context, nor define the meaning given to symptom, symbol, and sign respectively in this connection. A reader familiar with Swedish will find a full account of this in Matthis (1997). In English, and related to the work of Bion, Alfred Silver has presented a somewhat different semiotic model based on Peirce (Silver 1983).

and whose case is reported in *Studies on Hysteria* (Breuer and Freud, 1893–1895), was in this way cured from her attacks. Telling the stories, revealing their interconnections, and expressing their dammed up emotions proved to be an effective treatment:

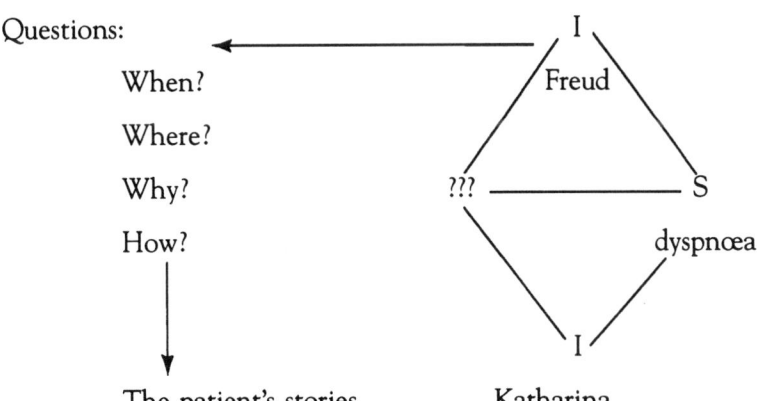

As we know from Freud, the symptoms in this process are looked upon as signs that refer to emotional states that occurred *in the past*. The famous statement: "hysterics suffer mainly from reminiscences" epitomizes Freud's view on the etiology of the hysterical symptom as presented in *Studies on Hysteria* (*Standard Edition* 2:7). The symptom arises due to a trauma, which in the case of hysteria usually is psychical and related to sexuality (in the case of Katharina, for example, the father's sexual seduction of herself and her cousin). The trauma has stirred up distressing affects that were not, for different reasons, allowed adequate expression. Instead the trauma—or rather the memory of it—remains in an unconscious form: it acts as a "foreign body which long after its entry must continue to be regarded as an agent that is still at work" (*Standard Edition* 2:6).

The hysterical symptom is thus based on and finds its affective matrix in a strongly cathected situation, where the details of the drama will provide the material for what later—*nachträglich*—and by way of conversion, will provide the bodily symptom-signs used to give expression to affects and sufferings felt but not known. To this well-known theory I would like to make an addition by reintroducing the concept of disposition for the corporeal matrix to which these affective "reminiscences" are attached. Our experience teaches us that psychic and mental phenomena (affects and thoughts) influence the physical, and, vice versa, physical disorders give rise to psychic disturbances. My assumption is that these exchanges work by way of a disposition.[3]

We shall shortly return to this issue, but first let me—as material for my argument—present the case of Rosalie, which Freud uses to illustrate the process of symptom-formation in hysteria (*Standard Edition* 2:169–173).

ROSALIE H

Fräulein Rosalie H. was 23 years old when she came to see Freud in Vienna, because of some difficulties with her voice. She was a good singer and had for some years been undergoing training. But, she complained to Freud:

> In certain parts of its compass [her voice] was not under her control. She had a feeling of choking and constriction in her throat so that her voice sounded tight. [. . .] At times the disturbance was completely absent and her teacher expressed great satisfaction; at other times, if she was in the least agitated, and sometimes without any apparent cause, the constricted feeling would reappear and the production of her voice was impeded. [*Standard Edition* 2:169]

---

3. In *Studies on Hysteria* Freud and Breuer talk about "dispositional hysteria" (*Standard Edition* 2:12) to designate a "liability to dissociation" so characteristic of the disease. And section 6 of Breuer's theoretical contribution is titled: "Innate Disposition—Development of Hysteria." He uses the term to replace the phrase "abnormal excitability of the nervous system" (*Standard Edition* 2:241). For both Breuer and Freud disposition is not only innate but acquired. "It is possible and perhaps probable that further observations will prove the psychical origin of one or other of these stigmata and so explain the symptom; but this has not yet happened" (*Standard Edition* 2:242).

The term disposition is a concept also used in the latest developments of cognitive theory (Johnson 1987, Lakoff 1987) as well as in the neuroscience dealing with the brain and its "brainstates" (Damasio 1994, Freeman 1995). Thus here we have a point where, at least in theory, the different perspectives of cognitive science, neuroscience, and psychoanalysis meet.

The difficulties could not be attributed to a defect in the organ itself, and besides, they only affected the middle register of her voice. Therefore we start out with the realization that there are no organic causes to be found behind the disorder. We might be mistaken, but so far we have no way to find out. This, of course, not only puts special demands on the doctor who is to treat the case, but also makes the situation for the patient more difficult by putting the blame on her. Fräulein Rosalie's guilt would thus be much greater, as it seemed she was the sole cause of the disorder. But if that was the case, she still could not by an act of will do anything about it.

Thus we can conclude: first, that the causal mechanism is not to be found in the physiology of the muscles and the organs of the throat. And second, that the reasons are not to be found among her conscious wishes, nor can she change the situation by simple willpower.

Where then are the causes to be found? "In the unconscious," would be Freud's conclusion. This realm of mental processes and psychic realities Freud explored by way of the cathartic method first introduced by Breuer in his work with Anna O. In this treatment the stories told by the patients, and the expression of affects related to these, were of fundamental importance. This will become clear, for example, in the case of Rosalie.

Within analytical philosophy the term includes properties of inorganic matter as well: a piece of iron will, for example, have a magnetic disposition. This cannot be judged by the exterior, but will show itself only when the iron is put in a certain context: among iron filings that will—if the iron is magnetic—arrange themselves in a certain pattern around the centerpiece.

The concept of disposition is thus a generally accepted one within many different sciences. Besides, it is a word of everyday use, and nobody has difficulties in understanding what is meant, when someone, for example, says that he has a disposition for a special illness or to certain acts. This does not imply, however, that it is possible to explain *how* a disposition is established or *how* it works. And when it comes to the type of psycho-physiological disposition with which we are dealing here, the explanation will of course be speculative and the models hypothetical. But in order to be able to even ask the question: why "words work wonders" on body and soul in the therapeutic process, we have to start by describing the clinical experience of it. This knowledge (which Aristotle called *phronesis*) precedes the question of why the word has effect, and even more so the answers to how (*episteme*) (Toulmin 1994).

She was the eldest child in a family of many children. The father was an abusive and violent man, both towards the mother and the children. Especially distressing for the family was the fact that he openly showed his sexual interest in and preference for the servants and the nursemaids in the house.

Then the mother died and Rosalie had to take over her responsibilities, defending herself and her siblings against the father's assaults. In order not to provoke him even more she had to keep back her disgust and hatred for him:

> It was at this time that the feeling of constriction in her throat started. Every time she had to keep back a reply, or forced herself to remain quiet in the face of some outrageous accusation, she felt a scratching in her throat, a sense of constriction, a loss of voice—all the sensations localized in her larynx and pharynx which now interfered with her singing. [*Standard Edition* 2:170]

A singing teacher came to her assistance and gave her lessons, to which she had to sneak in secret, often directly from an emotional scene at home. So a connection was established between a threatening situation, an emotional state, her throat, and singing. "The apparatus over which she ought to have had full control when she was singing turned out to be cathected with residues of innervations left over from the numerous scenes of suppressed emotion" (*Standard Edition* 2:171).

The Traumatic Process

In this description we recognize most of the elements that constitute a traumatic situation: violence, psychical or physical; strong emotions of fright or anger that have to be suppressed; in all, an overwhelming situation of too much anxiety and too little understanding. If we add to this the fact of the loss of the mother, we have a scenario designed for a traumatic impact on Rosalie's further development.

We can now give a first, simple model for the traumatic process, from which we can develop our argument:

External situation	Psychical and physical reaction	Aftereffect
physical or psychical violence or threat (traumatic situation)	affective states and bodily reactions	symptoms and dispositions

Whenever an external situation of traumatic effect occurs, internal reactions will take place that imply affective states as well as bodily reactions. We might feel angry and irritated, or afraid and desperate. These emotional states will always be accompanied by somatic reactions, whether we are conscious of them or not.[4] The heart will race or the eyes fill with tears, the hair on our arms will stand on end or our skin blush. Beside these easily detected reactions, a whole series of physiological and chemical reactions will also take place: signal substances are released and hormones and enzymes rush into the bloodstream. Emotional signs are in this way primarily linked to the body.

In Rosalie's case, Freud described some of the traumatic external situations and her emotional reactions to them. When, in our analytical practice, we are faced with situations like these, we tend to concentrate on the object relationships at the time and the affective links between the actors of the drama. We take the symptom to refer back to the psychological phenomena, with which we are generally concerned. This technique usually proves itself to be effective. But we tend to overlook, and even forget, the bodily reactions that took place at the moment of the event. However, these reactions are, I want to stress, important. In the case of Rosalie, for example, the bodily signs

---

4. It is a long-known fact that emotions and bodily reactions go together. William James wrote: "Instinctive reactions and emotional expressions thus shade imperceptibly into each other. Every object that excites an instinct excites an emotion as well" (1890 p. 1058). According to him, the bodily changes precede the feeling state, and the feeling actually "is our feeling of the same changes" (ibid. p. 1065). We do not run from the bear because we feel afraid; we feel afraid because we run from the bear. The relation between bodily reactions (having to do with objectively verifiable facts of physiology, chemistry, behavior, etc.) and emotional states (referring to subjectively experienced states of affect) is a complex issue. At this level of inquiry it is, however, enough for us to know that they always "go together" and all the time—in various ways—interact. I have elaborated this further in Matthis (2000).

were related to her throat. "It was at this time that the feeling of constriction in her throat started" (*Standard Edition* 2:170).

The external traumatic situation results in a symptom, based on the specific emotional and bodily reactions at the time (and they are always individually determined and context-bound). In Rosalie's case, her throat problems and vocal difficulties. The original reactions, however, did not only—in due time—give rise to symptoms which we can observe and analyze. Of equal importance is the fact that they created a disposition, a tendency to react in one way or another in the future. A disposition functions as a kind of anticipation: it is an *acquired expectation* founded on, and interacting with, an *innate condition*. The disposition cannot be investigated in the same manner as the symptom. The latter is obvious, something to be seen or heard by the subject himself or by an observer. The disposition, however, we can only make assumptions about. Only in the course of events will these show themselves to be true or false.

Rosalie's conversion symptom can thus be looked upon as both a symptom in the ordinary sense of the word, and as an indicator of the presence—in the unconscious, in the body—of a disposition, established on the same ground as that which caused the symptom. When we follow the course of treatment in Freud's presentation we will be able to see how this disposition will come to make itself known. Let us therefore return to the case history.

Rosalie's Treatment

Rosalie was soon to leave her family and move to Vienna. There she stayed with an uncle and aunt, while she continued her singing lessons. She was, however, not happy with her relatives. The uncle, a nice man—but old—took a liking to her. This made the aunt suspicious and she then made it her habit to spy on them. This made Rosalie avoid playing and singing when the aunt was around.

This was the situation when she came to see Freud because of her throat symptoms. Freud's treatment at the time included hypnosis as a part of the cathartic abreactive model. Thus he proceeded to hypnotize the young lady, in order to have her experience, once again and in his presence, the emotional states of the traumatic situations in her family of origin. But now,

Finger-Twisting and Cracked Voices / 153

instead of holding back her emotions, she was encouraged to vent them freely, to "abuse her [father],[5] lecture him, tell him the unvarnished truth, and so on, and this did her good" (*Standard Edition* 2:171).

To begin with, Rosalie did get better. But the tensions in her host family in Vienna worked against Freud's therapeutic efforts, and finally brought them to a premature end. But before this happened, Freud got a chance to observe the creation of a completely new symptom. One day Rosalie came to her session with a symptom that was scarcely 24 hours old.

Because of a disagreeable pricking sensation in the tips of her fingers, she made compulsory movements with her fingers. These movements came on as a kind of attack, that is, they could not be started by pure force of will. We can draw this conclusion because Freud first complains that he could not observe an attack, which he would have liked, as an aid to solving the puzzle. Well, in due time he would.

A semiotic model for this situation could look like this:

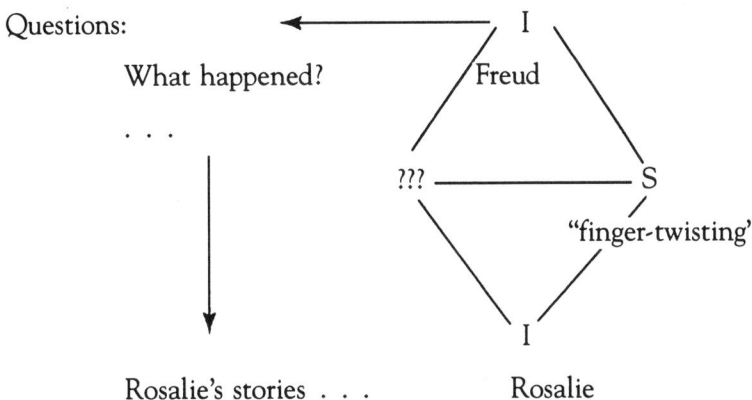

Freud now hypnotized Rosalie in the hope of finding out what had happened 24-hours previously—something, he guessed, that had precipitated the attacks. Instead he was astonished to

---

5. In the original text, Freud presented the offender as an uncle, while, in reality, it was the father. The reason was, as always, to cover up the identities of the persons involved.

find her starting to tell him about incidents dating from long before, and situations from far back in her childhood. One theme ran through all the narratives Rosalie now presented to Freud. It had to do with her having had some injury done to her, against which she had not been able to defend herself. For example, a schoolteacher had once hit her on the fingers with a ruler. But all the stories seemed to relate to very simple and ordinary occasions and, Freud writes:

> I should have been prepared to deny that they could play a part in the etiology of a hysterical symptom. But it was otherwise with one scene from her girlhood which followed. Her bad [father], who was suffering from rheumatism, had asked her to massage his back and she did not dare to refuse. He was lying in bed at the time, and suddenly threw off the bed-clothes, sprang up and tried to catch hold of her and throw her down. Massage, of course, was at an end, and a moment later she had escaped and locked herself in her room. She was clearly loath to remember this and was unwilling to say whether she had seen anything when he suddenly uncovered himself. [*Standard Edition* 2:172]

The Details of Bodily Involvement

So here again we find a traumatic situation, giving rise to an emotional state and to bodily reactions. Here too the sexual element is introduced, which was so decisive for Freud's argument concerning the traumatic process. To this I would like to add the importance of the details of the bodily involvement, in this case the fingers: they are being hit by the schoolteacher; they are being used to massage the father's body, and so forth.

> Only after relating the scene with the father does Rosalie come to the one of the day before, which had precipitated the new symptom "as a recurrent mnemic symbol" (*Standard Edition* 2:172).

> The uncle with whom she was now living had asked her to play him something. She sat down to the piano and accompanied herself in a song, thinking that her aunt had gone out; but suddenly she appeared in the door. Rosalie jumped up, slammed

the lid of the piano and threw the music away. We can guess what the memory was that rose in her mind and what the train of thought was that she was fending off at that moment: it was the feeling of violent resentment at the unjust suspicion to which she was subjected [. . .] The movement of her fingers which I saw her make while she *was reproducing this scene* was one of twitching something away, in the way in which one literally and figuratively brushes something aside—tosses away a piece of paper or rejects a suggestion. [*Standard Edition* 2:172–173, emphasis added]

The body reacts: it *reproduces* a scene, that is, it is what Freud sometimes calls a *Darstellung*, a putting on the scene, as it were, concretely: an embodiment. It creates a situation where the sign (S) coalesces with the object (O). The symptom in this situation is therefore not the creation of a *Vorstellung*, an idea of the thing, but the "thing" itself manifested. The quality of sign is in this case only ascribed to it from the position of the observer. Rosalie's body acts as if it was again at the father's bedside, where his body is demanding to be touched by her fingers. As the filings assemble around a piece of iron and thus it discloses its magnetic disposition, Rosalie's finger-twisting now reveals her bodily disposition. The finger-twisting is here not only a symptom in the narrow sense, but it reproduces a sign of a bodily inscription: a disposition to react in a certain way. Rosalie's finger-twisting symptom—that suddenly presented itself during the ongoing treatment—was not only related to the fingers that, at the request of the uncle, were playing the piano, but also to the bodily memory of the fingers that had massaged the father.

Freud believed "that a process of this kind is the rule rather than the exception in the genesis of hysterical symptoms." There is "not a *single* traumatic cause but a group of similar ones" (*Standard Edition* 2:173). Thus, we have a cluster of experiences that create a disposition. A few years later, in the *Project*, Freud will call it *Bahnungen*—a stimulation of certain synaptic connections and not others. Some of the traumatic scenes as reported by the patients seem rather harmless, but when they join forces with more dramatic instances, all this will work together to overdetermine the resulting symptoms. The symptoms arise, as Freud said, *from reminiscences.*

Given this evidence we have the right to ask whether it is the case that a bodily disposition (innate or acquired) is a prerequisite for the formation of a hysterical symptom? If the answer is "yes," a general model could look like this:

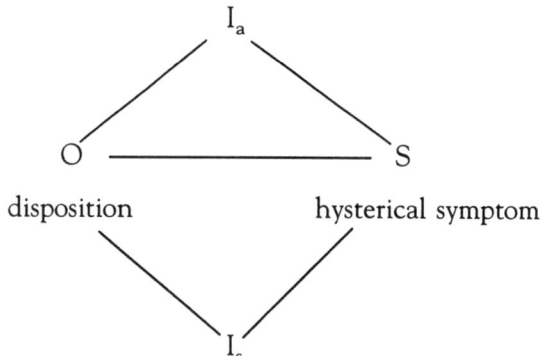

where O stands for an acquired disposition based on memories of traumatic situations—always connected to *bodily reactions* and *affective states* (sexuality), as described earlier; S is the presenting symptom (in this case the cracked voice and the finger-twisting); I_a an agent that in some way or other partakes of the interaction (the father, the uncle/aunt, Freud, and so forth); and I_s is the subject (Rosalie).

In the beginning of this paper I stressed the importance of the role of narrative in the patient's history of illness. The case of Rosalie, I hope, has illustrated this process, where the patient's stories are shown to constitute a kind of narrative of a bodily disposition. They actualize an anticipation by linking traumatic situations to perceptions and bodily movements, in which one or several elements are shared.

I also emphasized the often overlooked fact that free association is not only a psychological method to set this process going, but that it also has important theoretical and scientific implications, in that it reveals the intimate relation between the patient's words (conscious thoughts) and feelings (conscious emotions) on the one hand side and her bodily symptoms (signs of unconscious dispositions) and brain processes (unconscious mental states) on the other. The hysterical and psychosomatic symptoms cannot, to begin with, be controlled by the will; neither produced, nor stopped. The causative mechanism belongs to the unconscious and is constituted by a whole series of incidents which combine to create a bodily disposition. This disposition will give structure and form to our lived experience—in health and illness alike.

REFERENCES

Breuer, J., and Freud, S. (1893–1895). Studies on hysteria, G.W.I. *Standard Edition* 2.
Damasio, A. R. (1994). *Descartes' Error*. New York: Avon.
Darwin, C. (1872). *The Expression of the Emotions in Man and Animal*. Chicago, IL: The University of Chicago Press.
Edelman, G. M. (1992). *Bright Air, Brilliant Fire: On the Matter of the Mind*. New York: Basic Books.
Freeman, W. J. (1995). *Societies of Brains: A Study in the Neuroscience of Love and Hate*. Mahwah, NJ: Erlbaum.
Freud, S. (1900). The interpretation of dreams. G.W. II/II; *Standard Edition* 4/5.
——— (1914). On the history of the psycho-analytical movement. G.W. X; *Standard Edition* 14.
——— (1925). An autobiographical study. G.W. XIV; *Standard Edition* 20.
——— (1950 [1895]). Project for a scientific psychology. G.W. Nachtragsband; *Standard Edition* 1.
James, W. (1890). *The Principles of Psychology*. Cambridge, MA: Harvard University Press.
Johnson, M. (1987). *The Body in the Mind: The Bodily Basis of Meaning, Imagination, and Reason*. Chicago, IL: The University of Chicago Press.
Lakoff, G. (1987). *Women, Fire, and Dangerous Things: What Categories Reveal about the Mind*. Chicago, IL: The University of Chicago Press.
Matthis, I. (1997). *Den tänkande kroppen. Studier i det hysteriska symptomet.* (*The Thinking Body: Studies on the Hysterical Symptom.*) Stockholm: Natur och Kultur.
——— (2000). Sketch for a metapsychology of affect. *International Journal of Psycho-Analysis* 81:215–227.
Pally, R. (1997). How the brain actively constructs perceptions. *International Journal of Psycho-Analysis* 78:1021–1030.

——— (1998a). Emotional processing: the mind-body connection. *International Journal of Psycho-Analysis* 79:349–362.

——— (1998b). Bilaterality: henisperic specialisation and integration. *International Journal of Psycho-Analysis* 79:564–578.

Peirce, C. S. (1990). *Pragmatism och kosmologi*. Uddevalla: Daidalos.

——— (1991). *Peirce on Signs*. Chapel Hill and London: The University of North Carolina Press.

Penrose, R. (1994). *Shadows of the Mind: A Search for the Missing Science of Consciousness*. Oxford and New York: Oxford University Press.

Schacter, D. L. (1996). *Searching for Memory: The Brain, the Mind and the Past*. Hillsdale, NJ: Erlbaum.

Searle, J. R. (1997). *The Mystery of Consciousness*. New York: New York Review of Books.

Shevrin, H., et al. (1996). *Conscious and Unconscious Processes: Psychodynamic, Cognitive, and Neurophysiological Convergences*. New York: Guilford.

Silver, A. (1981). A psychosemiotic model: An interdisciplinary search for a common structural basis for psychoanalysis, symbol-formation, and the semiotic of Charles S. Peirce. In *Do I Dare Disturb the Universe?* J. Grotstein, ed. London: Maresfield.

Solms, M. (1997a). *The Neuropsychology of Dreams*. Mahwah, NJ: Erlbaum.

——— (1997b). What is consciousness? *Journal of the American Psychoanalytic Association* 45:3.

Toulmin, S. (1994). Teorins marginella betydelse för humaniora. *Dialoger* 30–32:85–92.

9

Setting Freud and Hysteria in Historical Context[1]

Harold Blum

We have read two fascinating papers that bring us back to the origins of psychoanalysis and the classical case histories, the *Studies on Hysteria* and the "Dora Case." To set these in their historical and cultural background, we have to understand how and why Freud has now been criticized—as well as "supervised." He has been criticized—by analysts, by people outside of analysis, by feminists, and so forth, but it is important to distinguish appropriate criticism from irrational censure. I would like to present this discourse on these case histories in the following way: Prior to Freud, these patients were not understood at all. One has to recognize what the treatment was of the hysterical patient in the late nineteenth century prior to Freud coming onto the scene. How were hysterics treated?

There were three main methods: One was the rest cure, pioneered by Weir and Mitchell in this country. Patients were ordered to bed.

---

[1]. Comments given by Harold Blum following the contributions of Imre Szecsödy and Iréne Matthis.

They were confined under "house arrest." They often suffered what amounted to seclusion and suggested bed rest, sometimes for months at a time. The second method was hydrotherapy. Patients were shocked by immersion in cold baths. This was thought to be the kind of shock that would help them to overcome their hysterical symptoms, so the patients would snap out of the illness. The third common method, to which Dora herself was subjected, was electric shock. Patients were given electric shocks, and if a patient like Dora had an aphonia, electric shocks were given directly to the larynx and the pharynx, sometimes inserted through the mouth, sometimes causing extreme spasms in the area and a great deal of pain, discomfort, and often nausea and vomiting. If the patient were constipated, as Dora was, she probably had electric shocks to her abdomen. And if that didn't work, an electric probe might be inserted into the anus. Some of the patients would, of course, have an immediate cure!

Along came Sigmund Freud. For the first time in history, someone really listened and took a history, heard the patients out, and began to understand them. This is the substance in a way, the core of Dr. Matthis's presentation. Freud began to understand patients in terms of the origin and *meaning* of their communications, not just in terms of the organic symptomology, particularly as an explanation of conversion hysteria. So Freud listened and learned from the patient, with the patient, and despite and through the patient's resistance. And that of course transcended what the patient could report. Because Freud not only took a history, he also began to engage the patient in the process of association and interpretation, and engaged his own reconstruction of that history. The patient that we heard about, the singer Rosalie, was a fascinating patient in many ways. She had some problems in common with Dora. She had a symptom around the problem of vocalization, a problem in her communication. Dora suffered from aphonia and coughing. Rosalie could not sing in her usual way. You can imagine Freud, as he was developing free association saying "sing whatever comes to mind," as well as "say whatever comes to mind." But, you may be interested to know that aphonias in that day were among the most common of all hysterical symptoms. That is quite interesting in terms of Freud's capacity to draw the patient into a dialogue, into presenting their history, because the patients had a great deal of difficulty speaking at all, as well as in speaking freely. Do you remember the Irma dream? In the Irma dream

(Freud 1900), the patient was embarrassed about opening her mouth. This was a disguised representation of a gynecological examination and a sexual encounter. However, if you look at that dream carefully, you will see that the patient is struggling to be able to talk to Freud. As he looks down her throat, she is embarrassed. She is reluctant to open her mouth. This is, of course, overdetermined. The symptom has many other meanings—for example, referring to ideals and values as well as sexual and aggressive meanings. What I am emphasizing here is the communicative aspect of these symptoms. The problem was in establishing communication between patient and doctor. The patients of that day, particularly the women—and most of the hysterical patients treated at that time were female patients treated by male doctors—the patients had a great deal of difficulty opening their mouths, speaking freely, and developing the method of free association. Not that we are free of resistances to free association today, but it was particularly difficult for these women. They have made an important contribution to our understanding of this problem. The girls of that day were raised not to be vocal but to be freely expressive. Their voices were passive and very soft; they certainly were not outspoken. They were supposed to be diffident, ladylike, to hold back their inner feelings and thoughts and to keep them essentially to and from themselves. They were to be submissive to authority; and with illness that authority was usually the male doctor. Given Freud's own unanalyzed countertransference, and his unconscious conflicts regarding women and femininity, it is not surprising that the resistance to free association was either not elaborated or overlooked at that time.

Some further comments: Here I draw upon my own research and my paper on Dora's conversion syndrome (Blum 1994). One may be interested to know that Dora, after she left Freud's treatment, married and had a child. This is also relevant to why Freud delayed publishing this case, delaying his own vocalization, his own bringing this pioneer case report out to the public. The treatment was terminated, as we heard, on December 31, the very end of the year, at the turn of the century, 1900. We are just now a century in commemoration of the Dora case. Freud waited almost five years to publish the case. He wrote it in 1901, but, the Dora case was only published in 1905. In that year Dora had become a mother. As soon as she became a mother, she converted to Christianity, and converted her child to Christianity. She, her husband, and her child all became Protestants at the same time. Religious conversion offered security and opportunity. Did she want to avoid having her child experience anti-Semitism? Freud probably assumed at that point that she had lost interest in the psychoanalytic approach, and in her relationship to Freud as a former patient. Freud wanted to protect her anonymity, and issues of informed consent were not yet confronted.

Dora did not anticipate she would become a museum piece immortalized by her therapist, Sigmund Freud. The understanding of this case has to be placed in the cultural context of Dora's being a Jewish woman treated by a Jewish analyst in Vienna at the turn of the century. And at that time and that place, being a woman and being Jewish were both psychosocially denigrated situations. This is relevant to the constant references to illness—to body illness and to being defective—which appear in the case. There was an apparent lack of appreciation of Dora's own interests and aspirations by her parents, and her being dismissed and disadvantaged. She was not given the social and educational opportunities bestowed on her brother. We know now that Dora was sent to a convent school when she was a little girl. I don't have time to develop that further in this essay, but her education in a convent school in Merano is part of the historical context that needs to be fleshed out in order to more fully understand her childhood development and some of her fantasies involved in conversion: conversion hysteria and religious conversion.

Some final observations on the cultural context in which Dora and Freud worked: The symbol of the burning house. The burning house figures in the famous first dream in the Dora case. At the time of the dream her father's factories had been nearly burned in anti-Semitic riots in Czechoslovakia, where the factories were located. There is an entire set of cultural, economic, and political meanings here. The meanings are in addition to the magnificent illustrations that Freud gave of Dora's intrapsychic conflicts and of the inner processes of the mind he described. We are in the process now, a full century later, of filling out so many dimensions of Dora's dream and case report. I will close with one great historical irony that concerns the anti-Semitic fires which would later threaten Dora and her analyst. Dora flees the burning house and her analyst flees with her! In 1938 analyst and patient, Freud and Dora, both fled the threat of being burned, as they left Vienna—almost together—as refugees from the Nazis.

REFERENCES

Blum, H. (1994). Dora's conversion syndrome: a contribution to the prehistory of the Holocaust. *Psychoanalytic Quarterly* 63:518–525.

Freud, S. (1900). The interpretation of dreams. *Standard Edition* 4.

——— (1905). Fragment of an analysis of a case of hysteria. *Standard Edition* 7:7–122.

10

Panel Discussion: Relating 100 Years of Psychoanalysis to Clinical Practice

Jill Savege Scharff (Chair)

Judith Chused, Steven Ellman, Ernst Falzeder, Iréne Matthis, and Imre Szecsödy (Panelists)

In this discussion, several speakers presented additional remarks in response to comments and questions from the floor. One speaker not otherwise represented in this volume joined the panel: Judith Chused (Washington, DC). She had given an unpublished paper "Why Theory?" in which she inquired into the origins of theory and its usefulness for the clinician. She concluded that what she valued most was theory she developed in the process of conducting clinical work. She preferred such an empirically derived framework to any slavish adherence to dogma, and spoke of the intertwining of personal growth with theoretical understanding: "Though our knowledge has increased, like Freud, we still must navigate from what we knew to what we know to what we have yet to learn."

Dr. Jill Savege Scharff began the panel by introducing the panelists and then opened the floor to participants' questions.

Jill Scharff: This afternoon we're trying to explore the relevance of psychoanalytic theory in clinical work over the last 100 years. We welcome contributions as well as questions from the floor.

Charles Schwarzbeck (Seattle and Vancouver): A little bit ago David Scharff said, "Psychoanalysis rests fundamentally on what we learn from our patients." I think of myself as rethinking almost everything from my developmental work with babies. I also notice that as we think together today, there is a lot of movement, more and more toward theories of affect. There is a lot of emphasis on how we think about affect in our clinical work and so forth. When Jill Scharff was talking, she started to move toward some of John Bowlby's thinking about attachment theory, comparing Freud's notion of impulses with some of Dr. Bowlby's thoughts. I wanted to add an idea here, pretty close to what has already been said, but I think it should be formalized a little bit. When we evoke attachment theory, we think about the person that we're looking at as motivated by fear. Attachment theory comes from motivations that have to do with fear. Susan McDonald and some colleagues a few years ago talked about another motivation—to seek warmth. So there is the idea of warmth versus fear. Much of what one sees with babies and mothers in healthy situations seems much better explained by the wish for warmth rather than by avoidance through fear. If we shift and think a little more theoretically, we start with babies with arousal. We don't really think about impulse or drive, and certainly not affect. Although many papers have been written about how we look at a baby's face, which we define as affect, we don't really know what we are doing when we do that. I would ask you to think about a hierarchy of development where we start with arousal, and then it is through the relationship with the primary caregiver—as the primary caregiver tries to help with transitions of state and eventually with the regulation of arousal—that the infant is able to regulate arousal on the right side of the brain. When that occurs attention is possible. Then the infant is able to do two things at the same time. The infant is able to focus on the primary caregiver, and at the same time the baby feels its body.

To hold these two events in mind, we need to look back at what Freud talked about when he talked about drive, and then see where we are today. The simultaneous feeling of the body and the capacity to pay attention to the primary caregiver allows for the development of affect. Only when we have the development of affect, can we think about whether the motivational system is one of seeking warmth, or one of fear about preventing separation or danger.

Jill Scharff: Let me see if someone on the panel would like to address that. Is anyone used to thinking in terms of warmth versus fear?

Steven Ellman: No, but I guess where I would start is the whole idea of Freud having multiple perspectives. For me, Edith Jacobson has said it best, and I think it comprised warmth and fear. Freud was really trying to talk about very early bodily states. We get lost in how they actually influence the infant. Freud didn't put in mother, and he should have. Winnicott makes a big point of a footnote of Freud's in the 1911 paper, where Freud writes that he should be talking about the mother and the interaction between the mother and infant, but he focuses on the infant. But Freud was talking about that in terms of a pleasure/unpleasure sequence. If the pleasure is going well, then it seems to me that the infant will look as if it's warmth seeking. But, if it's not going well, the infant is going to look much more like it is trying to avoid experiences of fear. But Freud put this in a much broader perspective in the era that Jill Scharff talked about today when she talked about his main theory of drive. For a longer period of time than he referred to eros and thanatos, or to sex and aggression, drive for Freud had to do with the survival of the self and survival of the species. That was his "drive theory" for most of the time when he was actually seeing patients. So, when he was talking about that, I believe he had an object relations theory. He was talking about a much more complex system. One of the things that could eventually evolve out of that would be warmth and comfort—positive experiences and the pleasure/unpleasure sequence. If it's not going well in terms of the attunement between infant and mother, then it would be fear.

Iréne Matthis: About this fear/warmth question: of course we would like that the warmth would be the primary affect between child and mother. But I agree with you, that if we look back in the evolution, it would be fear that would be the primary affect. In all the physiological responses and experiments that have been done, it has always been the negative affects that have had the highest amplitude, and that is the marker. I am also associating to William James, the great psychologist. He gave this example, as you probably well know, of the bear. You see the bear, you are afraid, and then you run. That's how we talk about it. That's how Darwin also talked about it. You get afraid and you run away. James reversed the two things—you get afraid because you run away! There are some unconscious processes that go on before the affect. Of course, this is what Freud brings up when he thinks about whether we can have unconscious affects or not. That is still an open question. But I think fear is the primary target, and the warmth will of course come in, too.

Barbara Cristy (Washington, DC): I wanted to address the issue of therapeutic trust. We were looking at the therapist and the holding environment, but what about the need for the therapist to trust the patient at some level? The ability to trust that the patient is telling you truth about the patient's world, the respect for the patient correlates with the sense of really working together and trusting each other.

Steven Ellman: I agree with you. I wrote a paper on that—a termination paper that came out in 1987, that indicated that in a long-term treatment it didn't really start to become an analysis until I understood that process of starting to trust what the patient was saying. I tried there to talk about my difficulties in doing that.

Harold A. Clark, Ph.D. (Brigantine, New Jersey): I have struggled with how to translate drive theory into object relations terms. The thing that keeps being a block for me is, "Where is the energy? Where is the passion? Or where does rage come in?" I think of this baby in a crib, when its needs are not being met, shaking the crib with righteous indignation. I am trying to figure out how that works from an object relations point of view.

Jill Scharff: Fairbairn's response to that situation is that rage is always secondary to frustration. It is a response to the needs not being met. That is precisely what it is. That is in contradistinction to some other views that would hold that the infant is born with a constitutional amount of rage. For instance, in the Kleinian version of object relations theory, that infant would be constitutionally endowed with aggression due to the force on it of a constitutionally determined amount of death instinct that the infant is having to deflect by this motoric expression of rage. But in the kind of object relations theory I was talking about today—the Fairbairnian approach—that expression of rage has the purpose of cueing the mother to pay attention, to meet the infant's needs, and to allow the infant to resolve the stress. To the extent that the mother doesn't do so, then, the infant takes in a bad object experience, splits off the unmanageably bad part of the bad internal mother, and represses that rejecting object into unconsciousness where it reverberates and causes further rage reaction.

David Levi (Washington, DC): I have two comments. First, I was reacting to the question of "Why Theory?" As somebody who doesn't feel very strong allegiance to one or another theory, I think that there's a kind of a theory about the clinical situation, that we have a place where something can be played out, where a patient can experience affect and you can be with the patient. But theory also connects me with a kind of professional identity—a sense of having something to offer there, and keeps me from getting completely taken over by my empathic identification with the patient's situation. It gives me some alternative perspectives to offer to the patient. Judy Chused talked about theories a lot in terms of conscious theories and I was struck. I'd been reading a piece by Joseph Sandler this week—strangely enough, the week after his death—in which he talked about unconscious theories. I think the theories we are *not* conscious of have a lot more to do with how we act in the clinical situation than some of the ones that we are conscious of.

I have another point. I was looking at the title of this discussion, which focuses on the evolution of psychoanalysis during 100 years. There has been a huge evolution even since I began in the late 1960s! In some ways the Dora case illustrates it. Freud had to have a theory, and he had to propagate the theory. He wasn't so interested in Dora being empowered to get with her own experience and express herself, or to help her develop her capacity to express herself. He was interested in getting the content of his theory over to her! You see this again in the Rat Man, which is a more elaborated case history in some ways. Some people would talk about Freud's promotion of theory as a phallocentric action, a man having to "put it out there" and show that he knows something, in contrast to a more maternal nurturing position where you try to help people express themselves, make it a safe place for them to express themselves. In this thirty years, there's been a tremendous shift from the analyst "having to know," to the analyst helping patients develop their own knowledge of themselves.

Imre Szecsödy: It's a very central question: What is the difference between prejudice and theory? I can't imagine that we can meet the world without having some kinds of preconceptions about it. Then it is important how you acknowledge what kind of unconscious preconceptions you have towards this patient. There is a fantastic study done in Switzerland. An interview with a patient was watched independently by eighty analysts. The question was how soon could they make up their minds about the patient's analyzability. Most of them made up their minds in six minutes. Surgeons would have made up their minds in two seconds, I think. For analysts it took six minutes. Then, the most important thing was, "How open were people to reexamine their preconceptions about such a judgment?"

David Tuckett wrote a very interesting article in the next to last *International Journal* about evaluating scientific papers. He writes that it's not so difficult for us to embrace new ideas, but we have terrible difficulties rejecting old ones. So, this is one of the problems. When I revisit the Dora case I try to empathize both with Freud and with Dora. I think that it is easy for us now to have perspective, to be critical. But I have seen us do many times as many mothers do. The important thing is to be able to give the child the possibility to "reflect herself in the mother's eyes," as Winnicott put it. But many times the mother is reflecting her own feelings and not the child's. To be able to be playful with the child, and to be able to be playful with your analysand or patient is extremely important. The question is: How can we maintain this platform—to remain playful—when our work is blood serious at the same time?

Jill Scharff: Since Dr. Levi's was a three-part question, we are going to have three responses. Dr. Chused, next please.

Judith Chused: You know, David Levi is obviously right. There are unconscious theories, and as I discussed, there are multiple unconscious determinants of theory. But there are also unconscious determinants of all kinds of points of view. I would like to address the last thing that you said. Yes, we want to enable patients to know themselves. But to refer only to a maternal nurturing point of view misses another task of the therapist. At some point the therapist, whether an analyst or psychotherapist, needs to be aggressive, assertive, intrusive in part. I think that is probably harder for many people than to be maternal and nurturing.

Ernst Falzeder: Regarding the question of whether theory affects our clinical practice, and whether it is at a conscious or unconscious level, I would like to highly recommend a book, *The Analyst's Preconscious*, written by Victoria Hamilton, from the Institute of Contemporary Psychoanalysis in Los Angeles, formerly from Scotland and London, as a very good book. She conducted interviews and sent out questionnaires to analysts in different countries with different orientations, about their preconscious theoretical background and how that affects their handling of transference, for instance.

Robin Gerhart (Washington, DC): I am grateful for object relations and the intersubjective approach and two-person psychology, because it has created a space for me in an analytic world where there once was no space for my theoretical orientation. But often as I hear these concepts discovered for the first time, I find myself thinking "where were you all twenty years ago?" when the existential therapies and humanistic therapies were flourishing, talking about the space between the therapist and the patient and the interactions—simple things, like Carl Rogers talking about taking an empathic reflective approach that allows the patients to develop their own voice. I was reminded, when Ernst Falzeder was talking about the repression of the origins of object relations, being in part due to a prohibition of the words of Ferenczi and Rank. We had to disavow those roots of our thinking. I wonder if there might not be a parallel process going on in the interpersonal theories, where analysts who in the past have denigrated the "supportive therapies" cannot now say names like Carl Rogers, Irving Yalom, or James Blumenthal. On the one hand I want to say, "Well, you must not have known." But then I realize that it was known, because it was criticized. So I am interested in your own awareness of these lines of thought.

Steven Ellman: Well, I, for one, was teaching Carl Rogers and Sullivan when I started as a professor in the graduate program at City University in 1971 or so. I still sometimes will refer to that, but I am still critical. I would say Kohut, in a more systematic way, has developed the space, yet I am critical of him, too. For me, the intersubjective position has brought up important issues that I think were present at that time as well, and that I tried to answer then. I'm still trying to answer them in a different way. But, there are some things they don't do. For instance, it's hard sometimes to be aggressive, interpretive, intrusive, or, at times, to allow the patient be alone. I have actually listened to many tapes of Carl Rogers, and I think he had difficulty doing that. He was effective in a variety of ways, but I think he still had a difficulty in allowing patients to be alone to hear their own voice more clearly, which to me is an important aspect of allowing transference to emerge.

The same caveat applies to a radical intersubjective approach, which I would guess not many people take now, although five years ago some people espoused it. That position is now being withdrawn. A radical intersubjective approach also does not allow patients to hear their own voice. It's always "the two of us." I said the same thing about Jodie Davies in a discussion, when she said, "It's always the two of us. We have to do it together!" at a time when I thought the patient really wanted to talk about himself and where he was, *without* her. I have to talk about development in the same way. When Allan Schore is talking about the mother-infant interactions all the time, he is not looking at the massive amount of development that is spent in sleep. Much of the time there is very little interaction except that the mother is holding the baby over her shoulder or trying to get the position right, and a variety of things like that. There are a variety of vegetative functions where the mother is not interacting—but is there much more activity toward what Winnicott described in his ideas about supporting absolute dependence?

Judith Chused: I would like to extend our thinking also. I know Carl Rogers, and I know Irving Yalom. I think Steve Ellman is right. I would put it slightly differently, but it's the same idea. One of the most difficult things when you are doing analysis is for a patient to develop a transference to you. It makes you uncomfortable, and it makes the patient uncomfortable. And to sit with it and allow it to develop, to not interpret it away and to not smooth it away, and to have the patient leave your office in pain, and have him come back still in pain—and to listen to it and to tolerate it. That is also something Winnicott talked about. All too often in some intersubjective approaches—although I'm very much an intersubjectivist I guess—and in some of the object relations approaches, there is an assumption that if one is a good object, that will do the trick. That doesn't do the trick!

Ernst Falzeder: I would like to second that, and to recommend Winnicott's paper, "The Capacity to be Alone." He describes how that capacity can develop when the infant is allowed by the caretaker to be alone in a safe environment without intrusions from the outside. To some extent, David Cooper expressed the same idea.

Imre Szecsödy: I would like to add that for me as an analyst the most important thing is to be available. But availability means also to be available as a dead object for the patient, not only to be there to be reassuring. I like very much the concept of the analytic trust. To me it would be translated into being available. And at the same time the enactment that the patient does is extremely important for the patient to be able to understand herself. Now, the analyst should try not to be too enacting, which we many times certainly do. Dora is a marvelous example of parallel enactment. What is crucial is to be able also to stand the patient becoming, and to stand being used as that object, and only then to make that understandable for the patient.

Jill Scharff: I would like to give Iréne Matthis the chance to answer the challenge of "where were you when?" if she wishes.

Iréne Matthis: We had nothing of object relationships in Sweden in the 60s and 70s, so it slowly evolved. We shall not be proud that we evolved in that way, because we still probably have some blind spots in our own views of the world. It is very important to learn from history. We will of course repeat the faults of our ancestors, but we will at least acknowledge it and be open to discussion and critique.

Jill Scharff: Now is the time for the audience to use the panel in discussion as that kind of background object in this setting. Please do give us your comments and questions. We'll move on now to one from Michael Moskowitz, one of tomorrow's speakers.

Michael Moskowitz: This is actually a follow-up to a comment by Allan Schore pertaining to the use of the couch. In his remarks, Allan was saying that particularly with patients with early self-pathology you have to meet face-to-face. I know I don't do that and I know that from my many discussions with Steve Ellman about this, he feels it's preferable at times to see these patients on the couch. So I wonder if I am answering correctly for you, Steve? And what do the other panelists think about that as a technical issue?

Judith Chused: One thing that Steve Ellman touched on in his talk is the value of the tone of the analyst's voice and of the mother's voice. I did two years of infant research with some blind infants when I was in training, and those that were relatively healthy had mothers whose voices were very soothing. To my mind, a patient with difficulty with self regulation or sense of self could do quite well on the couch. It's really what helps establish the trust, which doesn't have to be a careful following of the gaze. I think it can be following the tone of voice as much as anything.

Imre Szecsödy: There is research evidence that the baby does not always directly reflect the mother's facial expression of affect. When you look very closely at mother/baby interaction and how the baby is imitating or responding to mother's facial expression of emotions, there is a very interesting response: When mother shows disgust, the child shows disgust; when mother shows fear, the child shows fear; but when mother shows rage, the child smiles! That's a fantastic response, a very good defense. Secondly, according to the studies conducted by Rainer Krause, an analyst who is professor in Saarbrucken, Germany, on affect and nonverbal communication, therapists who are closely following the patient's facial expression have less success with treating psychotic patients. That is an extremely interesting finding.

Steven Ellman: Let me respond to these issues on the centrality of gaze and the difficulty with treating psychotic patients by saying two things. First, Goldie Alfassi Siffert did her dissertation with me on gaze aversion. One of the things we saw is that infants who seemed in particular distress had a very difficult time holding gaze with their mothers. They were only at ease when the mother really allowed them to look away and then gaze back spontaneously. Siffert tried to train the mothers to allow their infants to come back, because you would observe the mothers of these infants trying to stay continuously in front of the infant and keep their gaze fixed on the interaction. Secondly, something comparable is true for psychotic patients—who were most of my practice for the first 10 years. It is hard for them if the therapist is scrutinizing their gaze. I don't think you can set an absolute rule, but the idea that you have to be getting information and keeping emotional contact visually, I believe, is a mistaken idea on three grounds: (1) it may be very difficult for the patient to do it; (2) the therapist may find it difficult to contain the patient's responses when there is direct visual contact; and (3) psychotic difficulties and some borderline disorders may be much earlier difficulty than is encoded in terms of visual elements, particularly facial expression. The channels of expression may involve early sounds, smells, etc.

Imre Szecsödy: I would like to add a comment that follows on the importance of differentiating right and left hemisphere functions, as Dr. Schore did in his paper. I would like to refer to Peter Fonagy's studies on "mentalizing" or reflective functioning, which is a first capacity to conceive of oneself and others in terms of mental states: feelings, beliefs, intentions, and desires. Mentalizing also refers to the capacity to reason about one's own and another's behavior in terms of mental state, and to be able to reflect about it so one has this capacity to be able to see the intentionality in one's self and in others. This capacity involves a synthesis of right and left brain functions.

Warren Sibilla (South Bend, Indiana): This has been an amazing conference. My head is full of a lot of ideas, so please be patient as I try to formulate my comments. I have been thinking about this idea of the baby, and the blending of drive theory and object relations theory, and how the introjection of the object is the beginning of an unconscious. People have asked how does that fit? And in the spirit of the conference, I am wondering about some of the opposing ideas in psychoanalysis. For example, there is Jung's idea of an archetype—that there is an organizing center in the psyche, the self, that combines affect and image as a unifying force. In the Jungian formulation, what one sees on the surface is the complex, but underlying that there is a unifying force. That idea might be a useful idea to help bridge the two. Jungians are studying this material quite a bit, and talking neurobiologically about deep structures and how some of this fits in with their ideas. I wondered if I could hear a comment on that.

Jill Scharff: I think perhaps no one here is as qualified to respond as you were to ask the question, but I appreciate your comment, which will have to stand as its own contribution.

Stephen Skulsky (Omaha, Nebraska): I would like to take a stab at answering Warren Sibilla's question, because I have an interest in Jungian thought as well as psychoanalytic object relational thought. I would cite two brief quotes or paraphrases. One is from James Hillman, who said that the goal of dream work is not to bring the dream up to rational thought alone, but to pickle the rational mind with the dream juices of death. That notion reminds me very much of something I heard Arthur Hyatt Williams say in a workshop when talking about Bion. He said that the id is as much threatened by the ego, as the ego is by the id. Why am I saying that? I think one of the real struggles that we have going is that it is important to value words and the capacity to use words to process experience. But so much of what gets conveyed to us, especially if we use countertransference, does not have to do with words alone. According to Jung, it has to do with images. I don't think Jung paid enough attention to bodily sensations separate from images, because so much gets conveyed in that channel alone. But Warren was referring to the tough balance that has to be struck: "How do we stay open to what's preverbal or preconscious or unconscious when it's impinging on us in ways that aren't just rational, when we also value rational thought and capacity to process so much."

Jill Scharff: Thank you Steve. Now we'll take another question.

Michael Sharpston (Washington, DC): I would like to go back to the first speaker from the floor [Dr. Schwarzbeck], who was talking about arousal. Supposing there is sexual arousal. That could elicit pleasure, anxiety, or anger from the same primary source, depending on context, on perception, or on past experiences. I wonder if the panel could help me with how that relates to the different schools.

Judith Chused: Of course you are right. And it's not just sexual arousal that can elicit such different responses. A variable response to attachment is quite common. Patients have widely varying capacities to tolerate our helping them, to tolerate trusting us, or to tolerate being vulnerable. For some people that's quite a pleasurable state, or at least it is not unpleasurable. That's why Steve Ellman's response to the question about arousal is so important; the question is pleasure or unpleasure? I have certainly had my share—as I expect many of you have—of patients who as soon as you make a connection with them and they begin to feel some relaxation of their defensiveness, they feel enormous fear. That's a very painful state. One hypothesizes that these are people with difficulties with insecure attachments early in life. So, that would also be my answer about sexual arousal: It depends on whether it's pleasurable or unpleasurable and, as you said, that is determined by the context and its meaning to the person.

Iréne Matthis: I think that points out the kernel of the whole Freud Exhibition, which is titled "Conflict and Culture." What you pointed out is the conflict that is always aroused when there is any affective arousal. Because when culture is added to fear, pleasure, and lust you have this conflict. I would say that goes for any subject you could imagine. Not only sexuality, but we do emphasize sexuality because it is the basic force in evolution not only of human beings, but in every species.

Jill Scharff: Would any of the panel members like to offer a closing remark? Something you think is important to pick up or a question you wish you'd had a chance to answer?

Judith Chused: It's not necessarily a closing remark. But I would like to remind you of what was said a few minutes ago, which struck me as so important: that it is terribly important for the therapist to allow himself to be used as a bad object as well as a good object; to not deny the patient the opportunity to use us as fully as he wishes.

Steven Ellman: I feel lost in thought about two comments that have come up. One, I was asking myself why I don't know more about Jung. I realized it had to do with my own psychoanalytic history and the political difficulties in psychoanalysis that interfere with knowing alternative perspectives, even though I have tried to be informed about them. The second thing I would say, since this is a conference about Freud, is that Freud didn't really have a theory of the mind. He had a lot of questions about the mind. He had a theoretical scaffolding that was about the mind, and about the relationship between mind and bodily experiences. The trouble in the United States is that we prematurely give answers. We said, "Well Freud said this, so this is right." At one point in my psychoanalytic education I remember I couldn't believe that people seriously considered these ideas as correct. I had come from graduate school, and so I thought at first that they were kidding, that this was an elaborate joke. Surely, they were testing me just to see what I could believe, as opposed to considering Freud as a developing clinician/theorist who was asking a variety of questions. Freud was a very sophisticated version of William James in terms of this capacity to question—I think much deeper and more sophisticated. But his early formulations should be seen more in that light. I hope this conference does something to move us toward that end.

Jill Scharff: Please join me in thanking the panel and members of the audience for their stimulating examination of Freud's ideas and clinical practice.

PART IV

ART AND LITERATURE

Freud was interested in nearly everything, and especially in the lessons of literature for its knowledge of humanity. He wrote that the poets had always known those things that analysis only discovered by hard work. As **Norman Holland** notes, in his lucid essay "The Mind and the Book: Past, Present, and Future Psychoanalytic Literary Criticism," it was Freud who said from the first that there were three angles from which analysis could inform our understanding of literature—by understanding the writer, analyzing a character, or examining the response of the audience.

Holland is unusual in his thorough knowledge of literature and theories of literary criticism on the one hand, and in his real grasp of psychoanalysis on the other. In this essay, he gives us a look at the history of analytic literary criticism, and then inquires as to the purpose of the discipline of literary criticism in general and specifically the purpose of the psychoanalytic brand of criticism. His conclusion is both enlightened and pleasing! Personally, I find that his essay renews my pleasure in reading literary and artistic criticism because of the way it gives gentle reinforcement to the psychoanalytic credo, "Know thyself!"

Freud made few forays into writing about the visual arts. **Donald Kuspit's** "Freud and the Visual Arts" is an exploration of this medium, and finds Freud short on understanding because of his discomfort with a purely sensuous mode of appreciation. The difficulty in tolerating a wordless experience, as he felt forced to do when confronted with painting or music, left Freud bereft of words and at the mercy of the cauldron of chaos that the more unformed and intuitive visual or musical experiences presented. This intolerance contrasted with the love of literature he frequently voiced, and the comfort with the symbolic use of language of the poets and great writers, with which he identified. He was more comfortable with sculpture—as seen in his fabled love of the small sculptural artifacts of antiquity that was spoken of so movingly by Erica Davies in the first morning of the conference (see page xviii). He handled his discomfort with the wordlessness of art by translating the pictorial image into words that he could then assign symbolic meaning. Kuspit makes a convincing argument that Freud was intolerant of a kind of seduction offered by the sensuous quality of visual arts, and he examines the narrowing of experience that is in evidence when Freud makes Michaelangelo's Moses serve his own unconscious purpose. It remains a puzzle that Freud was so unconflicted about his collection of sculptural artifacts. It seems to me that sculpture, and most especially the special quality of these artifacts as beacons of lost cultures, found a narrow, almost secret, avenue into Freud's unconscious appreciation. The artifacts were stripped by their history from any intentionality of design by an identifiable artist. Freud may have felt free to make of them what he would, safe from contradiction by a known artistic history. The artifacts presented a lost world, as Davies said to us, "a world as in a dream," from which Freud felt inspired as by a muse, and for whom Freud felt he could speak without fear.

11

The Mind and the Book: Past, Present, and Future Psychoanalytic Literary Criticism

Norman N. Holland

The first thing to recognize is that the title above announces an impossible task. One cannot survey the field of psychoanalytic literary criticism in a mere essay. The field is immense. The classic bibliography, Norman Kiell's, is two volumes and refers to some 20,000 items (Kiell 1982), and, at that, it only covers up to 1980.

Moreover, there's not much point in trying to survey this field again. The subject has been covered many times by many people, several times just by me. (See Schwartz and Willbern 1982, Natoli and Rusch 1984, Wright 1998, Coen 1994, and Holland 1976, 1986, 1990, 1993.) Instead, I'd like to set out some general ways of thinking about psychoanalytic criticism. In particular, I'd like to suggest ways of thinking about the past, the history, of psychoanalytic criticism, where it should go in the future, and what psychoanalytic critics should be doing now, in the present.

PAST

In a nutshell, the key to understanding the history of psychoanalytic literary criticism is to recognize that literary criticism is about books and psychoanalysis is about minds. Therefore, the psychoanalytic critic can only talk about the minds associated with the book. And what are those? There are three, and curiously, Freud spelled them out in his very first remarks on literature in the letter to Fliess of October 15, 1897, in which he discussed *Oedipus Rex*. He applied the idea of oedipal conflict to the audience response to *Oedipus Rex* and to the character Hamlet's inability to act, and he speculated about the role of oedipal guilt in the life of William Shakespeare. Those are the three people that the psychoanalytic critic can talk about: the author, the audience, and some character represented in or associated with a text. From the beginning of this field to the present, that cast of characters has never changed: author, audience, or some person derived from the text.

Those are the three minds that the psychoanalytic critic addresses. How the psychoanalytic critic addresses those minds depends on the orientation of the critic. Is he or she a classical psychoanalyst, an ego psychologist, a Lacanian, a Kleinian, a member of the object relations school, a Kohutian, and so on? Each of the various schools in the development of psychoanalysis necessarily produces a different style of psychoanalytic literary criticism.

In the earliest stage of psychoanalytic criticism, the critics did little more than identify Oedipus complexes and the occasional symbol or parapraxis in one or another work of literature. Usually the critic would relate the complex or the slip of the tongue or the phallic symbol to the mind of the author, as in Freud's studies of Dostoevsky or da Vinci. Other familiar examples would be Ernest Jones' often-reprinted book about *Hamlet* (1949) or Marie Bonaparte's analyses of Poe (1933). (Relevant collections would be Phillips 1957, Manheim and Manheim 1966, and Ruitenbeek 1964.)

As psychoanalysts began to define the preoedipal stages—oral, anal, urethral, and phallic—the range of fantasies that one could identify in a literary text expanded from oedipal triangles to fantasies about money, devouring and being devoured, going into dangerous places, fantasies about control, ambition, rage, and so on, as in Phyllis Greenacre's well-known studies of Swift and Carroll (Greenacre

1955), Edmund Wilson's reading of Ben Jonson as an anal character (Wilson 1948), or Kenneth Burke's fine studies of *Antony and Cleopatra, Coriolanus,* and *Kubla Khan* (Burke 1966a,b,c).

In 1963 the French critic Charles Mauron made the important point that these different levels of fantasies were all transformations of one another, superimposed, so that one could imagine the human being as a series of geological levels with oral fantasies at the deepest level—then anal, phallic and so on—forming and leaving traces of themselves at the higher. This is, of course, consistent with the continuities we see psychoanalytically in the development of any human being. Mauron showed that one could read from a writer's repeated themes to the writer's *"mythe personel"* or, as I would say, "identity theme."

Then, as ego psychology developed further, and psychoanalysis acquired its complex theory of defenses, we literary critics became able in the 1960s and 1970s to trace defenses as well as fantasies in texts (see, for example, Kris 1952). Again, we often read both the defenses and the fantasies back to the authors, and the result has been distinguished biographies by Leon Edel (1953–1972), Justin Kaplan (1966, 1982), and Cynthia Griffin Wolff (1977, 1986), to name but a few of the many good psychobiographers.

Even more helpfully, we became able to see that literary forms functioned psychologically like various types of defense mechanism. Form works as a defense, both at the level of particular wordings and in larger structures. Our identifications with characters serve in this way, to modulate and direct our feelings as identifications do in life. The parallel plots of a novel or a Shakespearean play, for example, would act in the reader's mind and perhaps the author's as a kind of splitting. A shift of the sensory modality in a poem may serve as a kind of isolation. Symbolizing serves to disguise all kinds of content in literary works. And, of course, omission functions like repression or denial. (See Holland 1968a, Withim 1969–1970, and Rose 1980.)

The idea of form as defense meant that we could talk about literary works that had no characters at all, where one could only talk about form. We were no longer limited to plays and stories. We could talk about lyric poems (see, for example, Sullivan 1967 or Tennenhouse 1976). We could analyze nonfiction prose. Necessarily we related these to the mind of the author. We could say, for example, that Matthew Arnold's sentence structures expressed denial of physical contact, perhaps related to the general denial of sexuality in Victorian times (Holland 1968b; Ohmann 1968).

Today, in the 1980s and 1990s, I believe psychoanalysis has become a psychology of the self, although there are wide differences in the way different schools address the self: British object-relations, Kohut's self psychology, or Lacan's return to a verbal psychoanalysis. Various collections of essays use one or another of these familiar approaches: object relations (Woodward and Schwartz 1986, Rudnytsky 1993); self psychology (Bouson 1989, Berman 1990); and Lacan (Davis 1981, Stoltzfus 1996). In their various modes, these follow the general pattern of psychoanalytic criticism: applying object relations, self psychology, or Lacanian psychoanalysis to the reader, the author, or some person derived from the text. To me, the most significant breakthrough was the recognition that our relationship to a literary work is to a transitional or transformational object. Literature exists in potential space (Schwartz 1975, Bollas 1979).

There have been many failures of psychoanalytic criticism, mostly as a result of crudity in applying psychoanalytic ideas: labeling, pathography, id analysis. And there have been some successes.

Today, I think the liveliest psychoanalytic criticism addresses questions of gender and personality in the personality of the author and, to me, most interestingly, in the mind of the reader (Holland 1975, Flynn and Schweickart 1986). Nowadays we have psychoanalytically-oriented courses in literature and classes oriented to analyzing reader-response (Holland and Schwartz 1975, Holland 1977, 1978, Berman 1994). In such teaching, a critic or teacher can help readers understand what they are bringing to a given work of literature. How do you respond when you enter the obsessional world of Charles Dickens? How do you respond when you enter the oral world of Christopher Marlowe with its overwhelming rage and desire? How do you shape and change those worlds to fit your own characteristic patterns of fantasy and defense? In other words, what kind of person are you and how do you perceive the world of books and the world around you?

FUTURE

But what about the future? I've developed very briefly the century-long history of psychoanalytic literary criticism. What's next?

It seems to me that a large challenge faces psychoanalytic theory, including its theory of literature, in the twenty-first century. Psychoanalysis has to integrate its insights with the new discoveries coming from brain research and cognitive science. These are very powerful and, as I read them, often quite in harmony with what psychoanalysis has been saying about people from an entirely different perspective and based on entirely different evidence. It seems to me that what psychoanalysis or psychology in general has to do is to put together the clinical knowledge derived from psychoanalysis with the new knowledge of how the mind works in perception, memory, learning, bilateralization, and, most important for a literary critic, in the way we use language. I do not think this is an impossible task, or even, perhaps, a very difficult one. There have been several efforts so far: Reiser 1984, Winson 1985, Harris 1986, Modell 1997, and Kandel 1998.

What I think is rather more difficult is integrating with literary criticism the things we are finding out about the brain and how it acquires and uses language. MRI and PET scans enable us to get pictures of the blood and oxygen flow and other things in the brain as that person fears or perceives or reads or listens to language. Scientists like Gerard Edelman (1992) or Hanna and Antonio Damasio (1992) are showing how we understand words in our brains. There is no simple correspondence between signifier and signified, between word-sound and meaning, as Lacan claimed (following the nineteenth-century linguistics of Saussure). Rather, just to understand one word, the brain must bring together a variety of separate features, the sound of the word, its grammatical role, as well as other words that it is like and unlike.

Then, to arrive at a meaning for a word, the brain assembles or coordinates these different kinds of information from different places in the brain. Furthermore, and most important for the psychoanalyst, what information there is, where it is located, and what memories and emotions accompany it are all highly personal. For each of us, the meaning of a simple word like "dog" or "cat" results from our unique history with that word. And, of course, for complex words like "democracy" or "psychoanalyst," the results will be even more personal.

Thus, each of us interprets a word in an individual way, that is, a way that is both like and unlike everybody else's interpretation. If so, then *a fortiori* each of us will interpret a literary text consisting of a lot of words in an individual way. These new researches confirm what we reader-response critics have been saying for a long time. But more to the point, they confirm what every psychoanalyst has seen from behind the couch. Different patients will respond to an event—take, for example, national catastrophes like the Kennedy assassinations or the *Challenger* explosion—out of their different personal histories and characters. There is no fixed meaning "in" the event. Neither is there a fixed meaning in a literary text.

In a general way, then, I think the discoveries of brain science are confirming *the theory behind* psychoanalytic literary criticism, particularly reader-response psychoanalytic literary criticism. But how, if at all, can we apply this to individual works of literature? I'm not sure.

It may be that neuroscience will describe no more than the processes by which we read and interpret. If so, then neurosience will provide at most a framework within which critics, to be consistent with the science of the mind, should situate their claims. (No claims of "the" meaning "in" the text, for example.) Perhaps neuroscience will be able to go further, giving us a picture of the flow of someone's particular response to a film, story, or poem—as, back in the 1930s, I. A. Richards had hoped. That would yield a great deal more understanding of how we perceive and interpret literature—and life.

We don't know where neuroscience will lead psychoanalysis or literary criticism. What I am sure of is that the best future I can imagine for psychoanalytic literary criticism is a fusion of insights derived from psychoanalysis with insights derived from neuroscience.

PRESENT

I've described what psychoanalytic critics have done in the past, and I've suggested what I think they should do in the future. I'd like to say now what psychoanalytic critics ought to do today. I'd like to go back to a more fundamental question: What is the purpose of all this mental energy that people have put into psychoanalytic literary criticism over the past century? What was it all for? What *should* it be for? What is the purpose of psychoanalytic literary criticism? What, for that matter, is the purpose of any kind of literary criticism?

In the 1960s, literary critics vastly expanded their subject matter to include just about anything that involves language. Nowadays, in literature classes or scholarly journals, you find discussions, not just of this or that poem or story or play or writer, but of gender, race, politics, anthropology, sociology, linguistics, all kinds of sciences, and, of course, of psychoanalysis. Literary critics have become "cultural critics." Needless to say, few English teachers can qualify as the universal geniuses that such discussions require. Perhaps for that reason we might do well to focus on that part of this larger criticism that does talk about literature, particularly this or that particular poem or story or play or film or advertisement, as psychoanalytic literary critics tend to do.

What is the purpose, what is the use, of saying Hamlet has an Oedipus complex and maybe Shakespeare does too? What is the use of saying that Othello and Iago have a homosexual marriage? What is the purpose of psychoanalytic literary criticism? What is the purpose of literary criticism?

Literary criticism, any kind of criticism, rests on the purpose of literature itself, for, after all, criticism is, as the old saying has it, only the handmaiden to the muse. We come, then, to a much larger question. What is the purpose of literature?

Most, perhaps even all, theories of literature seem to me to agree in a general way on two purposes. They are most simply expressed by Horace in his *Ars Poetica: aut prodesse aut delectare. Delectare*—"to delight"—that's straightforward enough. We turn to literature for a pleasurable experience. We usually translate Horace's other term, *prodesse*, as "to instruct" or "to teach" or "to enlighten." That seems a little bit more problematic.

In the duller periods of literary history, people said that *prodesse* meant teaching better morals. That, I take it, would be the point of view of, say, Jesse Helms or McGuffey's *Reader*. Not a very sophisticated view and not very pleasurable literature. But then, in our rather phallic society, politicians rarely show interest in the arts (Apple 1998).

Another idea of *prodesse* would be that of a middlebrow book reviewer. "This novel tells us what life is like in an advertising agency." "This is a sensitive and perceptive account of life on a Minnesota farm in 1903." *Prodesse*, "enlightenment," means giving you factual information. But we do not prize Joyce's *Ulysses* for its picture of 1904 Dublin, nor Fitzgerald's *The Great Gatsby* for its geography of Long Island.

If we take a less narrow and fundamentalist view, and a less middlebrow view, I would suggest that the delight, the *delectare*, in Horace's formula is the experience of entering the imaginative world created by the writer. I can enjoy the manliness of Hemingway's hunters and soldiers. I can enjoy the intensely interpersonal mind of Woolf's character Mrs. Dalloway. I can enjoy the gallantry of Sir Walter Scott's romances or the avarice of Charles Dickens's world. In other words, I can take pleasure in the great human themes, both the good ones and the bad ones, by means of what I read.

If that be the pleasure side of Horace's formula, what is the teaching or instruction side? Again, if we take a less narrow and fundamentalist and politically correct view, I would suggest that the instruction literature itself offers is the understanding of these experiences, these writers' minds, these alien worlds. Not judging them morally, not downloading information from them, but understanding them as fully as we can so that they can become part of our own experience of living—vicarious living.

What is the purpose of literary criticism, then? Literary criticism, any kind of criticism, rests on the purpose of literature itself. The critic is also *prodesse aut delectare*, to delight or to instruct, but more narrowly than the writer. The critic delights or instructs in relation to literature. That is, the critic should give you ideas that enable you to add to your delight. The critic should be saying, "Watch this, notice that, see how this other thing works out. If you observe these aspects of the work, you will have a better experience of it. You will be able to enter the world of the book in a more imaginative, more exciting, more empathic, more satisfying way."

In this way, a critic can add to your pleasure in a book but also help you to understand your pleasure. Criticism should help us to understand both our experience of literary pleasure and to understand ourselves as the experiencers. The art gives us the experience. Criticism should give us some understanding of the experience. Criticism finally, then, should enable both critic and ordinary reader to obey the primary command above the temple of the Delphic Oracle: Know Thyself.

That is how literary criticism helps literature achieve both its pleasure and instruction. Very occasionally, literary criticism is an aesthetic experience in itself. More often it is not. At least, though, literary criticism should help us to shape and articulate some other aesthetic experience to ourselves, to take it from the author's words and put it into our own words and our own world of experience and understand what we are doing. In other words, instruction helps delight and delight helps instruction.

In that sense, all literary criticism would benefit from psychological wisdom. The better the psychology, the better the criticism.

I started by saying that literary criticism is about books and psychoanalysis is about minds. The reader-response critics and the brain scientists would add an important corollary to that: *The only way you can know a book is through a mind.* You can only know a book—you can only know a work of art of any kind—through some human process of perception, through your own mind or through some other person's telling you about the book or the painting. Inevitably then, there is a psychological component to any talk at all about books. Often, orthodox, nonpsychological critics don't talk about that psychological element. They leave it unspoken or even denied. But there is always an element of personality in what a critic says—otherwise, why would we sign our articles?

Now how does this ideal for criticism translate into psychoanalytic literary criticism in particular? Suppose I say that Dickens is an obsessional writer. That is the crudest kind of psychoanalytic criticism. I gave you no more than one word and that, jargon. Yet, you can now name a quality you may be experiencing. I gave you a way of thinking about it. You now have the opportunity of finding out what obsession is, what it feels like, what kind of world such a person inhabits, what kind of imagination. By evoking the psychoanalyst's clinical experience of obsession, I can sensitize you to the issues that dogged Charles Dickens, questions of control, aggression, possession, money, dirt—you can share his horrified fascination as he followed the Thames floating its filth and corpses down to the sea. In effect, I offer you another way of entering the imaginative world of, say, *Bleak House* or *Our Mutual Friend*.

I believe that the psychoanalytic literary critic's primary job is to foreground that psychological element in what he or she says about books. In other words, I think psychoanalytic critics should be interpreting their own, if you will, countertransference to the text, author, or whatever else they are describing, a point vigorously made by Stanley Coen (1994).

Good literary criticism can help us to shape and articulate that experience to ourselves, to take it from the author's words and put it into our own words and our own world of experience. Also, good psychological literary criticism can help us shape and articulate the psychological experience of the writer or the characters to ourselves, to form that psychological experience from the author's words and put it into our own words and our own world of experience.

Think back for a moment to Charlie Chaplin's movies. I think most of us would agree that, mixed in with all the delightful comedy, is a great deal of dreadful sentimentality. We could simply call it mush or treacle or schmaltz and dismiss it. But suppose I offer you a bit of psychoanalytic criticism. Suppose I say to you that Charlie Chaplin, as Stephen Weissman has recently written (1996), is dealing in his films with the problem of a promiscuous mother. At first, she had been a glamorous dancer onstage where the boy often admired her. At the end she was an impoverished seamstress, who perhaps prostituted herself, and who certainly suffered and eventually died from syphilis. The psychoanalytic critic combines this biographical information with the psychoanalystic insight that, as Freud put it about Chaplin, "He always plays only himself as he was in his grim youth" (Freud 1960).

We can understand why so often in his films his hero rescues and repairs damaged and fallen women. We can understand the ineptitude, the childishness of his tramp-hero, as he tries to attract these women, like a child playing up to an elusive mother. We, like most people, could simply write these episodes off as repellingly sentimental, but I think psychoanalytic insight offers us a chance to do better. We can enter into these episodes more fully, with better understanding and more empathy.

We can understand the Little Tramp as a recreation of the boy Chaplin. In *Limelight*, we can understand differently the appalling sentimentality of the last scene: the aged music hall star dying offstage as his protegée dances her way back to stardom. We can ask ourselves, how would *we* feel if we had had a prostitute for our mother? We can imagine a small boy giving his life to the rescue of that shamed and failing mother, making her into something different from what she was, erasing the reality through his own creativity.

As a psychoanalytic critic, I'm asking you to look at the women in Chaplin's films in a different light, not just as sentimentalized or demonized, but as detested and loved in a painful and complicated combination of fear, desire, and loathing. And through that understanding, we perhaps can experience these episodes more sympathetically, more empathically, more generously. We can rescue them by using our imagination, as Chaplin rescued his mother in imagination.

That to me, is the purpose of psychoanalytic criticism. To open up art to us. To add to our empathy and understanding and through our empathic understanding to add to the experience of art. In other words, what I'm suggesting is that good psychoanalytic criticism instructs and delights its readers in the experiencing of our own human nature.

In the past, psychoanalytic criticism has addressed the three persons involved in the literary transaction: author, reader, and textual person. In the future, I hope psychoanalytic literary critics will draw on the rich insights of cognitive science. But in that future, and right now, I hope even more that psychoanalytic literary critics will offer their readers both instruction and delight. No more pathography, no more id-analysis, no more symbol-mongering, no more jargon. I hope instead that psychoanalytic critics will keep open a royal road into the human possibilities offered by great literature.

REFERENCES

Apple, R. W. (1998). Elected bodies with hardly a cultured bone. *New York Times*, July 26, section 2, p. 1.

Berman, J. (1990). *Narcissism and the Novel.* New York: New York University Press.

——— (1994). *Diaries to an English Professor: Pain and Growth in the Classroom.* Amherst, MA: University of Massachusetts Press.

Bollas, C. (1979). The transformational object. *International Journal of Psycho-Analysis*, 60:97–107.

Bonaparte, M. Princess. (1933). *Edgar Poe, Étude psychanalytique.* Paris: Denöel et Steele.

Bouson, J. B. (1989). *The Empathic Reader: A Study of the Narcissistic Character and the Drama of the Self.* Amherst, MA: University of Massachusetts Press.

Burke, K. (1966a). *Coriolanus* and the delights of faction. In *Language as Symbolic Action: Essays on Life, Literature, and Method.* Berkeley, CA: University of California Press.

——— (1966b). *Kubla Khan*: proto-surrealist poem. In *Language as*

Symbolic Action: Essays on Life, Literature, and Method. Berkeley, CA: University of California Press.

——— (1966c). Shakespearean persuasion: Antony and Cleopatra. In *Language as Symbolic Action: Essays on Life, Literature, and Method*. Berkeley, CA: University of California Press.

Coen, S. J. (1994). *Between Author and Reader: A Psychoanalytic Approach to Writing and Reading*. New York: Columbia University Press.

Damasio, A. R., and Damasio, H. (1992). Brain and language. *Scientific American* 267(3):88–95.

Davis, R. C. (ed.). (1981). *The Fictional Father: Lacanian Readings of the Text*. Amherst, MA: University of Massachussets Press.

Edel, L. (1953–1972). *Henry James* [5 Vols.]. Philadelphia, PA: Lippincott.

Edelman, G. M. (1992). *Bright Air, Brilliant Fire: On the Matter of the Mind*. New York: Basic Books.

Flynn, E. A. and Schweickart, P. P. (eds). (1986). *Gender and Reading: Essays on Readers, Texts, and Contexts*. Baltimore and London: Johns Hopkins University Press.

Freud, S. (1960). Letter to Max Schiller, 26 March 1931. In *Letters of Sigmund Freud*. E. L. Freud (ed.), T. Stern and J. Stern (trans.), p. 405. New York: Basic Books.

Greenacre, P. (1955). *Swift and Carroll: A Psychoanalytic Study of Two Lives*. New York: International Universities Press.

Harris, J. E. (1986). *Clinical Neuroscience: From Neuroanatomy to Psychodynamics*. New York: Human Sciences Press.

Holland, N. N. (1968a). *The Dynamics of Literary Response*. New York: Oxford University Press.

——— (1968b). Prose and minds: A psychoanalytic approach to non-fiction. In *The Art of Victorian Prose*, ed. G. Levine and W. Madden, pp. 314–337. New York: Oxford University Press.

——— (1975). *5 Readers Reading*. New Haven, CT: Yale University Press.

——— (1976). Literary interpretation and three phases of psychoanalysis. *Critical Inquiry* 3:221–233.

——— (1977). Transactive teaching: Cordelia's death. *College English* 39:276–285.

——— (1978). With the members of English 692: Colloquium in

Psychoanalytic Criticism. Poem opening: An invitation to transactive criticism. *College English* 40:2–16.
——— (1986). Twenty-five years and thirty days. *Psychoanalytic Quarterly* 55:23–52.
——— (1990). *Holland's Guide to Psychoanalytic Psychology and Literature-and-Psychology*. New York: Oxford University Press.
——— (1993). Psychoanalysis and literature. *Contemporary Psychoanalysis* 29(1):5–21.
Holland, N. N. and Schwartz, M. (1975). The delphi seminar. *College English* 36:789–800.
Jones, E. (1949). *Hamlet and Oedipus*. New York: Norton.
Kandel, E. R. (1998). A new intellectual framework for psychiatry. *American Journal of Psychiatry* 155(4):457–469.
Kaplan, J. (1966). *Mr. Clemens and Mark Twain: A Biography*. New York: Simon & Schuster.
——— (1982). *Walt Whitman: A Life*. New York: Simon & Schuster.
Kiell, N., ed. (1982). *Psychoanalysis, Psychology, and Literature: A Bibliography* (2d ed.). Metuchen, NJ and London: Scarecrow Press.
Kris, E. (1952). *Psychoanalytic Explorations in Art*. New York: International Universities Press.
Manheim, L. F. and Manheim, E., eds. (1966). *Hidden Patterns: Studies in Psychoanalytic Literary Criticism*. New York: Macmillan.
Mauron, C. (1963). *Des métaphores obsédantes au mythe personnel*. Paris: José Corti.
Modell, A. (1997). Reflections on metaphor and affects. *Annual of Psychoanalysis* 25:219–233.
Natoli, J. and Rusch, F. L. (1984). *Psychocriticism: An Annotated Bibliography*. Westport, CT and London: Greenwood Press.
Ohmann, R. (1968). A linguistic appraisal of Victorian style. In *The Art of Victorian Prose*, ed. G. Levine and W. Madden, pp. 289–313. New York: Oxford University Press.
Phillips, W., ed. (1957). *Art and Psychoanalysis*. New York: Criterion Books.
Reiser, M. (1984). *Mind, Brain, Body: Toward a Convergence of Psychoanalysis and Neurobiology*. New York: Basic Books.
Rose, G. (1980). *The Power of Form: A Psychoanalytic Approach to Aesthetic Form* [Psychological Issues, Monograph 49]. New York: International Universities Press.
Rudnytsky, P. L. (1993). *Transitional Objects and Potential Spaces:*

Literary Uses of D. W. Winnicott. New York: Columbia University Press.

Ruitenbeek, H., ed. (1964). *Psychoanalysis and Literature.* New York: Dutton.

Schwartz, M. M. (1975). Where is literature? *College English* 36:756–765.

Schwartz, M. M. and Willbern, D. (1982). Literature and psychology. In *Interrelations of Literature,* ed. J.-P. Barricelli and J. Gibaldi, pp. 205–224. New York: Modern Language Association of America.

Stoltzfus, B. (1996). *Lacan and Literature: Purloined Pretexts.* Albany, NY: State University of New York Press.

Sullivan, R. E. (1967). Backward to Byzantium. *Literature & Psychology* 17:13–18.

Tennenhouse, L., ed. (1976). *The Practice of Psychoanalytic Criticism.* Detroit, MI: Wayne State University Press.

Weissman, S. M. (1996). Charlie Chaplin's film heroines. *Film History* 8(4):439–445.

Wilson, E. (1948). Morose Ben Jonson. In *The Triple Thinkers.* New York: Scribner's.

Winson, J. (1985). *Brain and Psyche: The Biology of the Unconscious.* Garden City, NY: Anchor/Doubleday.

Withim, P. (1969–1970). The psychodynamics of literature. *Psychoanalytic Review* 56(4):556–585.

Wolff, C. G. (1977). *A Feast of Words: The Triumph of Edith Wharton.* New York: Oxford University Press.

——— (1986). *Emily Dickinson.* New York: Knopf.

Woodward, K. and Schwartz, M. M., eds. (1986). *Memory and Desire: Aging—Literature—Psychoanalysis.* Bloomington, IN: Indiana University Press.

Wright, E. E. (1998). *Psychoanalytic Criticism: A Reappraisal.* London and New York: Routledge.

12

Freud and the Visual Arts
Donald Kuspit

As Louis Fraiberg noted in 1956, "Only twice did Freud essay . . . detailed analyses of painting and sculpture: most of his application to art was in the field of literature" (p. 88). Fraiberg gives two explanations for this fact: (1) "Literature . . . since its medium, like that of psycho-analysis, is language, lends itself readily to scientific investigation without the necessity of constructing a new symbolic foundation" (p. 82), and (2) "And in literature, the presentation of the themes which interested him was on the whole more explicit and lent itself more readily to study, being closer to the kind of material which he obtained from his patients" (p. 88). More particularly, Richard Sterba (1940) observes that "Freud uses poetry as a paradigmatic basis for his investigations in the field of the psychology of art because, of all the material employed to form the work of art, poetry stands nearest to the dream and the fantasy, those all-important objects of psychological research. It may also be that the art of poetry lay nearest to Freud's own creative expression" (p. 262).

Now I have the difficult task of insisting that while all this is so, there is more than meets the eye with respect to Freud's preference for the literary over the visual arts. I will argue that there is a certain calculated reluctance in Freud's withdrawal—as I want to characterize it—from the visual to the literary. It shortcircuits his analysis of Leonardo's paintings: the *Mona Lisa* (1503–1506), the *Virgin and Saint Anne with the Christ Child and the Young John the Baptist* (1500–1501), and Michelangelo's sculpture *Moses* (1513–1515), to name the works of visual art Freud dealt with most extensively. Freud himself said, at the beginning of his essay "The Moses of Michelangelo" (1914), that while he was "no connoisseur in art . . . works of art do exercise a powerful effect on me, especially those of literature and sculpture, less often of painting" (p. 211). The only explanation he offered was his need to "explain to myself what their effect was due to, noting, almost as an aside, that wherever I cannot do this, as for instance with music, I am almost incapable of obtaining any pleasure. Some rationalistic, or perhaps analytic, turn of mind in me rebels against being moved by a thing without knowing why I am thus affected and what it is that affects me" (p. 211).

Presumably works of literature and sculpture were easier for Freud to analyze and explain than works of painting and music, which no doubt had their effect but did not afford much pleasure. In a sense, he resisted being moved by them: the unpleasure of being unable to analyze them cancelled out the pleasure they could have given him. He became indifferent to them on principle. Sculpture escaped this fate because it was essentially three-dimensional literature for Freud. Indeed, it could be understood through literature, from which it was derived. It represented figures—for example, Moses—who were already celebrated in literature, whether for their deeds or ideas. Once a person was famous enough on paper, he would be represented—monumentalized—in space, as though to satisfy curiosity about his appearance—even if no one remembered what he actually looked like. Artistic fantasy would make him look important—and signal his superior place in society. Visual representation derived from literary representation—visual fame from literary fame. Visual fame consolidated literary fame, absolutizing it. Michelangelo's *Moses*, in effect, resurrected the body of the biblical hero, confirming his importance for civilization, the nobility of his person, and the authority of his mind, that is, the immortality of his ideas. The ideas were beyond criticism, and he was beyond reproach.

If, as Harold Blum (1991) writes, "Moses came to life, reborn as Freud's idealized self, object, and self-object, alter ego and ego ideal, replacing Fliess" (p. 516), Michelangelo's *Moses* also symbolized Freud's wish to be famous and immortal for his writing. When Freud relinquished Fliess, Blum writes, "the sculptured Moses was further utilized as a concrete 'living' presence, a partially externalized object and self-representation serving the remodeled internalization and consolidation of Freud's analytic ideals and identity" (p. 516). There was even more—competition with Moses, amounting to hubris: Moses's heroism led the children of Israel out of physical slavery, and Freud's ideas would lead them—all of mankind—out of mental slavery. Freud not only wanted to be larger than life, like Michelangelo's statue, but larger than Moses. Did he dare think that psychoanalysis was more important than the Ten Commandments, or at least as important? Both were received with great ambivalence, and continue to be.

Freud, then, wanted intellectual pleasure from art, not sensuous pleasure. I think he was interested in Leonardo because he had been stuck on the horns of the same dilemma as Leonardo—the choice between the sensuous pleasure of art and the intellectual pleasure of science—and like Leonardo, if with less agony and earlier in his life, he chose science rather than art, or rather subsumed the latter in the former. Like Leonardo, Freud (1910) had "an insatiable and indefatigable thirst for knowledge" (p. 75), "saw countless other problems arising" behind the first one (p. 77), "controlled and subjected [his affects] to the instinct for research" (p. 74), and "did not love or hate, but asked himself about the origin and significance of what he was to love and hate" (p. 74). Convert[ing] his passion into a thirst for knowledge, like Leonardo (p. 74), Freud discursively read what he saw rather than enjoying it spontaneously. Freud identified with Leonardo and Moses because they were both intellectuals who had repudiated the life of the senses and brought their emotions under control. According to Freud, Michelangelo showed Moses in the act of doing so. More precisely, they analyzed and bent the life of the senses and emotions to a higher, more mature purpose—the life of the mind. Two years after his study of Michelangelo's *Moses*, Freud declared, in his essay, "On Transience" (1916), that "it was incomprehensible . . . that the thought of the transience of beauty should interfere with our joy in it" (p. 305). But he could not enjoy beauty unless he could intellectually dissect it. As he said, he abhorred the "state of intellectual bewilderment" an aesthetician regarded as "a necessary condition" for a work of art to achieve its greatest effect (Freud 1914, p. 212). Such intellectual bewilderment was in effect capitulation to purely sensuous pleasure.

In dealing with art, only comprehension gave Freud pleasure, and literature gave him pleasure because it was, for him, the most readily comprehended art. It could be easily read and intellectually analyzed. In contrast, painting and music could not be read in the same straightforward intellectual way, however much music, like literature, used a comprehensible language, and thus could be systematically analyzed. As far as I know, Freud never learned the language of music, although the music he liked was accompanied by language, as though that alone made it meaningful. One of Freud's favorite works was Mozart's *Don Giovanni*, which, like all operas, involves a text the music presumably translates, or at least that is correlate with the music, making it easier to follow, if not comprehensible in its own terms.

As for sculpture, "the statues of ancient deities that adorned Freud's study and desk . . . had many meanings for Freud," as Blum writes (1991), "including concrete representations of images and of the past in the present; loss and replacement; death and immortality" (p. 524). In other words, they were important for what they symbolized and how they could be read—translated into words, into writing, into literature—not because they were beautiful works of art, all the more intriguing because of the way the artist who made them used the material medium to make them sensuously appealing. They were emotionally engaging because of their psychological meaning, not their aesthetic appearance, which is, as Freud himself acknowledged in his discussion of Leonardo, the real "artistic achievement."

But, as Fraiberg remarks, for Freud the "psychology of aesthetics . . . was explicitly ruled out as unprovable" (p. 86). Indeed, it was played down, if not dismissed as altogether beside the psychological point. As Sterba points out, while the "aesthetic side of the work of art has a . . . forepleasure effect" for Freud, that is, "it seduces the individual into the enjoyment of forbidden instinctual wish gratification without his even becoming conscious of the original sources of his pleasure." It is "at the same time . . . considerably overestimated. It is valued as if the entire quantity of pleasure caused by the work of art were brought about by the aesthetic features, while actually the real sources of pleasure remain for the most part unconscious" (p. 267). So aesthetics is deception and self-deception, all the more so because aesthetic qualities cannot be quantified; they get in the way of understanding the psychological truth, which affords intellectual pleasure. Clearly there is a parallel here between forepleasure and orgasmic pleasure and aesthetic pleasure and intellectual pleasure. Freud seemed to have experienced what Winnicott called an "ego orgasm" from intellectual analysis. The paradox of art for Freud is that just when it is most successful as art it hides, even falsifies, the psychological truth. It is the irony of sublimation: aesthetic sublimation is a big lie, psychologically speaking, however necessary socially.

In short, visual art was a form of text for Freud, or had to be turned into a text, or was dependent on some preexisting text, rather than an aesthetic experience of value for itself. It was always secondary to and derivative from something written, that is, to words, which could be readily understood and analyzed. Freud's analysis of Leonardo's art was heavily dependent on Dmitry Sergeyevich Merezhkovsky's *The Romance of Leonardo da Vinci*, one of his favorite novels, as Fraiberg notes. Freud read Leonardo's art through the book—saw it through the filter of Merezhkovsky's romanticization of Leonardo's life and fame—rather than looked at it with fresh eyes, in an unprejudiced if informed way. Similarly, Freud's Moses was the legendary, romantic figure in the Old Testament; Michelangelo's *Moses* was a secondary elaboration of this unusual figure, confirming his significance. The linguistic reduction of visual art, which was the first step in its de-aestheticization—one wonders how sensitive Freud was to the aesthetic character of literary works of art, how much he delighted in them, or whether he was even aware of them—was a matter of course for Freud, and works of visual art that could not readily submit to it were placed in the limbo of "unresolved riddles to our understanding" (Freud 1914, p. 211).

No matter how much Freud hoped, as he said in his Michelangelo essay, "that the effect of the work will undergo no diminution after we have succeeded in thus analyzing it" (p. 212), that is, reducing it to text or disclosing it as text, he was more interested in the analysis than in its effect. Indeed, the verbal analysis was a way of controlling the effect—keeping it from becoming overwhelming—and finally a substitute for it, and even, I dare say, in Freud's psyche, for the work of art. Freud's essay on Michelangelo's *Moses* is certainly more than an ordinary souvenir of an experience of art, and even more than the usual intellectual momento mori left after the murderous work of analytic dissection. On some emotional level it is competitive with it, and means to replace it by rationalizing it. If, as T. W. Adorno (1984) says, "works of art, do not, in the psychological sense, repress contents of consciousness," but "rather, through expression they help raise into consciousness diffuse and forgotten experiences without 'rationalizing' them" (p. 82), then Freud rationalizes artistic expression by naming and analyzing the diffuse and forgotten experiences it helps raise into consciousness, which in a sense is to undermine its purpose and neutralize its emotional effect. It is to treat the work of art as a means—a secondary *via regia* to the unconscious, the dream being the primary road—rather than a sublime end in itself. To put this another way, if, as Alfred North Whitehead (1955) wrote, "the work of art . . . unlooses depths of feeling from behind the frontier where the precision of consciousness fails" (p. 270), Freud thinks it is possible to treat the depths of feeling precisely without the special mediation of the work of art.

For Freud, it seemed, "the Word was God," as John 1:1 states, even if, as Freud stated (1900), "visual images constitute the principal component of our dreams" (p. 33), which are spokesmen for that dynamic god called the unconscious. Presumably when Sterba said that "the art of poetry lay closest to Freud's own creative expression," and characterized poetry "as nearest to the dream and the fantasy," he was calling attention to the abundance of images that can be found in Freud's writing. But these images are not strictly visual; they are words that describe and evoke what can be seen—word-pictures, not painted pictures, which, as Paul Gauguin said, present themselves all at once rather than in a logical, orderly way, like Freud's literary images. Freud really could not abide painting, or at least was seriously insensitive to it, as I hope to show in my discussion of the lacks in his discussion of Leonardo's paintings, because, in contrast to sculpture, it is forcefully and unmistakably visual, whatever its literary references. But even in his treatment of Michelangelo's *Moses* there is a serious lack of attention to the sculpture's appearance as a visual whole.

Artistically speaking, no element in a good work of art has priority over any other. Whatever hierarchy seems to be established by placing one element more front and center than the other elements is a rationalist illusion. Who, really, is to say that Mona Lisa's smile is more important and visually privileged than the raw landscape behind her, or for that matter that the smile is more complex and strange than the landscape? Who is to say that Moses' beard and hands, of which Freud makes so much, are more relevant to the plasticity of Michelangelo's sculpture than the muscles and tension of Moses' body, which modify those of the *ignudi* [nude] seated on the cornice projections of the Sistine Chapel ceiling—completed a year before (1512) work was begun on the *Moses*—without destroying their dramatic character? Only everyday perception, which determines what must be seen on the basis of its practical importance—rather than aesthetically attuned perception, which is ready to see whatever is to be seen without prejudging its importance—can prefer one to the other. Leonardo, as we know, was a master of landscape, and I believe that for him the face was simply another kind of natural terrain, and not the most difficult one to scientifically analyze. The swirl of water and the geology and topography of the Po valley took precedent over it. Similarly, Michelangelo was a master of the body, and it is the expressive positioning of the body that takes precedent over its religious narration in his art. Indeed, the unprecedented plasticity of Michelangelo's bodies is the point of his art.

As far as I know Freud never dabbled in painting, or for that matter wrote poetry, even as a hobby. In fact, we know that he was happy when his adolescent son Martin recovered from "his attacks of poetitis" (Young-Bruehl 1988, p. 44), which of course makes psychological sense in view of Freud's assertion that the mechanism of poetry is the same as that of hysterical fantasies, as he wrote in his analysis of Goethe's *The Sorrows of Young Werther* (quoted in Fraiberg, p. 94). One had to be cured of poetry, inasmuch as it was a symptom of hysteria. Or else one had to enlist it in the service of reason—psychoanalytic science—as Freud does by way of his use of analogy and metaphor. Horace said that art should serve morality; Freud suggests that it should serve psychology. It seems that he was more than happy to save people—and himself—from the fate of being an artist, literary, or visual, however much he admired such literary artists as Shakespeare, Goethe, and Arthur Schnitzler, and seemed to have regarded them as his most serious competition in the realm of psychological understanding. To Arthur Schnitzler he wrote: "Whenever I get deeply absorbed in your beautiful creations I invariably seem to find beneath their poetic surface the very presuppositions, interests, and conclusions which I know to be my own" (Rose 1987, pp. 14–15). Clearly Freud was conflicted about art.

Particularly visual art, as I am strongly suggesting. Freud's withdrawal, as I called it earlier, from the visual to the literary, is an example of what might be called the "downcast eye syndrome," to use Martin Jay's term (1994). It is responsible for the incomplete attention he gave to Leonardo's paintings and Michelangelo's sculptures. He did not see them in their visual completeness, but rather selected certain elements for psychoanalytic interpretation, because of a fear of being taken in by visual appearances, a certain resistance to accepting them on face value. Freud wrote (1900) that "a thing that is pictorial is, from the point of view of a dream, a thing that is *capable of being represented*" (p. 340). It is this unconscious thing—the dream's latent content—that is important, not its pictorial representation—the dream's manifest content. The issue for Freud is to reverse the "transformation from [unconscious] idea into sensory image" (p. 535), not to idolize the sensory image, as though it was a special achievement of unconscious art, a creative triumph of the imagination—even if it is.

Why did Freud castrate his vision, as it were—blind himself like Oedipus? Jay suggests an answer. Freud, he wrote, admired "Charcot's observational skills," which were clearly in evidence "in the theatricalized amphitheater and photographic studio of Charcot's clinic at Salpetrière" (Jay 1994, p. 331). As Freud wrote:

> Charcot was, as he himself said a "visuel," a man who sees. . . . He used to look again and again at the things he did not understand, to deepen his impression of them day by day, till suddenly an understanding of them dawned on him. In his mind's eye the apparent chaos presented by the continual repetition of the same symptoms then gave way to order. . . . He might be heard to say that the greatest satisfaction a man could have was to see something new—that is, to recognize it as new; and he remarked again and again on the difficulty and value of this kind of seeing. [Jay 1994, p. 331]

In a sense, Charcot, like an artist, studied his model—in his case a symptom—until it made pictorial sense to him, which is when he thought he understood it.

Now as Jay points out (p. 332), while Freud "steadfastly continued to value clinical observation . . . he gradually distanced himself from Charcot's ocularcentric method." He came to "stress . . . the interpretation of verbally reproduced phenomena such as dreams or slips of the tongue, as opposed to the mere observation of hysterical symptoms or physiognomies," which "meant that listening was more important than seeing" (p. 334). Looking stays on the outside—on the surface—while listening tells one what goes on in the inside—in the psychic depths. Literature, it should be noted, was Freud's preferred art because it deals with both the inside and outside—psychic activity as well as physical appearance. As Michel de Certeau writes, Freud in effect "adopt[ed] the style of the novel," that is, a kind of literature, which was "to abandon the case study as it was presented and practiced by Charcot in his Tuesday sessions. These consisted of observations, that is to say "coherent charts or pictures, composed by noting the facts relevant to a synchronic model of an illness" (Jay, p. 335). Similarly, Derrida notes "the movement from optical metaphors of the psyche ('a compound microscope, or a photographic apparatus') in *The Interpretation of Dreams* to more scriptural ones in his later work, such as what Freud called a 'mystic writing pad'" (Jay, p. 335). Thus Freud toppled another father figure, declaring his methods obsolete and his results inadequate, that is, his work pseudo-scientific.

But the change involved more than the rectification of a theoretical error, that is, "the temporality, spacing, and difference that had been banished from Descartes's famous ball of wax was restored as Freud 'performs for us the scene of writing,' an *écriture* that combined absence with presence and defeats any direct visual representation" (Jay, p. 335). Rather, the shift from the optical to the graphic involved technique and therapy; in distancing himself from what could be seen and emphasizing what could be heard, Freud was distancing himself from appearances and emphasizing associations. While he accepted Friedrich Schelling's definition of the uncanny as "the name for everything that ought to have remained secret and hidden but has come to light" (Jay, p. 332) and thus can be seen, what is in fact seen makes no psychological sense and has no therapeutic relevance unless it can be interpreted, and it cannot be properly interpreted unless one has associations to it.

As Freud stated again and again, dreams were to be approached by way of the dreamer's verbal associations to them. To be seduced by the dream's unusual appearance was to miss its psychological point.

For Freud, the dream was an "unconscious puzzle picture," to use Sterba's expression (1940, p. 262), with the weight on "unconscious puzzle" rather than "picture." One could best understand its logic by the apparently tangential approach through the associations of the dreamer. To admire its inventiveness, to be fascinated—taken in—by its exciting appearance, to aesthetically celebrate its perplexing details, was to defend against its psychological meaning, blind oneself to its psychological purpose. In a sense, the visual appearance of the dream distracted from its meaning, and was incidental and even accidental—contingent on circumstances, that is, the so-called "day residue," as well as unconscious wishes and conflicts. Freud made this point decisively in a letter to André Breton, who had asked Freud to write an introduction to *Les Vases communicants*, a collection of some fifty dreams by various surrealist artists dedicated to him. Freud rejected the idea, writing that "a mere collection of dreams without the dreamers' associations, without the knowledge of the circumstances in which they occurred, tells me nothing, and I can hardly imagine what it would tell anyone" (Davis 1973, p. 128). Thus, no matter how much Freud was aware of "the powerful symbolic resonance of the eyes," as Jay says (1994, p. 332), from the phallic "gaze of Medusa" to Oedipus's castrative self-blinding, and to his discussion of the "triumph of the eye over the nose" in *Civilization and Its Discontents*—no doubt in part a criticism of Fliess, who was stuck on the nose—therapeutic technique was more than a matter of exchanging glances with the patient, as Freud's position behind the couch confirmed. It involved detached intellectual analysis, whatever else might be emotionally involved.

Like a latter day Tieresias, Freud in effect sacrificed sight to insight. He turned away from the symptom toward the association, from the theatrical appearance to the psychological meaning, from the dream's manifest content—a theatrical symptom—toward its latent content. The symptom is visible to the naked eye, the association is visible to the mind's eye—reason's eye. In contrast, Charcot fetishizes and aestheticizes the hysterical symptom by photographing and staging it—giving it center stage, presenting it as a public performance—under the illusion that he thereby understands its significance. No doubt he partly does; it is a performance, theatrical. But the performance is its end, not its origin, its appearance not its inner reality.

Charcot is transfixed—dare one say hypnotized?—by its novelty—its artistic novelty, as it were—while Freud realizes that the symptom represents an ancient conflict, inherent to being human. The visible symptom is not there to be mirrored—its appearance clinically elevated, as it were, by being made rabidly public—but to be understood, and the way to do so—to access its psychological meaning—is through the verbal associations of the person who has it.

Now all of this emphasis on the verbal meant that Freud did not see certain things in visual art, or seriously attend to what he saw. He was undoubtedly a good observer, but when he observed something that he could not analyze or rationalize he turned away from it, ignoring it as though it did not exist. Thus, in his discussion of Leonardo's paintings there is no mention of the reason for their fame, indeed, the reason they are original and distinctive: their *chiaroscuro* and *sfumato*. As Marilyn Stokstad (1995) notes, "Leonardo created the illusion of high relief by modeling the figures with strongly contrasted light and shadow, called *chiaroscuro*," and he "unified his compositions by covering them with a thin, lightly tinted varnish, which resulted in a smoky overall haze called *sfumato*" (pp. 686–687). Is it that the painting's skin of light and dark is beyond association, being a purely visual phenomenon? Or does it evoke depths of feeling impossible to name and analyze—depths that can only be acknowledged rather than brought into focus, for to do so was to dissipate them? Similarly, Michelangelo's *Moses*, whatever moment it depicts—Moses about to hurl the tablets, breaking them to pieces, or restraining himself from doing so, as Freud ingeniously argued—shows a muscular hero of superhuman strength. It is one in a long line of Michelangelesque bodies—positioned somewhere between the *ignudi* and the figures of the Medici on their tombs—and it makes its point as a body, not as an idea.

Skin and body—Freud stays away from them, even though, as he himself stated, the body ego is the most fundamental ego, and, as Didier Anzieu asserts, the idea of the skin ego was already latent in Freud's comments about the skin as an erogenous zone. Skin and body are sensuous sites, and sensually engaging. With a certain puritanical forebearance, Freud (1910) neglects to deal with them in depth or otherwise, although he does acknowledge, agreeing with other observers, "the contrast between reserve and seduction, between the most devoted tenderness and a sensuality that is ruthlessly demanding" in the smile of the Mona Lisa (p. 108). But Freud misses the artistic point of the picture, namely, the contrast between light and shadow that gives it—and the smile—its elusive substance.

Freud (1910) says that "what interested [Leonardo] in a picture was above all a problem" (p. 77), and he emphasizes the incompleteness of many of Leonardo's works, or the delays attendant upon their creation, and the fact that several became ruins within his own lifetime because of technical problems in their production. But the fact of the matter is that despite all these problems—and Meyer Schapiro points out that Leonardo had one of the largest oeuvres of any Renaissance artist, and delivered works with greater promptness than most—Leonardo achieved original artistic solutions to the problem of representing atmosphere and volume which made him famous, and had enormous influence on the history of art. Similarly, Freud obsesses about the position of the hands of Michelangelo's *Moses*, ignoring the fact that he makes his impression through his body, of which the hands are only a small, however noteworthy, part. Of course the right one rests on the tablets of the Ten Commandments—a book—and the left one points toward it, clearly indicating that it is the most important part of the statue. But that is only narratively, not artistically; artistically, the body is all important. The book is its attribute, not its essence. The body is of primary importance, the book of secondary importance—just the opposite of what Freud, following convention, assumes. Indeed, I venture to say that the contrast between the textures of the muscles of Moses' arms and his beard—two kinds of skin—has more expressive, quintessentially artistic carrying power than the hands, whether pointing to the tablets of the law or by themselves.

There is nothing that can be "proven" about the aesthetics of Leonardo's *chiaroscuro* and *sfumato* and the dynamic textures of Michelangelo's *Moses*, but that fact is beside their qualitative point. No doubt their emotional effect can be analyzed, but they have to appreciated and enjoyed first. Freud doesn't do so. I want to suggest that the reason is akin to the reason he was reluctant to engage music. Kohut (1978) writes:

> Pure music cannot be translated into words. The world of pure sounds cannot be mastered with the main instrument of logical thinking—the

neutralizing, energy-binding functions of the mind—which Freud calls the secondary processes of the psyche. It surely is the explanation for the specific quality of pleasure in music. Stimuli which cannot be mastered through translation into words (or comparable symbols used in logical thought) mobilize much greater forces, and perhaps also forces of a different distribution corresponding to a very early ego organization. This energy is required to withstand the influx of a chaotic stimulation; it becomes liberated when the form of music transforms the chaos into an orderly stimulation that can be dealt with comparatively easily. [I, p. 145]

Kohut suggests that Freud could not tolerate the regression induced by music, which, I suggest, is also induced by such purely aesthetic phenomena as atmosphere and texture, that is, *sfumato*, *chiaroscuro*, and pure plasticity, all of which mingle surface and depth indistinguishably and illogically.

They cannot be translated into words, and what makes them particularly treacherous in Leonardo's paintings and Michelangelo's sculptures of the body is that they are not subsumed by form, but seem to exist for their own dynamic selves. However much Leonardo's *chiaroscuro* may create the illusion of high relief and model figures, and however much his *sfumato* may unify the composition, they are independent sensuous phenomena that can be appreciated apart from their pictorial purpose, that is, from the form-giving character of the figures and the composition. Similarly, however much the textures of Moses' body may serve to define its form, they are sensuous phenomena in their own right. They cannot be intellectually neutralized, but remain sensuously autonomous and arousing. For Freud they were unanalyzable; they could not be rationalized away into form, or even given psychological form. And thus Freud looked through and around them. He attended to the figures that had rational form rather than the seemingly formless irrational elements in Leonardo's paintings and Michelangelo's sculpture. The latter were threatening, and more subtle than the smile Leonardo formally depicted and the dramatic moment Michelangelo narrated, and, I think, offer a greater clue to their creativity than the figures they represented.

I want to conclude by remarking the striking difference between Freud's approach to Leonardo and Michelangelo and Karl Abraham's (1937) much more visually sensitive approach to Giovanni Segantini's paintings. Abraham's lively essay about Segantini is written in an altogether different spirit and with an altogether different sensibility than Freud's somewhat sober essays on Leonardo and Michelangelo. Abraham is not only interested in the psychological meaning of Segantini's art, that is, the way it can be interpreted—the words it can be translated into—but in Segantini's "disintegration of color," as he calls Segantini's particular brand of Impressionism (p. 482). It is what made Segantini famous, and it is not easily described in words. It is at best poetically evoked by them. Color is in fact ineffable, beyond being simplistically named. Experientially, it is a "chaotic stimulation," to use Kohut's phrase, however much it can be scientifically analyzed, that is, made to seem rational. Abraham repeatedly talks about Segantini's "yearning for light and color" (p. 482), his "luminous colors" (p. 497), his use of "the lightest and most brilliant shades of color" (p. 497). He associates Segantini's colors with his "eroticism"— with "sexual excitement" (p. 480)—but he also appreciates them as aesthetic phenomena in themselves, ultimately unanalyable—delightfully irrational.[1]

I don't know what Freud thought about Abraham's essay, which was originally published in 1925, but we do know that in a 1922 letter Freud found an expressionistic drawing of Abraham's head "horrifying," adding that the artist was "the all-too-undesirable illustration of Adler's theory that it is just the people with congenital defects of vision who become painters and draughtsmen" (Kofman 1988, p. 222). He also remarked that Abraham's "tolerance or sympathy for modern art" was "a trifling flaw in [his] character." I think that Freud's intolerance or lack of sympathy for it is a major flaw in his mind if not character. For it suggests how blind Freud was to the purely visual factor in art, if we accept Clement Greenberg's argument that modern art at its abstract best pursues aesthetic-sensuous quality—pure visuality—independently of any literary purpose.

NOTES

1. Freud says nothing about the colors in Leonardo's paintings, and it seems unlikely that he would have much tolerance for Segantini's impressionist use of gestalt-free color-gestures, as Anton

Ehrenzweig calls them. According to him, they are the carrier of unconscious affect in modern art. As Marion Milner (1987) points out, color "is very closely bound up with the feelings" (p. 225). For Freud, such physically raw, colorful gestures would probably have represented unchanneled or unbound id energy, and as such unintelligible and dangerous in itself. He would be defensively intolerant against its direct expression, even in symbolic form. This is no doubt why he preferred the clear and distinct—well-constructed, carefully controlled, intelligible—forms of Renaissance art to the more loosely constructed, often unclear, and indistinct forms of modern art. For him the former probably symbolized integration, the latter disintegration.

Also, since Impressionist works are more forthrightly and consummately aesthetic—sensuously explicit, as it were—than Renaissance works, they would seem to contradict Freud's devaluation of the aesthetic, that is, his relegation of it to a subsidiary role—in effect the sugarcoating on the bitter psychological narrative. Or else he would be faced with the unhappy possibility that works of art can be all regressive foreplay—lyric tour de forces of arrested sexual development, as it were.

Clearly epic, "well-armored" Renaissance works of art lend themselves more readily to Freud's intellectual approach to art, that is, his intellectual defense against it and the feelings it arouses. If, as has been argued, modern art is closer to the essence of art—transformative engagement with the material medium, as Milner says, involving intense emotional investment in it—than Renaissance art, then Freud's vituperative indifference to Expressionism and, implicitly, Impressionism, indicates that he completely missed the basic point of art. He missed the complex relational and even libidinal psychodynamics of Michelangelo's engagement with stone and Leonardo's with paint.

There is no doubt that the ego—Freud's ego—is entitled to its reflections on the finished work of art, but they tend to miss what is specific to art as art, however insightful they may be into its narrative and social import and function. No doubt it is those most people latch on to, because they are familiar, but in doing so they miss the fact that art is not simply a delivery system for known information and ideas. In mediating them art transforms them into something unfamiliar, at least if it is credible as art; transforms them into aesthetic substance, thus peculiarly transcending them. We do not look at Vincent van Gogh's wheat fields to learn how to plant wheat nor do we expect a familiar homey feeling from Paul Cézanne's still lives and interiors, at least if we are interested in experiencing them as art rather than as a kind of reporting, at which they no doubt miserably fail.

Freud offered a new reading of Michelangelo's *Moses*, for which we are grateful, but his reading does little to change our experience of the aesthetics of the sculpture—although it does remind us how subtly Michelangelo could work with fingers—which is what has given it a more prominent place in the history of art than other Renaissance and Mannerist representations of Moses. These include the Moses in Botticelli's *Punishment of Korah, Dathan, and Abiram* (1481–1482), Rosso Fiorentino's *Moses and Jethro's Daughters* (ca. 1523), and Tintoretto's *Moses Striking Water from the Rock* (1577–1581). Art history prefers Michelangelo's Moses to theirs for aesthetic reasons, rather than because Michelangelo's reading of the story of Moses is ingeniously novel—according to Freud—compared to theirs.

Incidentally, it is worth noting that the Renaissance scholar Frederick Hartt (1974, p. 457) thinks that "Moses holds the Tables of the Law . . . not in anger but with prophetic inspiration." This suggests that Freud, who thought Michelangelo's Moses was trying to control his anger at the children of Israel, and did so successfully, showing his ego strength, may have projected his own anger into Moses. Among other things, this would be anger at the fact that his inspiration—psychoanalysis—was insufficiently recognized and appreciated by the world, just as in dancing around the Golden Calf the children of Israel did not recognize and appreciate the hard-won achievement of Moses. Just as Moses' narcissism was offended—was it anger he experienced, or rage?—by the indifference of the children of Israel, all too eager for pleasure (dance is euphemism for orgy), which suggested the difficulty the Ten Commandments would have making their way in the world, so Freud's narcissism seems to have been injured by the difficulties psychoanalysis had making its way in the world, and even among its adherents, who offered alternative—non-Freudian—versions of it. But if, as Hartt says, Michelangelo's statue is "symbolic rather than anecdotal," as Freud thought, and Michelangelo shows us Moses in a state of inspiration rather than at a moment of anger—and Hartt offers convincing evidence that this is the case (it has in part to do with the fact that the statue was meant "to have occupied a corner position on the second story" of the tomb of Pope Julius II, and thus "seen sharply from below")—then Freud missed its basic meaning.

REFERENCES

Abraham, K. (1937). Giovanni Segantini: a psychoanalytic essay. *Psychoanalytic Quarterly* 6:453–512.

Adorno, T. W. (1984). *Aesthetic Theory*. London: Routledge & Kegan Paul.

Blum, H. (1991). Freud and the figure of Moses: the Moses of Freud. *Journal of the American Psychoanalytic Association* 39:513–533

Davis, F. B. (1973). Three letters from Sigmund Freud to André Breton. *Journal of the American Psychoanalytic Association* 21:127–134.

Fraiberg, L. (1956). Freud's writings of art. *International Journal of Psycho-Analysis* 37:82–96.

Freud, S. (1900). The interpretation of dreams. *Standard Edition* 4/5.

——— (1910). Leonardo da Vinci and a memory of his childhood. *Standard Edition* 11.

——— (1914). The Moses of Michelangelo. *Standard Edition* 13.

——— (1916). On transience. *Standard Edition* 14.

Hartt, F. (1974). *History of Italian Renaissance Art*. Englewood Cliffs, NJ: Prentice-Hall and New York: Harry N. Abrams.

Jay, M. (1994). *Downcast Eyes: The Denigration of Vision in Twentieth-Century French Thought*. Berkeley, CA: University of California Press.

Kofman, S. (1988). *The Childhood of Art: An Interpretation of Freud's Aesthetics*. New York: Columbia University Press.

Kohut, H. (1978). *The Search for the Self, Selected Writings of Heinz Kohut: 1950–1978*. 2 vols. New York: International Universities Press.

Merezhkovsky, D. S. (1928). *The Romance of Leonardo da Vinci*. New York: Modern Library.

Milner, M. (1987). *The Suppressed Madness of Sane Men*. London and New York: Tavistock.

Rose, G. (1987). *Trauma and Mastery in Life and Art*. New Haven, CT: Yale University Press.

Sterba, R. (1940). The problem of art in Freud's writings. *Psychoanalytic Quarterly* 9:256–268.
Stokstad, M. (1995). *Art History*. 2 vols. Englewood Cliffs, NJ: Prentice-Hall.
Whitehead, A. N. (1955). *Adventures of Ideas*. New York: Mentor.
Young-Bruehl, E. (1988). *Anna Freud: A Biography*. New York: Summit.

PART V

FREUD AND LOVE

The first two papers of this section on culture and society deal with love and romance. In the first, **R. Curtis Bristol** outlines Freud's fundamental contributions to a psychology of love, ideas that grew and developed through Freud's career. Each of Freud's contributions has something to offer a modern view of passionate and romantic love, to our study of the way in which love interacts with sexuality. Freud noted early on that finding the object of love was not a new finding, but was a refinding of the mother with her breast and her initial care for the infant. This earliest relationship always marked later object choices. Later he talked about the two basic forms of love as "anaclitic" on the one hand, and narcissistic on the other, describing the tension between needing somebody to meet one's needs and investing in a person because they were an object of identification. Later contributions have emphasized that it is not only a matter of refinding an old object, but also a desire to move on, to repair and sustain a lover. Recent literature has talked about the tension between intimacy and sexuality, and the way the two relate to each other, but are not synonymous. Bristol's paper comprehensively sums up ideas about romantic love and their relationship to other forms of love, intimacy, and sexuality.

Stefan Pasternack's paper applies Freud's theories of love to a clinical case. After briefly reviewing and summarizing some of the issues that Bristol takes up in detail, Pasternack shows how an understanding of the problems in love relationships can successfully be applied in analytic therapy. His case of a young man torn between two women presents treatment of a common problem carried out with finesse. He holds his neutral ground in order to facilitate the patient's search for the meaning of his agonized indecision about love. This case is a gem in psychoanalytic writing: It demonstrates the utility of good theory in the hands of a masterful clinician who also is able to describe his work to us in a way that reads like a short story.

13

What Freud Taught Us about Passionate Romantic Love

R. Curtis Bristol

> To enlarge or illustrate the power or effect of love is to set a candle in the sun.
>
> —Robert Burton, *The Anatomy of Melancholy* (1621)

Every psychoanalyst since Sigmund Freud encounters as he did the problem of love and how to understand it in the clinical setting and real life. Freud (1914c, 1930a [1929]) asserted that love is essential to the individual and to the collective society: without love there is neurosis and chaos. The philosopher-analyst Lear (1990) observes that "Analysts tend to dismiss love as cosmological speculation for which Freud had a predilection but which goes beyond the bounds or concerns of psychoanalysis" (p. 156). Yet ". . . no aspect of Freud's life work has been as little understood, and so misunderstood, as his contribution to the understanding of love" (Bergmann 1987, p. 156).

In matters of love, words are critical. Bergmann cites Stallworthy (1974) that poets write more about love than about any other subject.

Let me define some terms necessary to an objective discourse on passionate romantic love. The word *romance* derives from the meaning "to write" in Roman, the vernacular of Latin (Webster 1988). In medieval times romance was a narrative verse or prose about chivalric exploits by heroic knights, and later meant a fictitious, wonderful tale of adventure that idealized events and characters by use of the imagination. Later it took on the meanings of a love story in literature or real life. The imaginative overvaluation of the other remains evident in traditional and popular romance literature. And it is the narrative truth for love in reality. *Passion* is another word associated with romantic love (Webster 1988). It derives from *passio*, that is, suffering, especially of Christ and the martyrs, but also of any narrative of personal agony. It has evolved to mean extreme affect that may be sexual, but as well, fear, hate, rage, grief, or excitement. I will not dwell on the complex meanings of romance, or the contradictory meanings of passion; they are apparent to the attentive student of love. I will develop the meanings of *intimacy*, *longing*, and *desire* as they apply to passionate romance, and introduce two new terms, the "lover dyad" and "intimate dyad."

There is good reason to distrust romantic love in real life. Everyone knows that the experience may be brief or enduring, defeating or transcendent, deflating or enlarging. Those enthralled by romance do not act with precision or objectivity. Lovers are at one moment captured by the beloved, the next doubting, critical, and dismissive. Passionate love takes an irregular course and often appears foolish and has its ridiculous eruptions and misunderstandings. No matter its twists and turns, the absurdity is more evident to the outsider than the lovers themselves. Their emotional vitality is private, exclusive, and seemingly self-generated. Person (1988) observes: "The couple—'we'—accumulates its own history. The lovers delight in recounting it to each other, because all its milestones, however ordinary and inert when described to an outsider . . . are sacred to them by virtue of the power they have to revivify past emotions" (p. 62).

I refer to lovers and their couple as the *lover dyad*. I explicate the individuals and their intersubjective affects along with the sociocultural value systems that are conflated into the text of passionate romantic love. I assert that passionate romantic love provides the motive for individuals within the lover dyad to integrate diverse forms and experiences of love, intimacy, and sexuality. I believe that the adult feelings or romantic love originate and are first experienced within the *maternal-infant dyad*. Love and intimacy are also evident in diverse other pairings throughout life. These I identify as the *intimate dyad*, especially evident in latency without the sexual aim, and in adolescence where there are many trials of love, intimacy, and sexuality, but not yet the integrating motive of romance per se, a developmental task that awaits the adult. (Bristol and Pasternack 1988)

Romantic feelings unite actual lived experience with myth, fiction, and biography. Any theory of psychology that values unconscious motive and conscious affect, and the genetic (historical) and psychodynamic hypotheses, must take romantic love seriously. Feelings are what love is about. Lichtenberg (1989) observes: "In the century-old history of psychoanalysis, the aspect of psychic functioning that has been considered of central importance has shifted from trauma to instinctual drive and fantasy to ego functions and the structural hypothesis to object relations and now to affects" (p. 259). This paradigmatic shift in psychoanalytic theory is one reason that romantic love, given its complex regressive and progressive affect states, is more often written about today, for example, Bergmann (1987), Beebe and McCrorie (in press), Gabbard (1996), Kernberg (1995), Lear (1990), and Person (1988).

The psychoanalytic study of love begins with Sigmund Freud (1899a, 1905d, 1905e[1901], 1910c, 1910h, 1912d, 1914c, 1915a [1914], 1917e, 1918a[1917], 1924c, 1924d, 1927e, 1930a). He conceptualized that the biology of desire seeks an object for satisfaction. He made clear that eros has origin in the child's relation to the mother and others and has a pleomorphic course throughout life. Its manifestation in the choice of object and the unconscious motives for excitement and satisfaction are both normative and pathological depending upon developmental history. Freud looked to similarities and differences in the genders and their development from birth to adulthood to explain love. He understood the universality of eros and its manifestation in various transcultural historical epochs. To Freud (1905d) we owe the initial effort to understand the individual and interpersonal meanings of love based upon a developmental history and the dynamic unconscious. Since Freud, we look to the maternal-infant dyad to further explain attachment and its vast and complicated intersubjective affect experiences that differentiate into individual core gender identity, sense of self, and the defined object choices and identifications that set the stage for adult love and self-esteem (Bowlby, 1958, 1960, Jacobson 1964, Mahler 1979, Spitz 1945, Stoller 1968, 1985).

Freud (1930a) said that "People give the name 'love' to the relation between man and a woman whose genital needs (predominate); but they give the name 'love' to the positive feelings between parents and children, and between brothers and sisters of a family, although we are obliged to describe this as 'aim inhibited love' or affection" (p. 102). He described the origin of love and its pathway to adult romantic sexual union through the successive stages of the mother–infant dyad, love within the family—including oedipal love—a nongenital "affection" for siblings and friends, and "sublimated" love for sexual aim inhibited interests and causes expressed in social and cultural interests and pursuits. Intimacy—Freud used the word "affection"—is the emotional attachment to another absent a sexual aim; it is gender neutral throughout life. Intimacy is an essential component of romantic love when integrated with sexual desire. But other intimate dyads are independent of romance and sexuality.

Freud's views on love, eros, affection (intimacy), libido, object choice, sexual aim, and narcissism are not an integrated theory. His writings on love were not made a part of his structural hypothesis. Passionate romantic love as a topic to understand the structure, function, or motive for mental process was largely ignored by the ego psychologists. Nonetheless, Bergmann (1987) uses Freud's instinctual theory to explain that the adult search for romantic love has origins in the maternal-infant dyad. "The mother, or her substitute, becomes both the first love and the first sexual object" (p. 159). He considers Freud's (1910c, p. 222) ". . . statement that 'the finding of an object is in fact a refinding of it' to be Freud's most profound contribution to love" (p. 159). He adds: "Under the impact of Freud's dual instinct theory we are inclined to understand anti-eros as hate, but to the Greeks, the opposite of love was the wish to be loved. Eros also acquired the inseparable companions, Pathos, the personification of longing, and Himeros, the personification of desire. In language, the Greeks tell us that love is not love unless it is accompanied by both *desire* and *longing*" (p. 34, emphasis added). Romantic love becomes possible ". . . during adolescence (when) the libido (desire and arousal) makes a fresh start (after oedipal frustration and the latency period), searching for a new and nonincestuous love object, but the new love object must nevertheless in someway remain reminiscent of the old" (Bergmann 1987, p. 158).

Freud (1930a) observed that the union of lovers is stark: "At the height of being in love the boundary between ego (self) and the object (other) threatens to melt away. Against all the evidence of his senses, a man who is in love declares 'I' and 'you' are one, and is prepared to behave as if it were a fact" (p. 66). Freud's insight persists to this day: passionate romantic love is an intimately coconstructed mutual belief system of longing and desire, a "religion of two" (Person 1988). Romantic love is desire that searches to refind the emotions and conditions of the original maternal-infant dyad, yet has the confounding history of the oedipal triad, as well as the vicissitudes of the lover dyad. It also must fit more or less the demands of others expectations and condemnations, either individual, familial, peer group, societal, or religious.

The lover dyad appears unique, fresh, and spontaneously created to the lovers. Nonetheless, it has an intricate unconscious history that relies on the sensuous love and intimacy begun in the mother infant dyad, the subsequent influence of the Oedipus complex, and the experiences, fantasies, and longings with numerous others during latency and early adolescence in various intimate dyads. These experiences and subsequent memories and sources of fantasy will have been sometimes satisfying and other times frustrating, incomplete or traumatic.

Freud (1910c) called these vulnerabilities the "necessary conditions for loving." In romantic love, the unconscious "condition" associated with object choice and identifications from infancy or childhood sets the terms for the adult choice for the beloved. Bergmann (1987) notes that "One may differentiate successful from unsuccessful preconditions for loving." (p. 164) The particular and peculiar preconditions of love determine and narrow the range of object choices for the beloved, and broaden the risks of dissatisfaction. "When a precondition fails to resolve the intrapsychic conflict, it leads to the creation of a fate neuroses" (Bergmann 1987, p. 164). These are the failed adult lovers in an endless search for the elusive lover dyad, repeating compulsively the unconscious pathological "condition" of the maternal-infant dyad and oedipal triadic experience, haunted by their continued but unsatisfied desire and longing. They find lovers already committed to another, or promiscuous lovers, or ill lovers, and so forth. In some, the masochistic motive is unmistakable, in others castration anxiety predominates, yet in others a too critical superego condemns the lover or the beloved. A particular precondition is the failure to integrate intimacy (Freud's "affection") with sexual desire and psychophysical sexuality, the Madonna-Prostitute split: "Where they love they do not desire, where they desire they cannot love" (Freud 1912d, p. 183).

The time of falling in love is when the infantile unconscious preconditions that Freud described influence the individual's choice of lover. A particular risk to romance is a love choice that repeats the disasters of the Oedipus complex. Oedipal love is not the normative developmental predecessor to adult passionate romance, but one of its preconditions imposed upon the history of the maternal-infant dyad. Oedipal love, for those who overcome its repression, is recalled as betrayal, feeling small, insignificant, and vulnerable, caught in the conflicted triangularly of rivalry and competition, not taken seriously, ignored, or ridiculed for the ambivalent feelings of love and hate, and having no capacity for actual sexual expression, or worse, sexually exploited. The intersubjective love of the oedipal child is different from adult romance where self-esteem is enhanced by finding in the beloved the reciprocity of intimacy, love, and sexuality. By contrast, the Oedipus complex is a disruption of intimate attachment to each parent, as Bergmann (1987) makes clear: "During the oedipal phase, *the relationship to both parents is ambivalent.* The rival parent is also loved and homosexual wishes compete with heterosexual ones" (p. 158, emphasis added).

The original aims and objects of oedipal love are repressed when the child enters latency. It is a period rich with renewed opportunities for attachment in multiple intimate dyads: with each parent— representing a repair of the oedipal rupture of intimacy with each parent that is brought on by the oedipal sexualized object relation— and with siblings, and increasingly outside of the home with teachers, friends, and others.

The adult psychopathology of triangular love requires the condition of a real or imagined third party to enable the lover to love. It is a remnant of oedipal love, and the opposite of the lover dyad that is a twosome in structure and function. Some regard the latter as true romantic love, that is the absence of the disruptive influences of anger, jealousy, or competition with a feared superior rival. Thus defined, true love is impossible in the Oedipus complex and its failure is the motive force in adolescence and young adulthood to search again for dyadic love.

Bergmann (1987) describes love as ". . . a compound of many emotions, diverse memories, and many needs that remain ungratified in childhood that seek resolution in adulthood. People love on various levels of intrapsychic maturity. The level of development that a person has reached will to a significant degree determine the fate of adult love, and what he or she will find or will elude him." This view is especially useful for the therapist who has the opportunity to facilitate the adult capacities to work through the infantile and childhood genetic barriers to falling and remaining in love (Kernberg 1975, chapters 7 and 8).

Many adults have the ego maturity to achieve and progress in life's demands and opportunities but remain immature in romantic passion. They can not establish a lover dyad, nor use it as a bridge to further the goal of remaining in love. Others work through with each other, and not infrequently in therapy, the restricting preconditions that Freud described. The risks to the disruption of the lover dyad are the preoedipal traumata of frustrated intimacy, sexual over stimulation, perversion, and the threats about losses of the loved object or the object's love, as well as the experience of the oedipal love-hate polarity, castration anxiety, and superego self/other condemnation (Freud 1910h, 1921c, 1926d). The shift from the love, intimacy, and sensuous nurture of maternal attachment, to the threats of the Oedipus complex, represents the irreparable loss of the all-providing mother in fact and fantasy. This frustrated infantile wish is sometimes resurrected in the desire and longing for adult romantic love. But an all-providing other is impossible in fact in the lover dyad as in the maternal-infant dyad, but Mother Earth love fantasies abound in many would-be lovers. Examples of the all-providing maternal figure, an unconscious fantasy projected to the other of the lover dyad, is the man or woman who expects the total attention of the beloved. A modern variant in the expanded world of the real, nondomestic professional and work opportunities for women is that her lover be the domestic anchor for their relationship.

The lover's refinding the choice of love object and the conditions for loving have potentially harsh origins and must yield in the coconstructed renewed opportunity in the lover dyad. This is the work of romantic love. If infantile love holds too great an appeal or too great a demand determined by the maternal-infant dyad, that is the Freudian ideas of instinctual fixation or regression put in object choice terms, romantic love fails and the lover dyad can not be established or will not sustain.

One must mourn the loss of the ideal all good and providing mother, for it can not be realized in the lover dyad that depends upon reciprocity and mutual interaction. This is a paradox inasmuch as romantic love is emotionally enhanced for those who achieve the capacity for intimacy through the truly loving intimate and sensuous maternal infant dyad, but this original love must be abandoned and mourned to realize the new adult lover dyad.

Freud understood that the adult experience of romantic love — through its object choice and preconditions — had origin in the good (ideal) and bad (traumatic, devalued) actual experiences and fantasies of the maternal-infant dyad, and the subsequent Oedipus complex. These original identifications and object choices — and their respective preconditions — persist in unconscious representations that shape all subsequent love relationships, including transference love, romantic love, aim-inhibited "love" of siblings and friends, and the sublimated affiliations of loyalty and cause. To overcome the barriers to falling and remaining in love, to realize the favorable conditions for loving and avoid the bad, lovers — male and female alike — must find new, nonincestuous partners reminiscent of the maternal-infant dyad. My emphasis on object choice may surprise some that think of Freud's theories as dominated by the instinctual aim. This was true in his (1905a) first theory of love but was differently emphasized later on: "The object of the instinct is what is most variable about the instinct, and not originally connected with it but becomes assigned to it by consequence of being peculiarly fitted to make satisfaction possible" (1915c, p. 122). Thus, my emphasis on identifications, object choices, and their attendant preconditions for love, that is, the lover dyad as derivative of the maternal-infant dyad, are insights I owe to Bergmann's (1987) study of Freud.

The preoedipal and triangular traumata and psychodynamics of eros are familiar to psychoanalysts but the example of intimacy (Freud's term is "aim-inhibited" or "affection") is less understood. The word *intimacy* derives from the Latin *intimus*, meaning "close friendship." It is the superlative of *intus*, meaning "within." Intimacy is the inmost and fundamental structure of relation through private feelings, what is personal, familiar, and shared. We find intimacy within love and within friendship; it may be sexual, but not necessarily. Unlike the sexual intimacy in the adult lover dyad, intimacy from the beginning of life seeks appropriate partners for expression that becomes a self-capacity. Intimacy, like romantic love, is enriched by the diversity of experience, but it does not wait for adulthood. The intimacy of lovers derives from many intimate attachments before the adult choice of a lover, especially from the maternal-infant dyad, the numerous and diverse intimate dyads of latency, adolescence, young adulthood, and the intimacy with previous sexual but not romantic lovers.

The evolving affective experience of intimacy as a self-capacity and interpersonal experience before adult romance transcends the boundaries of age, gender, and ethnicity, and exists independently of sexual desire. These affective experiences are evident in the attachment pairings of an individual to nonparental caretakers, siblings, teachers, and friends. Companions in adventure and disaster, war buddies, friendships within the athletic team and within the workplace are a genre of the intimate dyad. Intimacy has more actual partners than sexual desire. In fact, sexual excitement and activity are frequently sought in fantasy and real life where intimacy is curtailed or impossible, examples being prostitution, pornography, and perversion.

A psychological task of adult loving realized through romance is the intimacy in the lover dyad, that is, to integrate it within love and sexuality from a diverse experience and associated affects. Romance generates new and unique dimensions for intimacy, including sexual intimacy. This is apparent in the private sexual passion of lovers, as well as their public behavior: giggling, touching, kissing, fawning, and so forth. Lovers are literally and figuratively in touch. Even their quarrels are intimate, so much so that outsiders strain to understand their content or meaning.

In existential terms, intimacy overcomes loneliness, separation, and mourning. Intimacy in romance creates a new edition of the self and appreciation for the other that transcends past fantasy and reality, a quality celebrated in the popular culture. Along with fictive characters, we yearn for the transformation of self into couple and enhanced self-definition. Lovers are absorbed by each other and the passion and intimacy that unites them. Romantic love provides a unique window into the intersubjective world. It is a motive force known to poets and analysts as well as to lovers: in order to know the subjectivity of the self and other one must find a way to observe and articulate the inner world of abstractness and conflict. Lear (1990) observes that: ". . . for an individual to come into existence, his archaic expression of subjectivity must be integrated into the rest of his life. An individual comes to be not by abolishing archaic life, but by taking it up into a higher level of organization" (p. 23). There is a vast archaic subjectivity from the maternal infant dyad and oedipal love to take up *before* the adult task to integrate love, intimacy, and sexuality in the lover dyad.

We must come to terms with who we were, who we are, and who we can become. These self views are each relevant to romance, but the last—who we imagine we can become—is rich to romantic fantasy and intersubjective experience within the lover dyad. To move into romantic love, we must give up—but not quite forget or ignore—the past maternal and oedipal loves, as well as those of siblings, friends, and sexual lovers, in order to flourish anew. For lovers there is a need to mourn and the fear of it. It is normative in romantic love to fear the loss of the overvalued object. The lover risks imagined losses of the beloved to a superior rival—a regressive oedipal anxiety—as well to the realities of age, illness, and death, even to one's own children as evident in family splits, feuds, and divorce.

We relinquish our past loves through the work of romance, by integrating them into the lover dyad. By focusing on the beloved, we mourn and work through the hold of past lovers and intimate dyads, including the maternal-infant dyad. Freud (1917e, 1930a) understood the relationship of love to melancholia. Lear (1990) interprets Freud's genius to understanding mental structures and dynamics as the consequence of his "dialectic of love and loss" (p. 158). Freud (1923b, 1926d, 1930a) recognized the preconditions to individual love established in the preoedipal actual loss of the object, or their love, and the loss of the superego love for the ego (self), a symbolic representation of the pervious threats and actual losses of the preoedipal objects that were compounded by the real and fantasy losses of the oedipal loves.

Adult love risks actual loss that is sometimes unconsciously created by the predetermined conditions for loving, as in a sick and dying parent from childhood, refound in a "new" love object who is ill, dying, or unfaithful. Other losses are those lovers who become absorbed in their career or with the family of origin, at a cost to the lover dyad, and for some men the loss of the wife to her maternal love and devotion to children (Pasternack 1988). Another condition in the phase of falling in love, according to Bergmann (1997), is the mourning for the past object of love when love begins anew. It is normal to romance to feel elevated self-esteem through the attachment and identification with the beloved. Yet some are unaccountably sad when falling in love, or angry rather than lonely when alone without the beloved. When a new love attachment is realized, some lovers fear inevitable loss. This "lowering of self regard feelings" and "self-reproaches" (aggression turned onto the self) as in melancholia— opposed to mourning—inhibits intimacy and sexuality (Freud 1917e).

Freud emphasized that for both genders the refound object and conditions for loving originated within the maternal-infant dyad. There are other influences on object choices too. Obviously the oedipal experience and identifications, superego formation, and the cross-gender traits of parents and siblings, contribute to what the lover unconsciously looks for in his or her "lover shadow," that is, the real life and fantasy connections from the past that are realized in the present (Wells 1984).

Bergmann (1987) documents that the Roman poet, Catullus, wrote of love and hate simultaneously toward the same person, and that Ovid wrote about the conflict of self love and love for another (p. 258). Freud (1912–1913, 1914c) transformed the ideas of ambivalence and narcissism into clinical theory. Ambivalence to Freud was bedrock, fundamental as bisexuality: each effects romantic love choice. Freud's (1914c) "second theory of love," according to Bergmann (1987), was on narcissism. It seems less relevant to me since Kohut: many analysts no longer believe the conversion of narcissistic libido into object libido is essential for the love of another. Nonetheless, Freud, like Ovid, recognized that in love one must overcome self-absorption to join with the other the co-creation of intimacy and sexuality.

According to Bergmann (1987), Freud's (1905d) first theory of love was the byproduct of the aim and objects of infantile sexuality that culminates in the Oedipus complex. This is the reason, I believe, that many analysts understand romantic love as if it was a variant of oedipal love. It is more likely that triadic disruption of the lover dyad is a pathology of dyadic love, or at the very least, an intrusion on it with historic meaning to the individual concerning the original transition from maternal love to oedipal love and the love of others. Freud's (1914c) second theory of adult love (the vicissitudes of narcissism) was also based on the object choice: "anaclitic love" or "narcissistic love." The anaclitic love is the dependency on the beloved for nurture or protection, thereby potentially compromising ego autonomy. Narcissistic love is to find in another what one is, once was or wanted to be, or someone who was once a part of him. There is a pathological example in the lover dyad where narcissistic expectation that the beloved must become what the lover wanted but failed to be. Too great a demand that the beloved be like the lover is one of the greatest disappointments in romance. These genetic dynamics in excess defeat the transcendent quality that passionate romantic love paradoxically enriches individuality and works toward mutuality *and* autonomy.

I believe that to varying degrees and in various combinations Freud's (1914c) original descriptions of the anaclitic and narcissistic object choices are normative to unconscious wishes in romantic love object choice. The expectation for some nurture and protection, and that the beloved share in what one is, has been or would like to be, are essential to the dynamics of the lover dyad. The "narcissistic" wish to find a lover who is a part of one's self experience of love and intimacy in the past is quintessential to the refound object choice that is derivative of the maternal-infant dyad. Freud (1914c) believed that the narcissistic object choice was more evident in women and the anaclitic object choice more so in men. In my clinical experience with lovers today, I do not find this distinction an easy demarcation.

Bergmann (1987) validates Freud's concept of the ". . . tension between refinding old love objects and the wish to move on to someone new." He adds a premise familiar to self psychology. Upon "refinding" the object of love, the lover will unconsciously make an effort to rework problems that are the "archaic" history of conflicts and deficits with their first objects of love. The lover who experiences renewed hope to magically correct past failures with the alcoholic, unfaithful, abusing, and so forth, parent that is refound in the adult lover is an example. A more pathological example is the lover who projects to the beloved the psychodynamic problems of their own past and is ready to attempt rescue by identification and projection, or to masochistically relive with the beloved the problems that belong to their unshared archaic past conditions for loving.

Some are transformed by romantic love; others are not. The attempt to magically undo childhood traumata apply to various love themes that attempt to reverse hate, indifference, or abuse into love and intimacy, and defeat and humiliation into success and triumph. There is often in such cases a confusion of self and other differentiation, a boundary already made fluid in romantic passion. The individual history of humiliation and suffering in the maternal-infant dyad, or the conditions established in the Oedipus complex, are sometimes acted out in the lover dyad through the lover's vengeance on the beloved, treating the other with the same sadism and contempt that they originally experienced. Alternately, others repeat the past and continue to masochistically suffer within the lover dyad according to their preconditions for object choice (Freud 1915c, 1924c).

I believe that the motive to repair and sustain a lover relationship is rarely based on sex, but more often on the desire to realize and sustain intersubjective intimacy. Bergmann (1987) points out that there is a "dialectic between refinding love similar to the original and the opposing wish to find another different from the original who will heal the wounds of childhood" (p. 264). In other words, the traumata of childhood doesn't necessarily predetermine a defeating condition in the choice of the beloved, but itself may be a motive to be healed or to heal childhood hurts of the beloved. We do see lovers who are initially well-matched for the need of repair and those willing to provide it, whether mutual or one sided. However, the condition of needing repair and providing healing as central to the couple's interrelated choice of lover has the potential to transform their lover dyad into a sadomasochistic dyad, marked ambivalence in one or the other of the couple, or Pygmalion love in a dominant individual of the dyad. Some are more frankly perverse in structure and function.

In this brief paper I have attempted to demonstrate Freud's view that we love in various stages beginning at the first stage of life. The infantile experience of love and intimacy establishes the conditions for the subsequent object choices and forms of love, including passionate romantic love that is an integrative developmental epoch of the adult.

REFERENCES

Beebe, B., and McCrorie, E. (in press). Intimacy: a model of love for the 21st Century. *Psychoanalytic Inquiry.*

Bergmann, M. S. (1987). *The Anatomy of Loving.* New York: Columbia University Press.

Bowlby, J. (1958). The nature of the child's tie to his mother. *International Journal of Psycho-analysis* 39:350–373.

——— (1960). Grief and mourning in infancy and early childhood. *The Psychoanalytic Study of the Child* 15:9–52. New York: International Universities Press.

Bristol, R. C., and Pasternack, S. A. (1998). *Intimacy in Love and Its Consummation.* 4th Annual Self Psychology Conference of the Institute of Contemporary Psychotherapy (recording).

Freud, S. (1899a). Screen memories. *Standard Edition* 3:30.

——— (1905d). Three essays on the theory of sexuality. *Standard Edition* 7:125.

——— (1905e [1901]). Fragment of an analysis of a case of hysteria. *Standard Edition* 7:3.

——— (1910c). Leonardo da Vinci and a memory of his childhood. *Standard Edition* 11:59.

——— (1910h). A special type of choice of object made by men. *Standard Edition* 11:164.

——— (1912d). On the universal tendency to debasement in the sphere of love. *Standard Edition* 11:178.

——— [1912–1913]. Totem and taboo. *Standard Edition* 13:1.

——— (1914c). On narcissism: an introduction. *Standard Edition* 14:69.

——— (1915a [1914]). Observations on transference love. *Standard Edition* 12:158.

——— (1915c). Instincts and their vicissitudes. *Standard Edition* 14:105.

——— (1917e). Mourning and melancholia. *Standard Edition* 14:239.

——— (1918a [1917]). The taboo of virginity. *Standard Edition* 11:192.

——— (1921c). Group psychology and the analysis of the ego. *Standard Edition* 18:67.

——— (1923b). The ego and the id. *Standard Edition* 19:3.
——— (1924c). The economic problem of masochism. *Standard Edition* 19:157.
——— (1924d). Dissolution of the Oedipus complex. *Standard Edition* 19:172.
——— (1926d). Inhibitions, symptoms and anxiety. *Standard Edition* 20:77.
——— (1927e). Fetishism. *Standard Edition* 21:149.
——— (1930a [1929]). Civilization and its discontents. *Standard Edition* 21:59.
Gabbard, G. O. (1996). *Love and Hate in the Analytic Setting.* Northvale, NJ: Jason Aronson.
Kernberg, O. (1975). *Borderline Conditions and Pathological Narcissism.* New York: Jason Aronson.
——— (1980). *Internal World and External Reality.* New York: Jason Aronson.
——— (1995). *Love Relations: Normality and Pathology.* New Haven, CT: Yale University Press.
Jacobson, E. (1964). *The Self and the Object World.* New York: International Universities Press.
Lear, J. (1990). *Love and Its Place in Nature.* New York: Farrar, Straus & Giroux.
Lichtenberg, J. D. (1989). *Psychoanalysis and Motivation.* Hillsdale, NJ: The Analytic Press.
Mahler, M. (1979). *The Selected Papers of Margaret S. Mahler,* Vols. I & II. New York: Jason Aronson.
Pasternack, S. (1988). *Passionate Cases—Dispassionate Treatment.* First National Conference on Love. Washington School of Psychiatry (recording).
Person, E. S. (1988). *Dreams of Love and Fateful Encounters: The Power of Romantic Passion.* New York: W. W. Norton.
Spitz, R. A. (1945). Genesis of psychiatric conditions in early childhood (Hospitalism). *Psychoanalytic Study of the Child* 1:53–74.
Stallworthy, J., ed. (1974). *A Book of Love Poetry.* New York: Oxford University Press.
Stoller, R. (1968). *Sex and Gender.* New York: Science House.
——— (1985). *Observing the Erotic Imagination.* New Haven, CT: Yale University Press.

Webster's New World Dictionary (1988). Ed. Victoria Neufeld and David Guralnik. New York: Webster's New World.

Wells, H. G. (1984). *H.G. Wells in Love: Postscript to an Experiment in Autobiography*. Boston, MA: Little Brown.

14

Freud's Theories of Love and Their Application to Treatment of Love Conflicts

Stefan A. Pasternack

Although Freud made many seminal contributions to the psychoanalytic theory of love, he never unified them into a single major work as he did with his studies on childhood sexuality, dreams, and psychoanalytic technique. This made his writings on love more difficult to understand and left Freud vulnerable to the criticism that he confused sexual instincts with love. In a detailed review of Freud's writings on love, Martin Bergman has identified three major theories of love contributed by Freud. Freud paved the way for subsequent investigations into love, and his theories have been useful in understanding and treating patients with various love pathologies. This paper will briefly summarize the highlights of Freud's basic contributions to love and their application to clinical work with a patient in the midst of a love triangle.

Freud's first theory of love was made possible by his discovery of infantile sexuality and of the impact of the child's early caretaking experiences on later adult love. In his "Three Essays on Sexuality" (Freud 1905a), Freud stated that in the early years of love the erotic desires of a child are focused on early caretakers, especially the parents.

The mother or her surrogate become both the first love and sexual object and serves as a template for subsequent loves. "There are good reasons why a child sucking at his mother's breast has become the first prototype of every relation of love. The finding of a love object is in fact a re-finding of It" (p. 222). This extremely important discovery about love, however, requires much greater elaboration. On the surface is his statement that the model of a child sucking at his mother's breast in the basic prototype might be taken to mean that the refinding process involves part objects and not complete relationships. Freud also implies that an incestuous fixation may interfere with later adult capacity to love. As Bergmann (1987) has pointed out, Freud thus explored a problem at the core of all love relationships. The next love must recall the old, but this will not result in happiness if incestuous guilt is also reawakened. A new love may triumph over the incest barrier, thus leading to mastery of conflict. Freud further elaborated that formative early-life experiences may cause an individual to develop "pre-conditions for love." When these preconditions are neurotically rigid, subsequent adult choices of love partners may also be neurotically determined.

Freud's second theory of love grew out of his studies on narcissism and his discovery that in love narcissistic cathexes are shifted from the self to the love object. A disappointment in the primary love object could result in a narcissistic object choice or in difficulty in loving. Freud's writings on narcissism also emphasize that identification plays a crucial role in the process of falling in love. In his 1914 essay "On Narcissism: An Introduction," he included a classification of love reflecting his awareness of the fluidity of self and object representations and of the importance of early identifications. In this classification, a person may love:

1. According to the narcissistic type
   a. What he himself is
   b. What he himself was
   c. What he himself would like to be
   d. Someone who was once part of himself

2. According to the anaclitic type (attachment type)
   a. The woman who feeds him
   b. The man who protects him

In the clinical case to be presented, this classification has some use. However, transfers of libido from self to object can result in various problems. Overidealization and excessive investment in the other can impoverish the lover's sense of self and set the stage for subsequent disappoint when expectations are not met. Similarly, unrequited love can be such a disappointment that the lover gives up the quest for a lover and remains narcissistically fixated on himself. Furthermore, Freud's theories of narcissism, ego, and ego ideal allow for an explanation of what happens when one falls in love. The normal tension between ego and ego ideal leaves the lover feeling incomplete and discontent with himself. When the love object is idealized and libido transferred, the ego ideal is projected onto the loved object just as in childhood the child idealized the parents. When love is reciprocated by the loved object, the self is loved by the ego ideal and elation and bliss may ensue. The exchange between ego ideal and the beloved, as Bergmann points out, takes place unconsciously: "Only the experience of bliss becomes conscious."

Freud's third theory of love is the most misunderstood and emerged in his paper "Instincts and Their Vicissitudes" (1915a). Bergmann (1987) has assessed Freud's struggle with the problem of how the drive for sex (a sexual instinct) can develop into love. Bergmann concludes that Freud never fully resolved this problem. Love could not be explained within the confines of instinct alone. However, Freud did make an important contribution to love theory as he struggled to get beyond instinct theory. He wrote:

> The case of love and hate acquires a special interest from the circumstances that it refuses to be fitted into our scheme of instincts. . . . We are unwilling to think of love as being some kind of special component instinct of sexuality . . . We should prefer to regard loving as the expression of the whole sexual current of feeling. . . . [1915a, p. 133]

Although Freud was discontent also with this idea of love as the whole current of feelings, this was nevertheless an extremely useful concept by which, as Bergmann (1987) carefully explains, Freud thereby has proposed that all sexual wishes have been concentrated upon one person. The lover only seeks those sexual pleasures which he enjoys with the loved object and has no interest in any other. The loved object is idealized as the source of all sexual satisfaction. This line of thought gradually evolved into the notion that love is not an instinct but that it is the total ego which loves its objects (Bergmann 1987). Bergmann's proposal has important clinical implications. The capacity to love may be viewed as an ego function. The individual's manner of loving and acting sexually provides insight into the lover's emotional history and patterns of ego functioning, sexual and relationship fears, and defenses. As an ego function, the capacity to love has understandable developmental origins, strengths and weaknesses, and specific characteristics that can be clinically evaluated.

Freud made another contribution to work with love problems through his discoveries of transference and countertransference issues (1915). As therapists for the lovesick and loveworn, we face many unique challenges; empathic immersion in the minds of the patient opens us to intense emotional pressure, and patients show up in our dreams and fantasies. We are required to process our own countertransference reactions carefully in order to maintain perspective and to help the patient master powerful emotional forces within. Thus, we have to balance introspection and countertransference management and attunement to the patient with awareness of expanding theories of love and be able to use current theory as a guide to understanding the patient's problems. This interplay between our theoretical views and our capacity for empathic interaction, I believe, is essential to a successful therapy. For we are both participants in the therapy as well as observers of it.

Thus, Freud's three theories of love enable us to understand different problems in loving and being loved. We can sort out the imprinting of early love experiences and the development of a "love template." We can assess the individual's preconditions for loving, different fixation points, and capacities for investment in the love object. We can understand what happens intrapsychically when one falls in love and how the ego functions in the process of love. We can evaluate various aspects of the individual's "re-finding process" and the unconscious motives for love choices. These ideas can be applied to a specific case, as will now be demonstrated.

CASE PRESENTATION

A 29-year-old graduate student sought my help because he was torn between two loves: his wife of 5 years and his girlfriend of 10 months. He began to feel distant from his wife shortly after the birth of their daughter, now 18 months old. He said he still loved his wife and did not wish to leave her. But he was never able to feel fully sexually satisfied with his wife. Now he felt passionately swept away by a 21-year-old woman in his program. They shared an immediate chemistry. One night when his wife had taken their baby to visit family, he and the younger woman went dancing and then made love. At first he thought of it as just a sexual diversion. She was playful and her lack of sexual inhibition seemed to liberate him sexually. He felt totally gratified. Then he became so obsessed with her that for the first time in his life work seemed unimportant, and he let his graduate research slip.

His wife complained about his frequent absences and his loss of interest in sex, but she did not voice any suspicions. She trusted him, he said with a sigh. He felt he had no justification for the affair because his wife was a loving, devoted, attractive woman and a good mother. Unlike so many people in the midst of these types of split-object love triangles, he did not devalue or blame his wife for his outside affair. In fact, he still loved and admired her, although he faulted her for his lack of sexual satisfaction with her.

He had a great deal of guilt about the affair, guilt magnified by his strong religious convictions. Thus tormented by conflict, he knew he could not indefinitely continue the involvement with both women. For several sessions, he compared the two women and sought a deciding factor with which to make a choice.

He described his girlfriend as colorful and sexually exciting, but also as immature, moody, and unpredictable. He had the uncanny feeling that he had known her before. She taunted him to flaunt their affair in public and to leave his wife. He could not.

Early in therapy he demanded that I give him an answer about whom to choose. "Doctor," he said, "you're the expert, so what do I do?" His question surprised me for I hardly knew him and did not feel I was in a position to offer him advice, even if I was inclined to do so. I could only guess at the origins of and the underlying motivations for his split-object love affair.

I said that I could not tell him what to do, but that I could help him to understand himself so he would know what choice to make. I also confronted him about his evasiveness and pressed him for more information.

He then revealed that I was his third therapist. The first had sided with his wife and lectured him about his duty to wife and child. The other seemed to accept his involvement in the affair so much that he feared the therapist was encouraging a lack of responsibility on his part. Now he openly wondered on what side I would come down.

I will pause here to make some observations about neutrality and preconditions for love. Experience with patients in the midst of various types of love conflicts cautions us against premature conclusions. Love-torn patients need, above all, someone who will maintain neutrality and help them confront their conflicts and assess their life circumstances. Freud, of course, spoke in favor of neutrality and also illuminated some of the dynamics of love triangles. His statement that "all love is a re-finding" made clear that adult choices derive from childhood experiences and unresolved oedipal-conflict "preconditions" for love. These preconditions could be more or less rigid and might compel a man to love only women in need of rescue, or compel woman to love exploitative men. One might be endlessly involved in replaying oedipal conflicts, and an incestuous fixation might inhibit adult love. In this case, the patient's motivations for his affair were concealed by his evasiveness. His preoccupation with his girlfriend had an obsessive quality. Furthermore, the likelihood that he might wreck his marriage led me to infer the possibility of a superego-instigated need for self-punishment. For it seemed he could not allow himself to fully enjoy the pleasures that his wife offered. I further wondered if he was one of those men described by Freud who had a Madonna-whore split and who could not blend love and sex in the same relationship. The uncanny feeling he had about the girlfriend, as if he had known her before, led me to the conjecture that she was a transference figure from his past, and represented an additional instance of re-finding that complicated his love life. There may be many "re-findings" in the course of one's life, subjecting every one to the need to master a variety of love and sexual temptations.

Before I could assess his underlying motivations, I had to better establish our working relationship and demonstrate to him how we could work together to advance understanding.

I then told him that he was ignoring the third alternative, which I had just outlined, and that suddenly coming down on any side would preclude careful understanding of what was going on and how his conflicts about love had developed. He was silent, and for awhile we sat quietly taking stock of each other. I reflected on the various possible meanings of his behavior and waited for him to reply. Then he reluctantly told me this story about his marriage.

He had met his wife after being jilted by another woman. His wife-to-be soon soothed his hurt feelings as she was apparently immediately smitten by him—it was easy to see why. He was a handsome, athletic, and intelligent man who, when not brooding, was very enthusiastic, especially about his research work. After almost a year of dating he agreed to marry his wife, although he did not feel romantic or passionate about her. He felt a strong affection for her, but married her mostly because she was so obviously in love with him and because she was a dependable caretaker who made him feel important. This reassured him, just when he needed it most. Deeply touched by her caring ways and also by her parents' affection for him, he felt he had acquired the love of a whole family. With this material one could infer that his marital love choice was "anaclitic," a love attachment based upon the Freudian classification of "the woman who feeds him."

With her consistent nurturing he did better than ever in his graduate research and studies. He emphasized the importance of his science career and his hopes for making original discoveries. He reported that his wife's one major complaint before the recent disruption was that he was a workaholic who put his research work before her. He joked that research was easier and more important to him than intimacy.

As we worked together he revealed that he was afraid of love—as if loving his wife would make him a "love hostage." He liked her to say that she loved him, but he could not reciprocate. He was plagued by fear that something would disrupt their relationship and he would have to leave. He began preemptively to withdraw and to push her away. Thus, he risked causing exactly what he feared.

When she became pregnant he was supportive and dutiful, but he felt himself becoming even more guarded and distant.

238 / *The Psychoanalytic Century*

With the birth of their daughter he felt abandoned, as if his wife cared only about the baby. His conscious jealously made him feel quite petty, and he expressed shame at what he called his "darker side." His attitude toward his wife also changed: he no longer trusted her. At the same time he realized that he was seriously overreacting to her. His account of the early years of his marriage highlighted what we regularly observe: that almost every quirk one has will be intensified during a long relationship. He became aware of his longing for but fear of love.

In Freudian terms, we would say his ambivalent reactions were overdetermined. It was clear he had no clue to the nature of his repressed conflicts and the life experience from which they were derived. His fears of being a love hostage bring to mind more recent analytic studies, such as Stoller's (1982) work on symbiosis anxiety in men and men's fears of loss of masculinity as they attempt intimacy with a woman; Stoller highlighted the regressive fear of feminization and castration through merger. Edith Jacobson (1971) also emphasized that the establishment of a solid self-representation would lead to a cohesive self. But fear of reengulfment by the intrapsychic representative of a parent might be displaced later onto a love object, causing anxiety and withdrawal.

Bergmann synthesized the work of Mahler on separation and individuation with accompanying clinical problems in loving. "The symbiotic phase leaves a residue in the form of a longing for merger. This is re-evoked when one falls in love" (p. 240). This may trigger irrational fears of engulfment. This is most likely when the relationship with mother was strained. When the rapprochement phase is not successfully resolved, lovers may repeat the need to love and return again and again setting the stage for endless cycles of getting closer, only to push away. These other developmental studies helped me to understanding the genesis of some of his problems in this patient's early difficulties with his wife.

To continue the clinical case, the patient could not make any sense out of his difficulties in loving his wife and his negative overreactions to her. He worried that he was just incapable of maintaining a serious long-term commitment. He wondered what I thought, and I reminded him that he had not told me much about his background and I would not conjecture. But I pointed out that if he left his wife for his new girlfriend, the same thing might happen with her. He was startled, but reluctantly agreed. This was really his first insight. And so he and I developed a pattern of working together, and in spite of periodic disruptions which caused him to become irritable, defensive, and withdrawn, our relationship deepened.

Let me emphasize this: I tried to discern his recurrent pattern of discontinuous intersubjective transactions with me. There was an underlying organization. His evasiveness, his demanding tendencies, and his extreme affective sensitivity helped me to understand the difficulties he experienced and caused in an intimate relationship. He was also a very appealing man whom I wished to help. It was obvious he had suffered some deep emotional wounds. His loneliness and his fearful longing for closeness were palpable. He then came to a session in a very angry mood and again demanded my opinion. "Should I stay in my marriage or leave?" This renewed pressure highlighted his underlying difficulty with self-regulation. Unable to tolerate his tension state he attempted to evoke it in me, and I tried to balance the tension state through insightful awareness of what was transpiring for both of us.

I tried to see the message in his demanding advice and to translate it back to him in words that clarified the motive for his pressure and the nature of his inner affective state. I conceptualized and interpreted this central theme: I am being forced to make a decision before I am ready. I then viewed this as a transference reenactment highlighted by intense affect. My dilemma was how to interpret this reenactment so as to engender insight and forestall acting-out.

So I told him that we should view his pressure on me to make his choice as a symptom of his problem, a clue to something he had been through before. I reminded him about his evasiveness concerning his past family experiences, a clue that he had to avoid something unpleasant. "Could it be," I said, "that you were forced to make a very important choice in the past before you were ready, a choice that had a big impact on your life and that you did not want to make?"

There was a dead silence and I thought I had missed the mark. He filled up with tears and then said, "Yes, my mom made me turn my back on my dad. He was a hopeless drunk and she hated him, so he left. But I loved him." Then we sat in stunned silence, together, and he seemed even more surprised by what he had said than I was. Then he outlined his traumatic childhood, one filled with frustrated developmental longings. These were events that which had distorted his "love map" and caused him many intrapsychic difficulties with intimacy, surrender, and love.

He was the younger of two children, with an older sister, born to a former combat marine and a fundamentalist Baptist woman. Father had impregnated mother before they married. They tried to hold their marriage together by having another child. His birth, when his sister was 3, not only distressed her but destabilized the family. Father was poor. Mother blamed father for wrecking her life. She degraded his father in front of him. Father became an alcoholic and flaunted his visits to local prostitutes.

But father adored him, his only son, and sought relief from mother's harangues by playing with him and teaching him about music, sports, and hunting. The patient tearfully recounted how father would perch him on his lap while they listened to records, especially songs of Sammy Davis, Jr. Father also regaled him with stories of his combat experiences in the Korean War. Father, thus, was a passionate and exciting figure with whom he could be a child. But father was also inconsistent and unavailable or drunk. Mother forced his father to leave and took her anger at father out on the patient. She dished out bible lessons and harsh punishment so that he "would not end up like your [his] bum father." She bluntly told him to "forget your father." Photos of him were removed; contact was forbidden. Father truly disappeared. Thus, there was a basic split in his love experiences with a fundamentalist mother and a hard-drinking marine father. It was impossible for him to integrate these conflicting object relationships. And, because mother forced him to be silent about his father, his disturbing memories were buried, where they formed the unconscious strata for later love problems. There was rage at his mother, and he lived in fear of losing control over his anger and being thrown out as well.

Shortly after his parents' separation, father was killed while driving drunk. His grief was compounded by humiliation when he was teased by schoolmates about father's drunken-driving death. This was a great blow and he felt he had to prove that he would not turn out like his father. He was troubled with intense shame and self-doubts, in spite of splendid academic and athletic achievements. He secretly blamed his mother for his father's death.

These basic interactional patterns with his mother were repeated with his sister and cast a shadow over his latency years and adolescence. He had many difficulties in negotiating all of the developmental tasks of his youth: serious problems mastering castration fears, establishing a positive image of his own body, forming a positive gender identity. Although he dated, he avoided intimacy, as it always seemed to threaten him with disappointment.

He felt liberated when he went off to college. He hung out with the guys and drank a bit. He had casual sex to prove he could do it. However, there was always a lingering sense of inadequacy and fear of rejection by women. So he mainly threw himself into his studies and excelled in science.

When he went on to graduate school he was extremely lonely and was more receptive to a relationship. He fell in love, only to be jilted. Wounded and disorganized by this loss, he first sought to steady himself by extraordinary efforts at his research. When he met his future wife, her immediate admiration and affection was immensely reassuring and helped him to bolster his injured self-esteem. He felt safe with and comforted by her. They had a quiet intimacy. But, he felt frustrated because he did not feel passion and he blamed her for his lack of response.

As our joint efforts continued, it was clear that as the clock of fate had ticked and as he had become a father himself, an intrapsychic upheaval was triggered. He recalled many previously repressed feelings about his own father. Similarly, the birth of his daughter disrupted his marital relationship, and it triggered a sense of loss and displacement similar to the feelings of his older sister when he was born. His wife could not appreciate the magnitude of the inner changes in him. He then was vulnerable to an affair.

We worked further on his conflict about therapy. His desire for treatment collided with his need to avoid the painful memories of his past. Therapy, as with his other intimate relationship, stirred his feelings up and was a traumatic reliving of his traumatic past. My interpretation about the reenactment gave him hope that the repressed memories of father could finally be addressed. His mother's prohibition about remembering his father was thus modified by his engagement with me. He felt closer to me.

We were then able to take another look at his feelings for both his wife and his girlfriend and to try to remove barriers to intimacy and its consummation.

He had the powerful feeling of literally being pulled apart, a reliving of the original childhood experience of being pulled apart by his parents. He could not bear the pain of having to give one of the women up. Anytime he felt a shift within himself or thought I was pushing him in one direction or the other, he became sad, then angry, and the work stopped. This divergence of desire reached all the way back to his earliest object relations and the shame he felt about obeying his mother's command to reject his father. Resolution of his current love conflict as well as its developmental roots required a careful elaboration of all his thoughts and feelings about each emotionally charged relationship, including his wife, his girlfriend, and in parallel focus his father and mother. The process in therapy, then, was of a slow, detailed remembering, repeating, and working through as described by Freud. This was also a process of mourning for the inevitable loss he would sustain.

Gradually, as he made connections between disappointment with his parents and his adult love dilemma, he achieved an inner-sense of awareness that the affair was motivated by his need to set up a situation in which, this time, he was going to make his own choice.

He needed the affair to reverse the painful humiliation and passivity of childhood. As a child he felt forced to give up his father and to endure pain. Now, he would choose and he would inflict the pain.

Fearful of rejection all his life, he now had an insurance policy should his wife leave. He was finally in command. Of course, the reality was sadly different than his unconscious fantasy.

The reworking of the past also led to his realization of his irrational negative and distorted feelings about his wife. He could see how he had projected the negative images of his mother onto her in a maternal transference and had scapegoated her with disavowed aspects of himself. He then worked through his long-denied rage at his mother. As this occurred he felt less resentment toward his wife and they grew closer. Next, he had to reassess his girlfriend and discover the special meaning she had for him.

He remembered when he first felt swept away. His wife was out of town with the baby. He and his girlfriend went dancing. She had picked a tune on a jukebox in the bar where they danced. It was the old Sammy Davis, Jr., tune "What Kind of Fool Am I?" The lyrics were the password to his heart. They danced, went to her home, made love, and in subsequent pillow talk she told him her life story. She, too, was the child of a troubled family and had suffered similar misfortunes. This impacted him quite powerfully as he had always been ashamed of his past and had not talked to his wife about it in any detail. In fact, out of shame he had kept his wife from having much contact with his mother and family. The girlfriend was the first person to whom he had ever confided details of his father's tragic death and his forced repudiation of his father. With his imperfect girlfriend, cut, as it were, from the same cloth, he felt a sense of acceptance. He recognized the uncanny feeling that he had known her before and that the girlfriend really understood him. This was a very powerful instance of refinding.

He then realized that he viewed his girlfriend as a reincarnation of his father. She drank, played games, acted crazy, and made him feel special. His girlfriend touched the taproot of father's love. The repressed returned—an old love refound in her. He felt grief for the disrupted years of his childhood, the losses caused by his parents' divorce, and the burden of having to forsake his father. His girlfriend was indeed a refound love object of childhood, as Freud wrote, and this example illustrated that there are many potential "refindings" in each of our lives.

He then became very defensive about his girlfriend, as if I was attacking her. He acted out by trying to provoke his wife into quarrels. Intuitively, she must have understood that something important was happening, and she was able to avoid being drawn into the conflicts that, in fact, were with himself. He wished she would act like a bitch so he would feel justified in being angry with her. His misperceptions of her became unmistakably clear. Instead, his wife held her composure and won his respect.

But his girlfriend grew frustrated, accused him of misleading her, threatened to tell his wife about the affair, and progressively alienated him. He saw he was testing each woman for constancy and came to appreciate his wife's maturity and true love for him. He then realized that he had fought his sense of disorganization, triggered when he became a father, with the affair. As he gained a heightened awareness of the multiple unconscious determinants of his attraction for his girlfriend, he was able to carefully think things through. He had to work his way through a great deal of anguish, the repressed memories of an unhappy child whose parents could not love one another and of a child who was forced prematurely to choose. He now understood that his research was sublimation of his need to search for answers and to find a precious and missing part of himself, namely his lost bond with his father and his identification with him. He was ready. He now was in charge and could make his choice. He sought to achieve intimacy and love with his wife.

The affair changed him in some positive ways. He had discovered that he had a capacity for sexual passion and could be playful and tender. He shed his split image of women as either mothers or whores, and could see his wife, not as a transference representative of his fundamentalist mother, but as the real-life person she was. His superego conflicts and his religious inhibitions were attenuated and the incest taboo avoided. Free also from anger at his mother he no longer worried about being a love slave and could relax with his wife. Furthermore, he was now able to concentrate all of his sexual and love feelings upon her, and his fantasies about sex with other women faded as his wife requited his passion.

Second, he needed secrecy no longer, and openly discussed his father's alcoholism and the family problems with his wife. She understood! Her compassion was quite touching. They grew closer. He felt love for her.

There were many other positive changes as well. Fortunately, his girlfriend found another lover and never retaliated against him.

One never knows exactly how a love triangle will work out. The human desires to love and be loved, to known and be known, will always motivate people to seek solutions to situations where love is compromised. While we cannot tell people what to do, with enriching psychoanalytic theories we can help them to understand their motivations and pursue happiness.

Freud's three theories of love—along with other seminal discovering on infantile sexuality, dreams, and psychoanalytic technique—ushered in a new era in the understanding of love problems. Love was now understood as a psychological phenomenon. Once love is clearly appreciated as an intrapsychic process and an interactive process, love can then be studied in greater depth. Further advances in the psychoanalytic theory of love would subsequently occur, making it possible to provide more effective therapy for those with problems in loving or being loved.

REFERENCES

Bergmann, M. (1980). On the intra-psychic function of falling in love. *Psychoanalytic Quarterly* 5:56–75.
——— (1987). *The Anatomy of Loving.* New York: Columbia University Press.
Freud, S. (1905a). Three essays on the theory of infantile sexuality. *Standard Edition* 7:123–245.
——— (1910). A special type of choice of object made by men (contributions to the psychology of love). *Standard Edition* 11:163–176.
——— (1912). On the universal tendency to debasement in the sphere. *Standard Edition* 11:177–190.
——— (1914). On narcissism: an introduction. *Standard Edition* 14:67–102.
——— (1915). Observations on transference love. *Standard Edition* 12:157–173.
——— (1915a). Instincts and their vicissitudes. *Standard Edition* 14:109–140.
Jacobson, E. (1971). *Depression.* New York: International Universities Press.
Stoller, R. (1982). The development of masculinity: A cross-cultural contribution. *Journal of the American Psychoanalytic Association* 30:29.

SUGGESTED READING

Dumas, D. (1998). *Sons, Lovers, and Fathers: Understanding Male Sexuality.* Northvale, NJ: Jason Aronson.

Gabbard, G. (1996). *Love and Hate in the Analytic Setting.* Northvale, NJ: Jason Aronson.

Gaylin, W. and Person, E., eds. (1988). *Passionate Attachments: Thinking about Love.* New York: Free Press.

Kernberg, O. (1995). *Love Relations: Normality and Pathology.* New Haven, CT: Yale University Press.

Person, E. (1998). *Dreams of Love and Fateful Encounters.* New York: W. W. Norton.

Stoller, R. (1979). *Sexual Excitement.* New York: Pantheon.

PART VI

RACE, ETHNICITY, AND INTERNATIONAL RELATIONS

Dorothy Evans Holmes's paper focuses on the role of race in psychoanalytic practice, and especially the way it affects the therapeutic dyad through its effect on countertransference, which, like race, is a relatively unexamined aspect of clinical experience. She holds that race is a factor not only when the race or ethnicity of analyst and analysand are different, but that it is often—and perhaps always—a factor because of the analysand's developmental course. An unknown inner-blackness that patients so often bring to treatment may be expressed by racist attitudes.

Since much of the effect of race in development and unconscious attitude affects the analyst's countertransference, the frequent lack of attention to countertransference—especially until the last few years—means that subtle but pernicious attitudes about race exert unnoticed influence in many analyses. These factors may carry unconscious themes central to the analysis that exert unrecognized influence because they ride on the backs of the unacknowledged racial issues. Not the least of these occur in cases in which analyst and analysand share the same race, so that a surface similarity and identification with the analysand disarms the analyst's awareness of racial transferences that exist nonetheless. Therapists often struggle with a confluence of countertransference blind spots and an unconscious blindness concerning race. Enhanced awareness helps bring these issues to the surface during the treatment so that they can more fruitfully be explored in the treatment situation, now given special access through the attuned countertransference of the therapist.

Michael Moskowitz follows Holmes's paper with a social psychoanalytic look at racism, anti-Semitism, and prejudice as features of individual and social psychology that have existed throughout history. He uses an analytic vignette from the literature to support Holmes's contention that race is an important factor in many analyses, and often plays a role even when there is no racial difference between analyst and analysand. He follows with a personal example of how awareness of racial imagoes in the transference in his own analysis helped to work out childhood issues deriving from anti-Semitic hazing, and the influence of this experience on his image of his father. Drawing on this powerful example, he raises the question of how analysis can contribute to an enhancing social awareness about the way prejudice promotes man's cruelty to man.

Freud's struggles with anti-Semitism evolved into an interest in the way group unconscious factors affect civilization through the tension between the individual and society. This strand of his legacy has been put to practical use in **Vamık D. Volkan's** work toward understanding the forces of social division, in order to facilitate resolution between conflicting groups. Here, just as in clinical work, psychoanalytic understanding is a practical tool for growth and healing.

Volkan has been in the forefront of the application of analysis to ethnic and international conflict for twenty-five years, so his experience constitutes a unique trove of understanding in a complex field that represents one of the most ambitious and intricate applications of psychoanalysis. This contribution on psychoanalysis and diplomacy is one paper in a four-part series published in the *Journal of Applied Psychoanalytic Studies* on the application of psychoanalysis to international relations. Freud's early writings on social psychology introduced the idea that analysis could be applied to social problems. Volkan reviews Freud's contribution, and the subsequent history of applying analysis to international relations, and briefly assesses their usefulness and limitations before illustrating some current efforts and frustrations in applying psychoanalytic principles to these exceedingly complex problems. While analytic principles constitute a useful set of ideas in international and ethnic negotiation, they fail when those who are guided by them do not also understand the very different realities of history and politics. His contribution sketches out the enormous scale on which analysis can be useful, but it also makes it clear that the lessons of psychoanalysis can only be usefully applied when accompanied by careful study of the fields of international relations and diplomacy.

15

Race and Countertransference: Two "Blind Spots" in Psychoanalytic Perception

Dorothy Evans Holmes

In this paper I propose an approach for the evocative use and resolution of racial and countertransferential manifestations in the treatment situation. When addressed with the interest they warrant, these phenomena can become powerful tools for the advancement of the treatment, rather than "blind spots." The therapist's own treatment is offered as the most likely means through which the evocative and pernicious effects of race and countertransference can be mastered.

Responses to race and countertransference reactions encompass complex cognition and emotion; both are likely to have highly conflicted components, and to mobilize defense. It is my position that race—whether in same- or cross-race dyads—and countertransference magnify each other's effects, can interfere with the ego resourcefulness of the therapist, and consequently, can limit the effectiveness

---

This paper was previously published in the *Journal of Applied Psychoanalytic Studies* 1(4):319–332.

of the treatment. These dire effects are not inevitable, however, and in my view, occur only when race and countertransference are not recognized to be the rich sources of therapy enhancing material that they are. What is likely to bar this recognition? In our culture, race continues to be a container for disavowed urges, a vehicle for distorted representations of those urges, and of the racial group onto whom they are cast. While a more open attitude towards countertransference is standard in training and practice now, recommendations on how to make optimal use of it in the treatment situation are still emerging and the topic remains controversial.

Alas, in my view, we are still faced with limiting effects of race and countertransference in most treatments. In our culture, race is ubiquitously linked to the worst of prejudices. That is, it is an all too familiar fact that one racial group (for example, African Americans) is often used by members of another racial group to fend off their own intolerable characteristics. As Mahon (1991) stated: "The tendency to . . . project one's instincts onto the scapegoated group suggests that it is more popular to use a group for id disposal and superego-disposal than to use a group . . ." (p. 373) for adaptive ego purposes. When a patient or a therapist is affected by rigid defenses against recognition of racial prejudice, he or she is limited in the ego resources necessary for psychotherapeutic work. As Mahon (1991) noted: "When a prejudiced person hates a [member of a] group without challenging his own self deception, . . . [he] . . . engages in . . . [an] affective, conflictual, defensive mind-set that obscures [his] error" (p. 377). Hence, when such an "error" occurs in a therapist towards his patient, his ego functioning is restricted, his effectiveness is reduced. It bears noting that race-based errors occur in same-race dyads, as a vignette presented later will show.

Regarding countertransference, Freud stressed its limiting effects. A good example of his point of view is found in his reference to Stekel. "There can be no reasonable doubt about the disqualifying effect of . . . [unrecognized countertransference] in the doctor; every unresolved repression in him constitutes what has been aptly described by Stekel as a 'blind spot in analytic perception'" (Freud 1912, p. 116). Careful reading of Freud clarifies that his cautions were directed to the *unconscious* influences of countertransference, *not* to its utility *in the therapist's mind* when conscious. More recent writings on countertransference, whether from a classical (Abend 1986) or intersubjectivist school (Hoffman 1994) hold in common, albeit with different emphases, that contributions to the therapist's subjective reactions, including countertransference, come from the therapist and patient. Still, there is much debate about how to make use of countertransference and enactments of it in the treatment situation (Gabbard 1995). Currently, no particular emphasis is placed on the therapist's own treatment as the primary experience in which the therapist consolidates awareness, understanding, and mastery of her countertransference potentials.

What has psychoanalysis offered to date about the relationship between countertransference and race? Writings in this area are sparse and most are dated. Schachter and Butts (1968) presented two case reports—one of a black male patient with a white female analyst and one of a white man treated by a black male analyst. They emphasized that race may have catalytic and evocative effects on transference and countertransference, but seemed to eschew the primacy of race to stir these reactions. In a richly textured paper, in which she discussed two cross-cultural cases of her own, Ticho (1971) demurred with Schachter and Butts by pointing out that race (that is, racial stereotypes) may have primacy in determining transferences and countertransferences. Bernard (1953) and Fischer (1971) focused on the difficulties (*and necessity*) of maintaining an analytic stance in the face of race prejudice, cultural biases, and countertransference reactions. Boyer (1977) and Boyer and Boyer (1979) explicitly stated that their countertransference contributions to impasse in conducting analyses with culturally-different patients were reduced through becoming familiar with culturally dissimilar patients by reading about their cultures and through their extensive field work as psychoanalytic ethnographers.

Most recent papers on culture and countertransference come from the psychodynamic psychotherapy literature and have focused on descriptions of the phenomenology of racial and countertransference effects (for example, Comas-Diaz and Jacobsen 1991), and on the utility of a process model of supervision in redressing interferences from such effects (Remington and Da Costa 1989). In an earlier paper (Holmes 1992), I raised the role of a countertransference identification with the patient as a limiting factor in an African-American female patient's gaining access to the links between her fear of becoming rageful and race. She came to treatment because she feared she would lose control of her rage in the race riots going on in her city when she sought treatment. In a recent paper by Leary (1997), postmodern perspectives and self-disclosure are discussed as helpful in freeing patients and therapists from barriers to effective therapy process linked to race. She aptly pointed out that silence in the face of race (such as allusions to race or unacknowledged racial difference) is not neutral. Leary presented the case of a married white woman who was given to outbursts of rage towards her husband and who suffered from identity diffusion. Leary's selective use of self-disclosure seemed to have the impact of stabilizing the working alliance with the patient, but the case material is ambiguous on the question of the impact of self-disclosure on gaining access to and resolving the patient's proneness to hostility and rage. In particular, the hostile, intrusive motivations for the patient's race-linked and non-race-linked questions (for example, the possibility that the patient was turning her passive experience of having been on the receiving end of her mother's intrusiveness into an active stance) did not seem relieved by Leary's answers. Nor was it clear how the therapist's answers clarified bases other than race itself for the patient's hostility. My present approach to working with race-linked expressions of drive derivatives—including questions the patient may ask me in which a social answer seems to be what is being demanded—emphasizes the utility of giving the patient ample opportunity to elaborate his feelings and thoughts as a foundation for eventual processing of them with the analyst, or to demonstrate to the patient that deflections away from continuing their race-linked associations occurred when unpleasurable affects arose signaling the danger of doing so towards me. An example of the recommended approach is given later in this paper, including the role of the therapist's systematic examination of her countertransference and race-based conflicts in her own therapy as a way of understanding the motivations for enactments. Leary's paper is silent on the value of such an examination.

The most frequently recommended approaches to race and countertransference have been didactic or post-treatment efforts (for example, self analysis). I think the following discussions will show that neither is sufficient when addressing the complexities of race and countertransference.

DIDACTIC REDRESS OF RACIAL AND COUNTERTRANSFERENCE REACTIONS

Increased Minority Representation and Culturally Sensitive Teaching Materials

No data exist on attempts to formalize the challenges related to race and countertransference into the curricula of psychoanalytic training programs. The most systematic data are available for clinical psychology. In a 1994 survey, Bernal and Bernal found that numbers of minorities and minority-focused curriculum offerings have significantly increased in mental-health training programs in the past fifteen years. However, in Cancio et al.'s recent comment on that survey (1995), it was pointed out that, "the results of the study did not convincingly provide evidence that graduates of culturally competent training programs are prepared for service and research with ethnic minorities" (p. 800). Relatedly, in my review of Dillard's book (1983) on multicultural counseling (Evans 1985), I pointed out the psychodynamic power of race to overcome the influence of education in the treatment situation. Specifically, Dillard provided useful information on the personal characteristics and socio-cultural problems particular to seven ethnically diverse groups of Americans. Such information did not, however, prevent certain insensitivities later in the book, such as repeated references to children born out of wedlock as illegitimate and the routine reference to adult patients by their first names.

Supervision

Case One: A Latin American Trainee Treating a Patient from a Rival Latin American Country

The insight-oriented psychotherapy supervisee was a young woman from a Latin American country who was treating a female patient from a neighboring country. I was the supervisor, and the supervision and psychotherapy took place in an urban, predominantly African-American university hospital. The therapy was conducted in the non-English language shared by patient and therapist since the patient had not learned English, even though she had graduated from college in her native land, and she had lived in the United States for seven years.

Early in the psychotherapy, the therapist began to express impatience towards the patient whose dependency conflicts were manifested in her not being able to move about the city on her own, a fact that contributed to her being erratic in her attendance to therapy. The therapist seemed to be at a loss to find an approachable surface to the patient's problems. Even though the patient's inability to read street signs played a role in her manifest problems, I noticed that the therapist showed little curiosity about her patient's lack of English fluency. When I brought this to her attention, at first she passed it off as a culturally-based personality characteristic, that is, as an aspect of dependency typical of women from the patient's country. In our discussions, partly for my own learning, and partly to stimulate thinking in the trainee about what I suspected were prejudices in her views, I asked her to inform me about the patient's culture. This supervisee's observing ego capacities came to life; she realized she was relying on a stereotype out of competitive feelings towards the patient's country of origin and towards the patient. She became better able to explore defensive aspects of the patient's dependency and identity problems that the patient had externalized onto her new country. That is, the patient's superego prohibitions against her own ambitions and liveliness had been attributed to her new country which she viewed as hostilely unwelcoming and demanding.

Case Two: A Black Trainee in a White and Then
a Predominantly Black University Hospital

The training situation involved a trainee in a large, predominantly black university hospital where I was a training program director. In his admission interview for residency training, Dr. Smith informed me that he had received his prior professional education in a virtually all-white setting. Also, he told me that his enthusiasm about coming to a minority-focused program was based on the feelings of isolation he had experienced at the university where he had received his professional degree. He wanted the experience of having black supervisors. When asked why this was particularly important to him, he recalled a painful experience with his first psychotherapy supervisor who was white, and who told him that he did not know anything about cross-racial therapy. I asked the applicant if the supervisor's admitted ignorance might have been promising. The prospective trainee countered that *that* possibility had been eliminated because the supervisor had hastened to suggest that he talk to somebody else about it. This young man was greatly offended by this; he felt that the supervisor had not been interested in him because he was black—unknown and unknowable. In that early formative experience, he was discouraged from thinking about the relevance of race in the treatment situation and supervision. He had taken a certain pride in deflecting what he felt was a kind of racial provocation from his supervisor; he thought he had contained the pain of that experience, and looked forward to the new training situation. He said that he was particularly drawn to it because I and others on staff were psychoanalysts.

It became clear early in the trainee's experience that his conscious aims were significantly undermined by unrecognized countertransferences and racial conflicts. For example, when a highly repressed young black woman was presented in a case conference, I noticed that Dr. Smith was frowning when the patient's failure to remember any specifics of an appendectomy at age six was described as repression. When he was queried, he offhandedly said that he thought the patient must have been lying. He was contemptuous and deeply mistrustful of her account. He took her coyness and playful allure to be signs of a "get over" mentality he described as "typical in the ghetto she had come from." ("Get over" refers to seeking an advance on a nonearned basis.) Multiple subsequent training experiences showed Dr. Smith to be quite strained by an attitude of open inquiry concerning the interplay between psychopathology, race, and social-class background. He often slept in seminars and missed many training exercises. When these problems were confronted, he expressed disappointment in himself and dismay, inasmuch as he had not experienced these problems in a more racially repressed setting from which he had come. Clearly, the earlier supervisor's attitudes had buttressed Dr. Smith's own defensive tendency to deflect pain associated with race and countertransference. Consequently, in the new training situation that discouraged such a defense, he showed contempt for a patient whose dynamics he misconstrued in terms of his own "get over" tendencies. Also, he did not recognize his countertransference reactions to her hysterical features, and miscast the patient's dynamics into a racially prejudiced sociological portrait of her.

Given that Dr. Smith and his former supervisor "agreed" that race was not knowable between them, any value of such knowledge was lost, and Dr. Smith's own aversion to various meanings of his and his first patient's different races increased. The possibilities for accurate perception of, and associated acquisition of knowledge about the role of his blackness in his early psychotherapy training were subverted, and his faulty perception was extended to the new training situation and to a patient *of the same race*. In addition, his own prohibitions against reflection and introspection regarding race in relation to his work were reinforced in his earlier training and seemed to generalize to and augment a hostile and suspicious countertransference reaction to the hysterical features of his new patient.

The portrait of the misguided first supervisor and the mental-health trainee just reported is not to conclude that training is not helpful in addressing the interaction of countertransference and race. Both of the training experiences described led to a necessary crisis in his career. However, I think the vignette illustrates that supervision alone, no matter how "culturally competent," does not have the full power to relieve and make positive use of race and countertransference, since typically, both involve strong and complex defenses against one's most conflicted impulses. The various meanings of race are especially difficult to reach in supervision since internal prohibitions to learning about thoughts and urges connected to race are reinforced by a generalized cultural bar to becoming aware of the meanings of race. Supervision is not powerful enough to overcome this factor. Also, the irreducible superego factor necessarily involved in a supervisory process is another limiting influence in supervision in terms of definitively reaching conflicted issues having to do with race and to some extent, countertransference. In both of these supervisions, one might wonder whether the cultural attributes cited by the supervisees (such as a "get over" attitude) represented important cultural values to be understood in their own right. Surely so; at the same time, I believe the examples illustrate that the supervisees adopted them in a defensive way that had limiting effects on their work. In Case One, when the supervisee had the opportunity to reflect upon her patient's use of the cultural value of dependency, the supervisee went beyond a reflexive and defensive reliance on that value.

SELF-ANALYSIS

Published accounts of Freud's responses to his Jewishness, and of his countertransference responses to patients and to colleagues, are instructive with respect to the limitations of self-analysis. He is known to have thought of his Jewishness as a boon to his work. For example, Freud wrote to Ernest Jones:

> The first piece of work that it fell to psychoanalysis to perform was the discovery of the instincts that are common to all men living today—and not only to those living today but to those of ancient and of prehistoric times. It calls for no great effort, therefore, for psychoanalysis to *ignore the differences* [italics added] that arise among inhabitants of the earth owing to the multiplicity of races, languages, and countries. [1929, p. 249]

Freud is also said to have commented to an analysand: "My background as a Jew helped me to stand being criticized, being isolated, working alone" (Blanton 1971, p. 43). Thus, Freud disavowed any vulnerability as a therapist on account of his Jewishness. His point of view is illustrated in Iwasaki's (1971) quote of Freud as saying in 1919: "I have been able to help people with whom I had nothing in common, neither nationality, education, social position nor outlook upon life in general" (p. 334). Freud's view of himself as racially neutral stands in contrast to Jones's recorded recollection of Freud's initial reaction to him, which revealed Freud's *unanalyzed* racial feelings. Jones (1955) reported that Freud said, "from the shape of my head . . . I [Jones] could not be English and must be Welsh. [Jones added:] It astonished me, first because it is uncommon for anyone on the Continent to know of the existence of my native country, and then because I had suspected my dolichocephalic skull might as well be Teutonic as Celtic" (pp. 42-43). There is ample irony here in Jones's own bent toward a language of racial biology.

Pointedly, Freud's conscious aspirations to be a racially neutral psychoanalyst was in some measure defeated by unconscious forces strong enough for him to have enacted a feeling of "racial strangeness" towards Jones when they first met (McGuire 1974). The examples already cited from Freud's life warn us of the potential for race and countertransference to interact harmfully. Another, more vivid example can be taken from Jones's challenge to Freud over whether he had thoroughly analyzed the resistances of his daughter, Anna. The challenge arose as part of a criticism of Anna Freud's technical approach to the analysis of children, which Jones and others thought was too superficial. Antagonized by Jones's criticism, Freud wrote to Jones in 1927: "Who, then, has ever been sufficiently analyzed? I can assure you that Anna has been more deeply and thoroughly analyzed than, for instance, yourself" (Freud 1927). Sometime later, while still reeling from Jones's adverse comments, Freud wrote to Max Eitingon, "I don't believe that Jones is consciously ill-intentioned; but he is a disagreeable person, who wants to display himself in ruling, angering and agitating, and for this his Welsh dishonesty . . . serves him well" (Freud 1960). In this correspondence, there is clear evidence of a confluence of racial and countertransference feeling which resulted in an enactment of ethnic disparagement. Such enactments may have had ramifications for Freud's theory construction. This possibility was proffered by Gilman in his discussion of the impact of the racist Viennese scientific community in which Freud worked. Specifically, Gilman (1993) pointed out that Freud was repeatedly faced with virulent racism in Vienna in the late nineteenth century; in that milieu, Jews were defined as an inferior race. How did Freud resolve or otherwise dispose of the sense of inferiority his adopted community sought to impose on him? Freud's response was to argue that race was of tangential importance. Apparently, such minimization was Freud's way of coping with the racist scientific community of his time, a community in which he defined himself. Gilman (1993) has suggested that there was a self-deluding element in Freud's minimization of race; and he has proffered that the errors and distortions in Freud's theories of female psychology represented a displacement from race to women and a projection of Freud's own conflicted feelings about his Jewishness. Clearly, self-analysis alone is not the answer.

RACE, COUNTERTRANSFERENCE, AND THE TREATMENT SITUATION

Having reviewed the opportunities and limitations associated with didactic approaches and self-analysis in making productive use of race and countertransference, I will turn to the treatment situation itself as the source of the greatest opportunities for full positive utilization of race and countertransference. How does the therapist achieve the capacity to aid patients with conflicts expressed in racial terms? The obvious but least explored means is through the therapist's own therapy. Therapists who achieve conscious, voluntary management of racially conflicted affects and drive derivatives are optimally suited to help patients who express their conflicts in racial terms.

Dias and Chebabi (1987), in their elegant paper concerning psychoanalysis and blacks in Brazil, frankly discuss the failure of analytic therapies to address the impact of race in the treatment situation. They particularly noted the inescapable and inevitable importance of race in the conduct of every analysis in that culture. Their wisdom is ours to heed, as there are many parallels between the Brazilian situation and the United States in terms of racial issues. As they noted:

> Making the unconscious conscious in Brazil means being able at a deep level to acknowledge racial prejudice as a phobia related to one's own instinctuality. . . . This will require the institution of a new dialectic . . . in place of the *master-slave* dialectic. . . . This [maturation of psychoanalysis] will enable us to overcome the narcissistic formula whereby strangers are stamped as enemies, [as] put forward by Freud. . . . [p. 200]

It is important to remember that when race enters into the therapy process, it often involves projected hostility or sexuality. The therapist's own discomfort, influenced by countertransference and race, may too quickly lead him or her to interpret the patient's defensive uses of race. I caution that to interpret defensive use of racial comments or allusions *early on* may defeat the purpose of defense analysis, which is to enlarge the ego's capacity to know and to voluntarily control that which has threatened its functioning. Demonstration to a patient of his or her defenses against awareness of the meanings of racial feelings needs to await the fullest possible elaboration of those feelings, or allusions to them, lest the defenses be redoubled (Evans 1985), often by the use of superego prohibitions. That is, patients and therapists are quick to be influenced by guilt or shame in the face of their racial feelings, since, on a conscious basis, most patients and therapists find their racial feelings unacceptable. As Gray (1994) has richly described, the primary threat to adaptive ego functioning comes from the superego, and patients re-externalize threatening superego activity onto the person of the analyst. Thus, the therapist's attempts to highlight the defensive aspects of racial comments or allusions may miscarry if they occur before the patient experiences a full opportunity to express racially-loaded thoughts and affects. For example, a therapist-to-be-patient may approach his or her prospective analyst or therapist with the expectation that he or she will not be helpful and—let us assume that the two are of different races—expresses the wariness in terms of the racial difference between them. In such a case, the therapist has the challenge—and I think the responsibility—to convey that he or she will not judge, or seek to persuade, the patient against such feelings. Rather, should the prospective therapist-patient decide to give the work a chance, he or she and the therapist will learn together how the expectations weight out over the course of the work. This kind of message lets the patient know that he or she will have the opportunity to express racial feelings and fears fully, and this approach minimizes the excitation of inhibiting superego forces. Thus, the therapist's own forbearance and open-ended curiosity in these matters will aid therapists in training to resolve their own racial conflicts and thereby, in work with their own patients, to show necessary patience and tolerance when race or other somewhat similarly affecting factors (for example, gender and class) come to the fore.

Case Three: A White Woman in Psychoanalysis with
a Black Female Psychoanalytic Candidate

This case was previously reported by me in a paper focused on race and transference (Holmes 1992). The patient entered analysis at age 31 because of difficulty deciding to marry her live-in boyfriend of several years. Similarly, she had not resolved conflicts over choice of career. Having graduated from college, she was working in a part-time business with her boyfriend and as a part-time concert violinist. Ms. Elliot grew up in a circumstance of privilege, with two professional parents and a brother who was 2-years older; yet, she took great pride in living a meager existence. Initially, in relation to her self-imposed impecunious state, my blackness seemed to appeal to her because, as she said, "Well, uh, as a black woman, I thought you would understand about low income." My awareness of some discomfort about this emerging transference to me, into which she incorporated my race, led me to ask her to expand on her impression. I commented thus, "I will try to understand, but right now, you do not make it clear why either one of us should be pleased with such low pay." What emerged over time is that Ms. Elliot used altruism to buttress masochistic tendencies to hold herself back. By the midpoint of her nearly five years of analysis, and after she guiltily acknowledged that she had been fascinated with the Civil War Confederacy during adolescence, Ms. Elliot expressed dread that she might express hostility in racist attitudes.

My countertransferences and racial responses toward Ms. Elliot came to light in the following way: Ms. Elliot noted with pleasure that frequently when I came to the waiting room to get her, I was humming, which she liked. She surmised that I must have a lovely singing voice, and she took my humming to mean that I was in a happy mood and glad to see her. In fact, until she brought the humming to my attention, I had not been aware of it, which led me to discuss it with my analyst. What I came to understand was that my humming represented a countertransference wish to be praised by the patient—a very accomplished musician. I wanted her to be a substitute for the musically talented members of my family who were critical of my extremely modest singing ability. In addition, I believe I began to hum at the time this patient began to anxiously link her hostile feelings to race. Since humming in my family represented a quasi-religious ritual for "calming the demons," I came to know that I was also using humming to quell my own anxiety about working with the patient's racial conflicts. Coming to understand my uses of race enabled me to make my blackness more available to the patient for the associative and projective uses to which she needed to put it. She became freer to express herself in racial terms, and thereby, to better understand her defenses against hatred, the origins of which had to do with her mother suppressing her ambition in favor of the patient's brother. The following exchange shows how this more forthright work began:

> **Ms. Elliot:** (The patient began by speaking of a black professor teaching her in graduate school.) Professor Jones, well—should I say this?—he just is not very good; nothing like you, of course. I mean you're excellent at what you do. I, uh . . .
>
> **Analyst:** You seem to strain to protect me from any possible criticism you have of me.
>
> **Ms. Elliot:** If I speak in racial terms, I'll be out on a limb. I'll fall off. You'll criticize me. I'll say the wrong thing and boom! In recent years I have been a champion of poor people and blacks. I don't want to recognize how angry I am, and it's still hard for me to believe that I can criticize anybody I want to in here. . . . If I cling to my love of the poor and blacks, and get you to join me, I don't have to face those feelings.
>
> **Analyst:** So, the "boom" is an alarming way of being aware of angry feelings you don't want to have. Fearing my objection to those feelings, is it easier to focus on blacks other than me and to remind me that you champion the rights of blacks and the poor?

This case presentation was offered as a way one's own treatment can and optimally should work to be sensitive to and useful in the resolution of racial and countertransference feelings such that the therapist becomes more usefully available to patients in their conflicts expressed in racial terms. In terms of my countertransference toward Ms. Elliot, I came to realize that I had enacted a fantasy of using her to elicit a favorable review of my meager musical ability, and with respect to race, I had been incomplete in analyzing her aggressive conflicts because I, at first, unknowingly shared with her a dread of race used as a vehicle to express hostility. My own analysis during training became the effective vehicle in which I could address these issues.

CONCLUSION

This paper was written to demonstrate the power of race to organize defenses against awareness of drive derivatives and to show how race and countertransference operate similarly and synergistically. Both may impede treatment, but when either is made available for the therapist's reflection and analysis, the therapist will be better able to assist the patient to grapple with his or her own racially expressed issues. It is my position that racial reactions are more potent and potentially more destructive of therapy than countertransference reactions in general since responses to race are determined and reinforced externally, that is, in the culture at large *and* intrapsychically. Given the ego-distorting effects which stem from the ubiquitous use of race for primitive defensive purposes, I have argued that neither didactic approaches nor self-analysis *alone* are likely to gain the therapist- or analyst-to-be sufficient mastery over racial "blind spots." The therapist's own therapy is likely to be the most effective means by which to resolve such conflicts. Since racial reactions are so heavily and universally relied on to fend off one's own instinctuality—as Dias and Chebabi (1987) and Mahon (1991) have previously pointed out—the resolution of racial reactions may serve as a prototype for the resolution of other "blind spots" in the therapist, such as those which may develop from countertransference feelings.

Heretofore, when race has been considered as a factor in psychoanalysis and psychotherapy, the emphasis has been on the phenomenology of it in terms of transference, and to a lesser extent, countertransference. Its unique role and its relationship to other variables such as countertransference have not been explored in depth previously in the United States, nor has the technique of how to analyze it as an important influence on the therapist been previously probed.

It needs to be highlighted that people in general, including therapists and patients, use racial groups to flee from the "bad" internal darkness of their instinctuality. In the United States, and in many other places, blacks serve this purpose. That is, through the use of externalizing defenses, blacks become a marginalized and impersonalized group onto whom unwanted urges are cast. In this paper, I have proposed a way for therapists to address such mechanisms so that race can be transformed from an "ambiguous, abyssal blackness . . . [into a conscious] container of insight, enlightenment and hope" (Tien 1993, p. 17). I think that it is within the analytic therapist's capacities and obligation to explore this realm in his own treatment and thereby, to gain the courage, sensitivities, and skill to be alert to and ready to work with its inevitable emergence in the treatments she conducts. It is a difficult but necessary calling.

REFERENCES

Abend, S. (1989). Countertransference and technique. *Psychoanalytic Quarterly* 48:474–495.
Bernal, M., and Castro, F. (1994). Are clinical psychologists prepared for service and research with ethnic minorities: report of a decade of progress. *American Psychologist* 49:797–805.
Bernard, V. (1953). Psychoanalysis and members of minority groups. *Journal of the American Psychoanalytic Association* 1:256–267.
Blanton, S. (1971). *Diary of My Analysis with Sigmund Freud.* New York: Hawthorn.
Boyer, L. B. (1979). Countertransference with severely regressed patients. In *Countertransference,* ed. L. Epstein and A. Feiner, pp. 347–374. Northvale, NJ: Jason Aronson.
Boyer, L. B., and Boyer, R. M. (1977). Understanding the patient through folklore. *Contemporary Psychoanalysis* 13:30–51.
Cancio, R., Corbett, C., Stanton, Y., and Soucar, E. (1995). On culturally competent clinical psychologists. *American Psychologist* 50:800–801.
Comas-Diaz, L., and Jacobsen, F. (1991). Ethnocultural transference and countertransference in the therapeutic dyad. *American Journal of Orthopsychiatry* 61:392–402.
Dias, C., and Chebabi, W. (1987). Psychoanalysis and the role of black life and culture in Brazil. *Internaltional Review of Psycho-analysis* 14:185–202.

Dillard, J. (1983). *Multicultural Counseling: Towards Ethnic and Cultural Relevance in Human Encounters*. Chicago, IL: Nelson-Hall.

Evans, D. (1985). Psychotherapy and black patients: problems of training, trainees, and trainers. *Psychotherapy: Theory, Research and Practice* 22:457–460.

Fischer, N. (1971). An interracial analysis: transference and countertransference significance. *Journal of the American Psychoanalytic Association* 19:736–745.

Freud, S. (1912). Recommendations to physicians practicing psychoanalysis. *Standard Edition* 12:109–122.

—— (1929). Dr. Ernest Jones (on his 50th birthday). *Standard Edition* 21:249–250.

—— (1960). Sigmund Freud to Max Eitingon, November, 27, 1927. In *Letters of Sigmund Freud*, ed. E. L. Freud. New York: Basic Books.

Gabbard, G. (1995). Countertransference: The emerging common ground. *International Journal of Psycho-Analysis* 76:475–486.

Gilman, S. (1993). *Freud, Race, and Gender*. Princeton, NJ: Princeton University Press.

Gray, P. (1994). *The Ego and Analysis of Defense*. Northvale, NJ: Jason Aronson.

Hoffman, I. (1994). Dialectical thinking and therapeutic action in the psychoanalytic process. *Psychoanalytic Quarterly* 63:187–219.

Holmes, D. (1992). Race and transference in psychoanalysis and psychotherapy. *International Journal of Psycho-Analysis* 73:1–11.

Iwasaki, T. (1971). Discussion of G. Ticho's cultural aspects of transference and countertransference. *Bulletin of the Menninger Clinic* 35:330–334.

Jones, E. (1955). *The Life and Work of Sigmund Freud*, vol. 2, pp. 42–43. New York: Basic Books.

Leary, K. (1997). Race, self-disclosure, and "forbidden talk": race and ethnicity in contemporary clinical practice. *Psychoanalytic Quarterly* 66:163–189.

Mahon, E. (1991). A note on the nature of prejudice. *Psychoanalytic Study of the Child* 46:369–379.

McGuire, W., ed. (1974). *The Freud/Jung Letters: The Correspondence between Sigmund Freud and C. G. Jung*. Princeton, NJ: Princeton University Press.

Remington, G. and Da Costa, G. (1989). Ethnocultural factors in resident supervision: black supervisor and white supervisees. *American Journal of Psychotherapy* 43:398–404.

Schachter, J., and Butts, H. (1968). Transference and countertransference in interracial analyses. *Journal of the American Psychoanalytic Association* 16:792–808.

Ticho, G. (1971). Cultural aspects of transference and countertransference. *Bulletin of the Menninger Clinic* 35:313–334.

Tien, S. (1993). *Old lines, new boundaries: a case of psychoanalysis with analyst and patient of different sexuality and ethnicity.* Paper presented at Division 39, American Psychological Association, New York, April 14–16.

16

Our Moral Universe
Michael Moskowitz

Psychoanalysis has a long history as a progressive social movement dedicated to the alleviation of common misery. In a letter to Putnam, Freud wrote, "the recognition of our therapeutic limitations reinforces our determination to change other social factors so that men and women shall no longer be forced into hopeless situations" (Turkle 1978, p. 142).

And in *The Future of an Illusion* (Freud 1927):

> One thus gets the impression that civilization is something which was imposed on a resisting majority by a minority which understood how to obtain possession of the means to power and coercion . . . [p. 6] . . . It is to be expected that these underprivileged classes will envy the favored ones their privileges and will do what they can to free themselves from their own surplus of privation. Where this is not possible, a permanent measure of discontent will exist within the culture concerned . . . [I]t is understandable that the suppressed people will develop an intense hostility towards a culture whose existence they

make possible by their work, but in whose wealth they have too small a share. [p. 12]

Freud's radical analysis of civilization and its illusions, which was the major focus of his later work, was continued by Reich, Fromm, Marcuse, and others in a loose association that became known as the Frankfurt school. The work of Adorno and colleagues (1982) on the authoritarian personality stands as perhaps the most influential research projects in the history of psychology. Yet for the most part, psychoanalytic political writings are untaught in the psychoanalytic institutes and remain outside the scope of clinical discourse. The powerful tools for social research, cultural analysis, and change that psychoanalytic theory offers have been largely ignored.

In its withdrawal from the social realm, psychoanalysis in the United States has come to be viewed as politically conservative and socially impotent. To make matters worse, the clinical field has been subject to internal and external forces that further diminish its social relevance and even threaten its survival as a therapeutic modality accessible to more than the elite few.

One way in which we can return psychoanalysis to the social arena is to assist in the understanding of psychological phenomena underlying racism. As analysts we are in a privileged position to view the complex interplay between personal and cultural factors that support both racism and the denial of racism. Studies confirming that there is no acceptable genetic basis for the concept of race (Cavalli-Sforza et al. 1994), make it all the more apparent that dividing the world into black and white is a delusion of civilization. People are not black or white. Where the line is drawn is politically and psychologically motivated. Skin color is a relatively changeable local variation and phenotypically similar populations may be genotypically quite different while genotypically similar populations appear phenotypically similar. That "race" is the only ethnic grouping in this culture that does not allow for the possibility of dual identity, belies its delusional rigidity. While "race" has powerful psychological meanings, it was important not to lend the word continuing scientific respectability, as other than a social construction tied to particular times and cultures. Furthermore, it is becoming clearer and clearer that all humans, as a species, developed in Africa less than 250,000 years ago, and that the genetic diversity of the entire world is contained in that continent.

Other disciplines, such as history and anthropology, raise questions about the danger of reifying concepts like culture and ethnicity (Wolf 1982). Alba (1990) has concluded that for the vast majority of whites living in America, ethnic identity had become a symbolic identity, a vestigial attachment to a few ethnic symbols imposing little cost on everyday life. Nearly two-thirds of all native-born white Americans view themselves as having mixed ethnicity. However, on a not quite conscious level, a new ethnic identity is emerging, that of a European American. From that group, which has little real connection to the customs of Europe, Asians, Latinos, African Caribbeans, and African Americans are excluded. The new European-American identity becomes, once again, an ethnicity of privilege and exclusion.

These issues can enter the clinical realm in various ways. A patient became more self-consciously Italian as our work progressed. His dream of me as a moose led to associations to his father's wondering about his analysis with a big-nosed Jew. The moose/Moskowitz/Jew image was a recurring image in the analysis. Often it seemed that subtle anti-Semitic images and feelings and a heightened sense of being Italian were used as a way of distancing me and making my interpretations foreign and less relevant.

A child patient was the son of a black American soldier and a Japanese woman. Before the age of 2, he was adopted into a middle-class family with a black father (who soon died) and a white mother. My patient looked "black." His new mother considered him black and talked with me about the problems of raising a black child in this culture. Several years into the therapy, in a context I do not remember, I mentioned something about the difficulty of being black in this racist world. He responded angrily: "I am not black!" It then became clear that he viewed himself as Japanese, which suddenly gave new meaning to his longstanding kung-fu fantasies.

If a general statement can be made regarding how psychoanalytic treatments can respond to race and ethnic issues, it is that a primary transforming aspect of analysis is the analysis of transference, and that racist and anti-Semitic transferences and countertransference are analyzable in much the same ways as other transferences with one important caveat. Since racism and anti-Semitism are touchy subjects, difficult to talk about, and since one's attitudes about these issues are packed with secret and potentially embarrassing meanings, both analysts and patient may be more reluctant to talk about and analyze these issues than they would other issues.

In a recent presentation, Dorothy Evans Holmes (1997) stated that even though there is increased willingness to admit to the ubiquity of countertransference reactions, and a deemphasis on their being bad, there is still debate about how to make use of countertransference reactions, and no particular emphasis is placed on the use of a therapist's own training analysis as the arena in which one's countertransference potential is mastered. (In my own informal survey, some analysts spent much of their training analysis talking about patients, while some spent very little.) Joining with Holmes on her point, I would add that most countertransference narratives in the literature have a moral: this is how my countertransference helped me understand my patient. Not, this is how I've been blind, I've missed something, I've hurt my patient.

Holmes goes on to state that racial feeling and defenses against them, which I think she sees as a more generic or culturally universal countertransference, should be explored in every training analysis. This seems to imply that racism can be a topic of every analysis. I think this is a radical position that deserves extensive consideration.

Holmes takes the further—and I think even more controversial position—that the usually didactic approaches to understanding one's racial fantasies and prejudices may be worse than useless in that they reinforce distance from scary feelings. Though supervision provides the opportunity for some change, Holmes feels that supervision alone is inadequate and that self-analysis also falls short. To be adequately addressed, these issues must be dealt with in the therapist's own therapy.

If Holmes is correct, and I think she is, one should be able to see racist elements in all analyses. Yet there is a notable paucity of writing about race-related issues that arise in a white-white analytic dyad. There is an interesting case (Rodgers 1960), powerfully presented, in which a white southern middle-class male psychoanalyst discusses the short (five-month long), unsuccessful treatment of a southern middle-class man. The patient, a 43-year-old bachelor who lived with his mother, started out as a professional pacifist and active member of an organization devoted to the abolition of capital punishment, and ended treatment as a leader of the White Citizens Council, an organization devoted to segregation and capital punishment as a way of "keeping the Negroes in line" (p. 241). One might call this a negative therapeutic reaction.

This upper middle-class white man was primarily raised by a black woman, who also served as cook and maid. While his parents were obsessional, uptight neatfreaks, his babysitter was permissive and indulgent. The patient's sexual life was divided into permissible sex with easy, degraded women and a phobic avoidance of sex with forbidden women—virgins, wives, and widows. Early in the therapy, after some analysis of his sexual inhibition relating to his fear of being like a black man—"Negroes were like animals about sex" (p. 240)—the patient allows himself to be seduced into a sexual encounter with a respectable widow. He could not believe that the analyst did not condemn this misbehavior, and that respectable people could be so casual about sex, which he associated with black people. Was his analyst really a black man who was making him into a black man?

He then had a dream in which his mother was lying helpless on the ground about to be gored by a huge bull with black horns. Rousing himself from momentary paralysis, and with a feeling of unlimited strength, he leapt at the bull and pulled off his horns with his bare hands. He felt a great sense of exhilaration. He associated the back horns to black men, his father's black cane, and the analyst's black horned-rimmed glasses. He had the thought that maybe it would be a good thing if all black men were castrated. Two days later the analyst received a letter terminating the treatment. Six months later, he received from the patient the first of several mailings of racist literature from the organization of which he was now a leader. As a complex racial transference had evolved, in which, without either patient or analyst identified as black, both patient and analyst were experienced at different times by the patient as being black, lending support to Holmes's hypothesis that the racial dynamic is present in all therapies.

Rodgers comments that his patient's relationship to two mothers: one white, uptight and unavailable, the other black, permissive and indulgent, provide ready-made templates for his tabooed and degraded sexual scripts. He goes on to say that white children brought up by black nannies not only have two mothers, but by extension two fathers, with the black male becoming the oedipally feared and hated father who can take way the source of sexual pleasure. He notes that this situation was once common in the South. While it may be somewhat less common, it is still common. How many white middle-class children are raised by women of color who leave their own children sometimes thousands of miles away? It is not surprising that someone raised by mothers of two colors would bring these representations to analysis. However, in other cases where color was not particularly present in childhood, racial representations still arise. I'll give a personal example.

>I remember vividly a dream from my therapy. In it I was denied access to a building by an imposing black doorman. My therapist pointed out that his own name was Schwartz, which I needed him to remind me means "black" in Yiddish. The associations and interpretation that followed related to my oedipally viewing him like my father, by denying me access to my mother's body and not providing me with the key that would give me the power to turn her on. He was my "Schwartz-father," my black father of the night. That I portrayed him as a doorman, with its racist stereotypes, was an attempt to diminish his power. Other dreams and fantasies about black men led back to my analyst, and I'd like to say that this in turn led me to further insights into my fear and envy of black men. And it did, but not in that analysis. The image stayed with me over the years and got elaborated and further analyzed, and I still work on it.
>
>I grew up in a rundown, impoverished white town, in which direct interaction with black people played no part in my early life. Being a Jew was never far from my mind. Being called "Christ-killer" and "dirty Jew" as I walked to school made it hard to escape. My father's ready explanation was that we were envied, we had a culture, a history, had survived for millennia. This was not my experience. I did not feel envied. I felt attacked. Seeing the civil rights struggle, I felt more identified with blacks fighting against oppression (Malcolm X, Eldridge Cleaver) than with my father's version of triumphant Jews.
>
>My father would get angry whenever "ghetto" was used to designate black communities such as Harlem. He would say no

one stops anyone from walking in or out of Harlem—that's not a ghetto. In a ghetto, Jews were locked in at night. What I was not able to see until recently is that by not asking my father about his life, what he knew of oppression, and the ghetto, I was denying his strength and my envy of his knowledge and ability to survive, which I displaced onto blackness.

Maybe I was lucky to have a therapist named Schwartz. I know many men who secretly wished they were black, who were, in Kathleen White's term, "black-identified white men." Black men were fantasized to be more athletic, sexual, and the like, but as importantly they are seen as standing in angry opposition to contemporary culture. We know that by far the largest buyers of rap music are white adolescents.

Yet again, when whites' fantasies of blackness come up in the literature, they are almost invariably reported by analysts of color. What makes these issues so difficult to talk about? And why when they get talked about do they get so often forgotten? Rodgers's paper was written in 1960, and it was proceed by papers on racism by prominent analysts like Brian Bird and Richard Sterba. Many papers on anti-Semitism were written following World War II. But these issues seemed to go largely underground in the psychoanalytic world. They now being revived and supported by a multicultural consciousness which is, of course, under attack. The analysis of the phenomena of lost or repressed knowledge is one that Russell Jacoby undertakes in *The Repression of Psychoanalysis* (1983). In brief, he states that knowledge gets repressed when it threatens the class and power relationships of a culture. I have continued this analysis in a 1996 paper (Moskowitz 1996).

Another factor that inhibits our analysis of racism is the moral universe we inhabit. Goldhagen drew our attention to this in relationship to the Holocaust. He claimed that to try to understand the Holocaust from our moral perspective only leads to dead ends and confusion. To understand how ordinary Germans could willingly and zealously brutalize, torture, and murder Jews, we must place ourselves in their moral universe and understand what Goldhagen calls the absurd beliefs at the center of a society's view of life.

Throughout history, most societies have been governed by absurd beliefs, such as the Aztec view that human sacrifices were necessary for the sun to rise, or the preliterate belief that trees were animated by good and evil spirits. Of course such beliefs do not seem absurd to the cultures that hold them. Only in retrospect or from a different vantage point do they seem so. Goldhagen argues that at the core of pre-Hitler Germany was eliminationist anti-Semitism, which viewed Jews as less than human and responsible for all the evils of society; as such they *should* be eliminated. In this moral universe the murder of Jews was not a conflicted, crazy, or guilt-ridden act. This view has certainly struck a chord in Germany where Goldhagen is treated like a rock star or a prophet. In a sense, he seems to be granting Germans expiation. He has given them an interpretation of their actions that shows that they were not crazy or evil, but acting understandably in an different moral universe.

Closer to home, when psychoanalytic societies refused admission to homosexuals, who then thought of it as mad? I assume we now think of it as mad, since we cannot now think of it as ever having been being reasonable.

Writing years before Goldhagen, Eugene Genovese asked a similar question about slaveholders: how could well-educated, intellectual Christians, who perceived themselves as thoroughly modern and moral, justify the keeping of other human beings as slaves? He too described a different moral universe. Genovese argues that slaveholders carried forth a feudal view of the world in that God meant some men should be rulers and others should be ruled. Since there had always been slaves, God must want it to be that way. It was often argued, and seemingly passionately believed, that the slaves of the South were better off than the laboring poor of the North.

Genovese has not been treated like a prophet and a rock star in this country. For reasons we do not clearly understand, we still occupy a moral universe not so different than the one he describes. Racism continues as a justification for slavery by a different name.

To repeat a few facts: We now imprison a larger share of our population than any other nation (tripled since 1970). There are 1.8 million people in prisons; 58 percent have minor children. About 46 percent of prisoners are black males—eight times their representation in the general population. One out of 4 black men in the U.S. between the ages of 20 and 29 is either in prison, on parole, or on probation.

The life expectancy for young black males in the inner city is lower than that in most developing countries.

We all know this . . . and don't. We can only hope our psychoanalytic discourse can contribute to further understanding so that in the future, the not-too-distant future, we will be able to look back in disbelief at the moral universe that makes these abominations possible.

REFERENCES

Adorno, T. W., Frenkel-Brunswik, E., Levinson, D. J., and Sanford, R. N. (1982). *The Authoritarian Personality*. New York: W. W. Norton.

Alba, R. (1990). *Ethnic Identity: The Transformation of White America*. New Haven, CT: Yale University Press.

Cavalli-Sforza, L., Menozzi, P., and Piazza, A. (1994). *The History and Geography of the Human Gene*. Princeton, NJ: Princeton University Press.

Freud, S. (1927). The future of an illusion. *Standard Edition* 21:1–56.

Genovese, E. (1972). *Roll Jordan Roll: The World the Slaves Made*. New York: Vintage.

——— (1992). *The Slaveholders' Dilemma: Freedom and Progress in Southern Conservative Thought 1820–1960*. Columbia, SC: University of South Carolina Press.

Goldhagen, D. (1996). *Hitler's Willing Executioners: Ordinary Germans and the Holocaust*. New York: Knopf.

Holmes, D. E. (1997). Race and countertransference: two blind spots in psychoanalytic perception. Presented at the NYU Postdoctoral Program in Psychotherapy and Psychoanalysis, New York.

Jacoby, R. (1983). *The Repression of Psychoanalysis*. Chicago, IL: University of Chicago Press.

Moskowitz, M. (1996). The social conscience of psychoanalysis. In *Reaching Across Boundaries of Culture and Class: Widening the Scope of Psychotherapy*, ed. R.M.P Foster, M. Moskowitz, and R. A. Javier, pp. 21–46. Northvale, NJ: Jason Aronson.

Rodgers, T. C. (1960). The evolution of an active anti-negro racist. *Psychoanalytic Study of Society* 1:237–243.

Turkle, S. (1978). *Psychoanalytic Politics: Freud's French Revolution.* Cambridge, MA: MIT Press.

White, K. (1995). Biracial psychoanalysis: a consideration of dissociated across race identifications. Presented at the CUNY Minority Association Annual Conference, New York.

Wolf, E. (1982). *Europe and the People without History.* Berkeley, CA: University of California Press.

17

Psychoanalysis and Diplomacy: Potentials for and Obstacles against Collaboration
Vamık D. Volkan

Given the pervasive influence of Realpolitik over government and the study of international relations, and some inherent difficulties within the field of psychoanalysis, it is not surprising that political science and psychoanalysis remain distant cousins. This chapter discusses obstacles against collaboration between these two disciplines, but also points to areas where collaboration is possible and can be useful.

FROM RATIONAL ACTORS TO PSYCHOANALYSIS

Encouraged by the work of Sigmund Freud and a few other pioneers, psychoanalysts have sought to venture beyond the couch and apply their expertise to interconnected aspects of human behavior and the external world. But given the pervasive influence of Realpolitik over government and the study of international relations, and some inherent difficulties within the field of psychoanalysis, it is not surprising that political science and psychoanalysis still remain distant cousins.

The origins of Realpolitik can be traced to Ludwig von Rochau, who introduced the concept in *Grundsätze der Realpolitik* (1853). Rochau advised politicians to estimate carefully what the opposition *really* wanted, not what they *said* they wanted, and to be prepared to exert force when necessary to support one's own or thwart another's objectives. Eventually the term came to mean the rational evaluation and realistic assessment of the options available to one's group and one's enemies. In the United States, especially after World War II, this latter interpretation of Realpolitik, named the "rational-actor Model," became prevalent in political analysis. This model (in its various forms) assumes that people make decisions by engaging in a rational calculation of costs and benefits, and that leaders, governments, and nations are rational "actors." (For various studies of this model, its modifications and criticism, see Etzioni 1967, George 1969, Allison 1971, Janis and Mann 1977, White 1980, Barner-Barry and Rosenwein 1985, Jervis et al. 1985, Achen and Snidal 1989, Volkan et al. 1998).

The so-called "deterrence" theories characteristic of the Cold War era depended on this type of rational approach, and many political analysts believe that decisions made according to rational-actor models prevented the Soviets and the Americans from using their nuclear arsenals. This is most likely the case, but policies based on deterrence have also failed, and research in a variety of disciplines demonstrated that decisions were not always predictable based on rational assumptions. For instance, Egyptian President Anwar Sadat surprised both Israeli and U.S. military intelligence by launching a massive attack across the Suez Canal on Yom Kippur on October 6, 1973. Based on the rational calculations of deterrence, policy analysts did not believe an Egyptian offensive could be launched before 1975, and reports of Egyptian troop movements in September 1973 were regarded as only exercises. Therefore, Egyptian forces were able to overrun poorly manned Israeli defenses and drive deep into the Sinai, although Sadat's army ultimately suffered heavy losses before a cease-fire. As the shortcomings of various rational-actor models became evident, some political scientists, and even some government decision-makers and diplomats, began to borrow concepts from cognitive psychology in the late 1970s and early 1980s to explain "faulty" decision-making. But they did not look to psychoanalysis for insights.

The application of cognitive psychology nevertheless expanded the scope of political analysis. But the limitations of this approach, which focused primarily on conscious considerations, also became evident. This shortcoming was recognized by Janis and Mann (1977), who discussed the relevance of unconscious motivations in their application of cognitive concepts to decision-making. They suggested a link between disciplines when they noted that, "If the study of unconscious motives that affect decision-making is to proceed, it is necessary to take into account of other types of research, including psychoanalytic case studies" (p. 98). One of the psychoanalytic cases Janis and Mann examined was Freud's (1901) case of Dora, an 18-year-old woman whose "decisional conflict," to use the terminology of Janis and Mann, concerned whether or not to have an illicit love affair with Mr. K, who was married and a friend of Dora's family. After deciding against the affair, Dora had much post-decisional regret and remained in "post-decisional conflict." Through their review of Freud's findings on the unconscious reasons why Dora could not "work through and resolve the post-decisional conflict in a normal fashion" (Janis and Mann 1977, p. 100), Janis and Mann noted that psychoanalytic insights were in fact needed to fully understand decision-making.

While both cognitive psychology and psychoanalysis consider the influence of previous historical events in decision-making, the nature of psychoanalytic theory takes into account more than conscious motivational factors and analogous associations; it examines defensive alterations of early experiences, layered personal meanings of events, condensations of unconscious motivations, transference distortions, and the personality organization of decision-makers. The principle of multiple function and over-determination, first described in detail by Waelder (1930) in regard to an individual's decisions and perceptions, also must be considered in the evaluation of diplomatic and political processes of decision-making.

Although politicians and diplomats began to broaden their horizons in order to understand "faulty" decision-making, and political scientists cautiously explored the relevance of psychology, psychoanalysts themselves did not quickly respond to the opportunity to contribute. Instead, it was two diplomats who indirectly invited psychoanalysts to apply their knowledge of internal psycyhodynamics to international issues. In 1974, following the division of Cyprus into

Turkish and Greek sectors, Turkish Prime Minister Bülent Ecevit noted the role of psychology in the long-standing conflict between these two neighboring nations. In response to this pertinent observation, I began to study the Cyprus problem, and later, with historian Norman Itzkowitz, I studied 1,000 years of Turkish-Greek relations through a psychoanalytic lens (Volkan 1976, Volkan and Itzkowitz 1984, 1993, 1994).

A few years later, Egyptian President Anwar Sadat further encouraged psychoanalysts to become involved in the study of international relationships. In 1977, Sadat made a historic visit to Israel, and in a speech before the Knesset, he stated that 70 percent of the problems between Arabs and Israelis were psychological. This statement, backed by Sadat's international reputation and popularity in the U.S., prompted a committee of the American Psychiatric Association (APA) to sponsor a 7-year project (1979–1986) that brought together groups of influential Egyptians, Israelis, and Palestinians for a series of unofficial dialogues. The American team, serving as neutral facilitators, consisted of psychoanalysts (including myself), psychiatrists, psychologists, and diplomats. The Israeli and Arab groups also included psychiatrists and psychoanalysts, but mostly were comprised of influential citizens—ambassadors, a former high-level military officer, journalists, and others—attending the meetings in an unofficial capacity. As a member of the APA team, and later as the project's chairman for its final 3 years, I was able to observe at close range how such dialogues were exceptionally useful in examining the psychological aspects of international conflict and the ubiquitous expression of ethnonational identity.

Three years later, inspired by my involvement in international and interdisciplinary projects, and encouraged by the writings of German psychoanalyst Alexander Mitscherlich (1971), who urged psychoanalysts to move beyond their clinical offices and become part of interdisciplinary work on societal and political issues, I founded the Center for the Study of Mind and Human Interaction (CSMHI) at the University of Virginia. For over ten years the faculty of the Center, which includes psychoanalysts, psychiatrists, former diplomats, political scientists, historians, and others from both social and behavioral sciences, have conducted research and projects in locations such as the Baltic republics, Georgia, Kuwait, Albania, Slovakia, Turkey, Croatia, Germany, the U.S., and elsewhere. In addition, CSMHI faculty have been invited to present our findings to organizations such as the International Psychoanalytic Association, American Psychoanalytic Association, American Academy of Psychoanalysis, and the American College of Psychoanalysts, as well as the UN, World Federation of Mental Health, and others. As far as I know, this Center is the only organization that specializes in directly applying psychoanalytic concepts to ethnonational conflicts, postwar adjustments, and facilitation of intergroup dialogues to encourage democracy and peaceful coexistence.

I must clarify, however, that there certainly are others who have significantly contributed to interdisciplinary work and the examination of history, politics, and social movements and relationships through a psychoanalytic lens. Peter Loewenberg, for example, a historian as well as a psychoanalyst at the University of California, Los Angeles, for many years has combined his expertise to analyze both domestic and international political issues (Loewenberg 1995). In addition, Afaf Mahfouz from Washington, D.C., has worked for some time to promote links between psychoanalysts and the UN. Similarly, in 1998 South American psychoanalysts Moises Lemlij and Max Hernandez organized a large and successful meeting in Lima, Peru that brought psychoanalysts together with high-level diplomats and politicians, and there are numerous other examples as well. But collaboration remains problematic.

OBSTACLES PREVENTING EFFECTIVE COLLABORATION

It has proven difficult to define specific areas where cooperation between psychoanalysis and political science or diplomacy can occur in useful and mutually satisfying ways. One reason stems from psychoanalytic traditions and previous attempts to apply psychoanalysis to other disciplines. Starting with Freud, psychoanalysts have written on a variety of topics relating to the diplomatic and political realms, but their contributions have thus far been mostly theoretical in nature, and of little practical use to diplomats and politicians. Psychoanalysts have studied group psychology, political leaders and their relationships with followers, mass violence and war. They have developed theories on the aggressive drive as the root cause of war, the perception of a state or nation as a mother, groups who respond to a leader as to a father and identification of group members with one another, and other applications of an individual's intrapsychic experience to societal phenomena. Furthermore, frequently and unfortunately, they applied psychodynamic observations on small groups, such as therapy groups composed of six to twelve individuals or organizations with members in the hundreds, to the psychodynamics of large groups composed of millions of individuals. There was little emphasis on understanding large-group identity in its own right, and few theorists accounted for differences between the processes that occur in a stable large group and those that occur when a group is collectively regressed, or when a group is preoccupied with a neighboring group.

Many of these earlier efforts at applied psychoanalysis and the theoretical constructs that resulted are valid, however, when they are utilized to understand specific aspects or limited features of large-group interaction. Freud's (1921) well-known theory on group psychology, for example, which reflects an oedipal theme, should not be abandoned. The behavior he described can be seen in regressed groups today: the members of the group sublimate their aggression against the leader in a way that is similar to the process of a son turning his negative feelings toward his oedipal father into loyalty. In turn, the members of a group idealize the leader, identify with each other, and rally around the leader.

Some recent international events can be illuminated by applying Freud's ideas. In 1998, tension between the U.S. and Iraq increased over the issue of inspection of some of Saddam Hussein's numerous presidential "palaces" in which illegal weapons were reportedly being manufactured. Some Iraqis responded to the increased tension and possibility of U.S. military action by creating a "human shield" around his palaces and other important sites. These individuals were literally rallying around a leader. Although autocratic persuasion and propaganda played a role in their response, many reputable policy analysts believed that a majority of these Iraqis acted voluntarily.

But we also must remember that Freud, as Waelder (1971) stated, was only speaking of regressed groups, and his theory does not provide a full explanation of large-group psychology. Given such shortcomings, in the last decade or so, some psychoanalysts who study large groups and their leaders have shifted their approach from emphasizing the leader as an image of an idealized father to the leader as an image of an idealized and nurturing mother. For example, Anzieu (1971, 1984), Chasseguet-Smirgel (1984), and Kernberg (1980, 1989) have written on regressed groups and the shared fantasies of their members in which the group represents an idealized, all-gratifying early mother ("breast-mother") that repairs all narcissistic lesions. The members of such regressed groups, according to Anzieu and Chasseguet-Smirgel, will choose leaders who promote such illusions of gratification, and the group may become violent and try to destroy external reality that is perceived as interfering with this illusion. Thus, there seems to be a growing emphasis on preoedipal rather than oedipal issues on this subject among some psychoanalysts. Kernberg has stated that Freud's description of libidinal ties among the members of a group, in fact, reflects a defense against preoedipal tensions.

I tend to agree with these formulations. Nevertheless, they basically represent individuals' intrapsychic perceptions of large groups and political leaders, and therefore remain theoretical constructs that political scientists or diplomats find difficult to use in their own analysis of day-to-day events or important incidents. My own study of large-group psychology began with my participation in small meetings where representatives of large enemy groups were brought together. I noted that besides speaking about their own individual identities, expectations, and anxieties, and besides the evidence of small-group dynamics such as those described by Bion (1961), participants from antagonistic groups became spokespersons of the large groups to which they belonged. Each individual participant in a dialogue, regardless of his or her personality organization, professional or social standing, or political orientation, felt that his or her side was under personal attack and was compelled to directly or indirectly defend their large group. Since individuals seemed determined to protect the identity of their large group, I came to believe that *large-group identity* needed to be studied more fully. The details of my investigation of this topic are summarized elsewhere (Volkan 1999b,c), but rather than further discussing such concepts, my emphasis in this paper is on how others in the psychoanalytic professions may best direct their energies if they are interested in contributing to the understanding of international relationships and psychopolitical issues.

Given the safety of strictly clinical issues, and the limitations of applied psychoanalysis, there is no simple answer to the question of how political and behavioral scientists or diplomats and psychoanalysts can best collaborate. In his letter to Albert Einstein (1932), Freud was pessimistic about human nature and the role of psychoanalysis in stopping wars or war-like situations. Although Arlow (1973) also found some cautious optimism in Freud's later writings on this subject, Freud's pessimism was mirrored by many of his followers, and this also may have played a role in the limited contributions made to diplomacy by psychoanalysts. Having seen what man is capable of doing to his fellow man in many parts of the world over the last two decades, I cannot help but join Freud in his pessimism. Groups of human beings cannot completely refrain from committing acts of violence, mass destruction, and atrocity. Thus, it is better for us, as psychoanalysts, to consider a more practical approach to international relationships.

In certain cases we may be able to contribute to the prevention of mass aggressive expressions. We may be able to offer insights on helping large groups and their leaders cope with traumatic events so that enmity between groups will not repeat in endless cycles of violence. And maybe we can encourage greater understanding of decision-making and more flexibility when political attitudes and policies become narrow and rigid.

But in considering how we can contribute to and influence international relationships, there is one more aspect of Freud's legacy which we must consider. It seems evident that he had assimilated, possibly without being aware of it, a degree of European ethnocentrism and a tendency to stereotype and denigrate other cultures. In his correspondence with Einstein, Freud made certain racist remarks about "Turks and Mongols," and also jokingly referred to his patients as "Negroes" (Tate 1996). These were not necessarily vicious or hateful attacks, and racism in general was especially prevalent and to a degree accepted in late nineteenth and early twentieth-century Europe. Freud may have identified with the aggressor in an attempt to defend against mounting anti-Semitism. But nevertheless, his remarks serve to remind us that our own personal analysis, self-analysis, and our extensive study of and training in human nature do not easily free us from investment in certain cultural norms, the attitudes of our own large group, or even racism. To be most effective in the psychoanalytic examination of large-group processes, and to appropriately apply certain psychoanalytic insights to international or interethnic issues, we must become involved in interdisciplinary work, we must gain first-hand experience with many cultures, and we must work through, as much as possible, our own prejudices. Furthermore, I long ago concluded that, just as I would not enter into analysis with a friend or family member, I would not become directly involved in an unofficial diplomatic project in which my own original large group was a party.

So far I have summarized some of the theoretical considerations and traditions that have prevented psychoanalysts from significantly contributing to the understanding of human relations beyond the couch. But other differences between the disciplines of psychoanalysis and diplomacy have presented difficulties that also should be mentioned.

The nature of the two fields, as they typically are practiced, creates obstacles that prevent psychoanalysts and diplomats from working together. In his or her clinical work, a psychoanalyst becomes involved in a long process that aims to help the patient resolve conflicts, be more realistic about everyday life, and become more flexible and playful without experiencing excessive anxiety, depression, or guilt. The aim of the psychoanalyst is to find a best possible solution for the patient's problems. A psychoanalyst typically needs to make money through his or her profession, and hopefully receives personal satisfaction from helping others, but otherwise is not primarily driven by self-interest.

Much of diplomacy, on the other hand, with the possible exception of those aspects that seek only to encourage cross-cultural understanding, concerns defining the "national interest" in a given situation and bargaining to protect or extend this interest. Although others may benefit from policies implemented through diplomacy, it is in essence self-serving. In some cases, it may be in the national interest to encourage, maintain, or ignore a conflict rather than seek its resolution.

Psychoanalysts who have worked with diplomats have been appalled when some diplomats demand short, simple, and quick advice or solutions. Such an approach goes against the psychoanalyst's training and thinking since in clinical practice he or she focuses on multiple internal and external motivations and their intertwining and is in favor of an open-ended process. On the other hand, most psychoanalysts do not put themselves in the shoes of diplomats and have no experiential knowledge of diplomatic training, practices, and traditions. Diplomats' aims need to be clearly understood by psychoanalysts if a collaboration between them ever will be fruitful. Furthermore, going through psychoanalytic training does not fully prepare a psychoanalyst to act as a consultant in diplomatic efforts. He or she needs to gain in-depth knowledge of the political, economic, military, and social issues at hand, each group's shared mental representations of past events that have been transmitted over generations (their chosen traumas and chosen glories—see Volkan 1997, 1999a), and be able to tolerate and enjoy interdisciplinary cooperation.

There are accepted rituals when the diplomats of opposing groups come together, and diplomacy depends heavily on obsessional patterns that try to keep anxiety from interfering with intellectualized considerations. Prejudice and transference distortions are inevitably absorbed in this obsessional process, especially when the large group that a diplomat belongs to is under stress, threat, or is regressed. In effect, under stressful conditions, at official negotiations every component of large-group identity is enhanced and dominates motivations. This leads to even more ritualizations where "playfulness" and the search for creative solutions often dissolve into resistances to change or the slow process of change. And even those diplomats who might want to negotiate creatively or have "orders" from their governments to try to reach agreements may adopt rigidified ritualizations.

Such problematic dynamics are further compounded by other motivations. Vasquez (1986) wrote "the most persistent philosophical question" that has plagued official diplomats has been "whether the foreign policy of a state ought to be based on the norms and principles of moral conduct" (p. 1). Official diplomacy speaks of *Fiat justitia, pereat mundus* (Let justice be done, even though the world perish) and seeks to galvanize its constituency by invoking images of glory and honor as they devalue the opposing group or take up arms against a foe. Ethnic, nationalistic, religious, economic, and social issues are often used to fuel such "truthfulness" of one's position and "immoral" aspects of the opposition's views and activities. The Christian Crusades and the Muslim holy wars were each pitched as a high purpose in which the Almighty was a partner. When the U.S. invaded Panama in 1989, which resulted in the capture of a drug lord at the expense of countless innocent victims, the incursion was called "Operation Just Cause" in an echo of Thomas Aquinas. The precise definition of morality can become not only ambiguous but also corrupted when threatened by the loss of power, self-esteem, and self-determination that are often connected with the reactivation of chosen traumas and other components of large-group identity.

Morality, formed at the oedipal age, begins as a matter of feeling, thinking, and behaving in ways to avoid being punished (Brenner 1983). The child's oedipal conflicts bring fears of losing loved ones and/or their love and of being punished. The child then becomes "moral" in the way his or her fantasies dictate in order to minimize anxiety and depressive feelings. Children may identify with their perceptions of a forbidding parent or remove themselves from competition in an effort to avoid expected punishment. And, since the beginning of morality is linked to anxiety or depressive feelings, the more anxiety and depressive feelings the child has, the stricter the superego he or she may develop: the outcome is a compelling sense of morality that is equal to the compelling need to avoid punishment. Children, of course, also develop moral codes that are unrelated to the fear of punishment, such as those related to efforts to please parents. Furthermore, as they grow, they find more sophisticated anxiety-reducing mechanisms and take into account the moral code of whatever group they come to owe allegiance to and, reciprocally, the group's code either corresponds to their psychological needs or is rejected. One is not surprised, however, to find that moral sense is not to be relied upon in situations in which there are regressive tendencies.

At times of stress, nations or other opposing large groups may undergo mass regression (see Loewenberg 1995) in that collectively experienced unconscious fear becomes condensed with a fear of "others." When large groups in conflict are regressed, their negotiators are more prone to hold on to the components of their large-group identity, to utilize more externalizations and projections, and to protect themselves more stubbornly from the return of their externalizations and projections (boomerang effect). These defense mechanisms lead to less empathy for the opposing group's problems and create resistances to attitude changes and the willingness to compromise. The "therapeutic regression" that is part of our clinical vocabulary and is necessary for a successful clinical outcome does not exist in diplomatic negotiations.

A therapeutic regression refers to taming a patient's existing and chaotic regression so that initial steps of progression can be made. There is no parallel concept or technique in diplomatic interactions for evolving such a process of change. Typically, opposing sides reach agreement not through a therapeutic regression followed by progression, but instead through the utilization of denial and repression of aspects of the existing conflicts, isolating oneself from emotions pertaining to conflict, and rationalizing the acceptance of terms of negotiation. Transference distortions also often occur in diplomatic interactions between the members of opposing groups, but although psychoanalysts are trained to deal with them, diplomats typically accept such distortions by utilizing rationalizations.

When agreements are reached and signed by opposing groups, the conflicts and emotions exacerbated by regression during crises do not altogether disappear and are not fully tamed, but are pushed into the shadows. These conflicts and emotions may erupt later to create new crises. The rule of law and reality testing, such as not having the resources to remain at war, force the parties in conflict to adjust slowly to the terms of agreements and remain at peace. Nevertheless, the legal documents do not change substantially the enemy relationships as far as internal perceptions and mental experiences are concerned. War-like situations, and even wars themselves, therefore, can remain an imminent but repressed threat. But diplomatically negotiated terms of peace are not necessarily always doomed. New events, such as a friendship between the leaders of enemy groups, internal change, or a revolution within one large group, can lead to the modification of perceptions, emotions, and expectations of the other at a psychological level. Furthermore, if the parties in conflict ask the help of a third, "neutral" team from another country, the third-party representatives may constructively interfere with the malignant effects of the existing chaotic regression among the representatives of opposing groups.

ROOM FOR COOPERATION

The examples briefly discussed above indicate that various phenomena appear in both the daily work of psychoanalysts and diplomats, but are perceived and reacted to differently. In spite of such inherent difficulties, however, there is still room for cooperation. Sometimes, when diplomats facilitate negotiations between enemy groups, they become frustrated when rituals associated with maintaining and protecting large-group identity (Volkan 1999a) are activated and create resistances to fruitful talks. For example, minor differences (Freud 1917) can become significant obstacles in negotiations. When such seemingly pointless discussions arise, psychoanalysts may help to design strategies that allow individual identities and group identities to be maintained and avoid the anxiety that can be experienced when too much "sameness" is perceived by opposing groups, causing them to seek the "protection" of minor differences. Psychoanalysis also can advise diplomacy about the importance of psychological borders—"togetherness" between ethnic groups, for example, can work better when some form of psychological border between the opponents is maintained. In addition, psychoanalysts can provide consultation when transference and countertransference reactions between opposing parties become very sticky.

In areas where there are chronic conflicts between two large groups, facilitators may become frustrated because leaders or diplomats of opposing large groups keep talking about past events instead of focusing on current issues. When conducting a dialogue, facilitators typically want the representatives of the groups in conflict to focus on "real" issues and make progress toward concrete objectives, but representatives often insist on enumerating in detail their group's historical grievances—their chosen traumas. For example, U.S. diplomats are periodically assigned to the "Cyprus Problem," and typically begin their task of negotiating a long-term settlement between Cypriot Greeks and Cypriot Turks with enthusiastic plans and strategies. In a short time many such diplomats complain that the two opposing sides cannot get beyond their preoccupation with past grievances and enter into a discussion of current issues, let alone future scenarios. A psychoanalytic perspective can be useful in such situations since our training and practice has taught us that no progress will be made on present issues if past ones are not understood and explored. A psychoanalyst, therefore, can help those in the dialogue understand the necessity of discussing chosen traumas and help to expand time when past and present have collapsed, and also assess when the time is right to attempt to move beyond them.

Most importantly, psychoanalysts can team up with former diplomats, historians, and others in certain suitable projects that are often called "unofficial diplomacy" or "Track II diplomacy" (Montville 1987, Volkan et al. 1990, 1991). For example, an interdisciplinary team from CSMHI has worked for over five years on bringing together

Estonian, Russian, and Russian-Estonian representatives, including high-level diplomats who attend in an unofficial capacity, to discuss the nature of post-Soviet relationships and practical means of promoting community and coexistence. This extended process of psychopolitical dialogue resulted in three indigenously designed and sustainable community projects to promote collaboration between Estonians and Russian-Estonians (Volkan 1997, Neu and Volkan 1999).

CONCLUDING REMARKS AND PREFACE

The tense situation in Estonia after the fall of the Soviet Union, like many other conflicts spawned by the collapse of the Communist empire, concerned groups within a sovereign state: one-third of Estonia's population is Russian (Russian-speaking). A struggle for "large-group identity" followed as those who defined and differentiated themselves from others sought to protect their large group from real and perceived threats. As we all witnessed in former Yugoslavia, governments and the UN are better equipped to deal with conflicts between states rather than within them. Diplomats and political analysts were puzzled by the intensity and irrationality of such large-group identity conflicts. How does the powerful and necessary force of ethnic pride lead to ethnic cleansing? What constitutes large-group identity, how does it come to contaminate legal, economic, military, and other real-world issues, and why does it become a significant and even dominant political force itself? In order to answer such critical questions, psychoanalysts must find appropriate ways to contribute to the general understanding of the role of large-group identity in interethnic and international relationships, and its specific influence in negotiations.

REFERENCES

Achen, C. H. and Snidal, D. (1989). Rational deterrence theory and comparative case studies. *World Politics* 41:143–169.

Allison, G. T. (1971). *The Essence of Decision: Explaining the Cuban Missile Crises.* Boston, MA: Little Brown.

Anzieu, D. (1971). L'illusion groupale. *Nouvelle Revue de Psychoanalyse* 4:73–93.
———— (1984). *The Group and the Unconscious.* London: Routledge & Kegan Paul.
Arlow, J. (1973). Motivations for peace. In *Psychological Basis of War,* ed. H. Z. Winnik, R. Moses, and M. Ostow, pp. 193–204. Jerusalem, Israel: Jerusalem Academic Press.
Barner-Barry, C., and Rosenwein, R. (1985). *Psychological Perspectives on Politics.* Englewood Cliffs, NJ: Prentice-Hall.
Bion, W. R. (1961). *Experiences in Groups.* London: Tavistock.
Brenner, C. (1983). *The Mind in Conflict.* New York: International Universities Press.
Chasseguet-Smirgel, J. (1984). *The Ego Ideal.* New York: W. W. Norton.
Etzioni, A. (1967). Mixed scanning: a "third" approach to decision-making. *Public Administration Review* 27:385–392.
Freud, S. (1901). Fragment of an analysis of a case in hysteria. *Standard Edition* 7:3–122.
———— (1917). Taboo of virginity. *Standard Edition* 11:191–208.
———— (1921). Group psychology and the analysis of the ego. *Standard Edition* 18:63–143.
———— (1932). Why war? *Standard Edition* 22:197–215.
George, A. L. (1969). The "operational code": a neglected approach to the study of political leaders and decision-making. *International Studies Quarterly* 23:190–222.
Janis, I. L., and Mann, L. (1977). *Decision Making: A Psychological Analysis of Conflict, Choice, and Commitment.* New York: Free Press.
Jervis, R., Lebow, R. N., and Stein, J. G. (1985). *Psychology of Deterrence.* Baltimore, MD: Johns Hopkins Press.
Kernberg, O. F. (1980). *Internal World and External Reality: Object Relations Theory Applied.* New York: Jason Aronson.
———— (1989). Mass psychology through the analytic lens. Paper presented at Through the Looking Glass: Freud's Impact on Contemporary Culture meeting, Philadelphia, September 23.
Loewenberg, P. (1995). *Fantasy and Reality in History.* London: Oxford University Press.
Mitscherlich, A. (1971). Psychoanalysis and aggression of large groups. *International Journal of Psycho-Analysis* 52:161–167.
Montville, J. V. (1987). The arrow and the olive branch: A case for

track two diplomacy. In *Conflict Resolution: Track Two Diplomacy*, J. W. McDonald, Jr. and D. B. Bendahmane, eds., pp. 5-20. Washington, DC: U.S. Government Printing Office.

Neu, J. and Volkan, V. D. (1999). Developing a methodology for conflict prevention: The case of Estonia. *Special Report Series: Winter 1999*. Atlanta, GA: Carter Center.

Rochau, A. L. von (1853). *Grundsätze der Realpolitik*. Frankfurt, Germany: Ullstein, 1972.

Tate, C. (1996). Freud and his "negro": psychoanalysis as ally and enemy of African Americans. *Journal for the Psychoanalysis of Culture and Society* 1:53-62.

Vasquez, J. A. (1986). Morality and politics. In *Classics of International Relations*, ed. J. A. Vasquez, pp. 1-8. Englewood Cliffs, NJ: Prentice-Hall.

Volkan, V. D. (1979). *Cyprus—War and Adaptation: A Psychoanalytic History of Two Ethnic Groups in Conflict*. Charlottesville, VA: University Press of Virginia.

—— (1997). *Bloodlines: From Ethnic Pride to Ethnic Terrorism*. New York: Farrar, Straus & Giroux.

—— (1999). *Das Versagen der Diplomatie: Zur Psychoanalyse nationaler, ethnischer und religiöser Konflikte*. Giessen, Germany: Psychosozial Verlag.

—— (1999a) Psychoanalysis and diplomacy part I: Individual and large group identity. *Journal of Applied Psychoanalytic Studies* 1:29-55.

—— (1999b) Psychoanalysis and diplomacy part II: large group rituals. *Journal of Applied Psychoanalytic Studies* 1:223-247.

Volkan, V. D., Akhtar, S., Dorn, R. M., et al. (1998). The psychodynamics of leaders and decision-making. *Mind & Human Interaction* 9:129-181.

Volkan, V. D, and Itzkowitz, N. (1984). *The Immortal Atatürk: A Psychobiography*. Chicago, IL: University of Chicago Press.

—— (1993). "Istanbul, not Constantinople": The western world's view of the Turk. *Mind and Human Interaction* 4:129-140.

—— (1994). *Turks and Greeks: Neighbours in Conflict*. Cambridgeshire, England: Eothen.

Volkan, V. D., Julius, D. A., and Montville, J. V., eds. (1990). *The

Psychodynamics of International Relationships, Vol.I: Concepts and Theories. Lexington, MA: Lexington Books.
——— (1991). *The Psychodynamics of International Relationships, Vol. II: Unofficial Diplomacy at Work.* Lexington, MA: Lexington Books.

Waelder, R. (1971). Psychoanalysis and history. In *The Psychoanalytic Interpretation of History*, ed. B. B. Wolman, pp. 3–22. New York: Basic Books.

White, M. J., ed. (1980). *Managing Public Systems: Analytic Techniques for Public Administration.* Scituate, MA: Duxbury.

18

Closing Panel: Psychoanalysis, Culture, and Society

David E. Scharff, Chair

Curtis Bristol, Paula Ellman, Dorothy Evans Holmes, Donald Kuspit, Michael Moskowitz, Stefan Pasternack, Vamık Volkan (Panelists)

The presentations of the second day included a video case presentation of an African-American woman artist who spoke of her own struggles and those of her family with race, and of her difficulties in loving. This presentation had the purpose of lending a tangible clinical example to the issues of creativity and the uses of art, psychoanalytic explorations of problems in loving, and the effects of race on the individual and the culture. There was also a jointly authored paper read by Paula Ellman, Ph.D., "The Riddle of Femininity"[1] written by a study group of women analysts, which explored the application of the two concepts of "primary femininity and the castration complex in the clinical treatment of women." The paper described a woman who used phallic identifications as a defense to deal with her developmentally compromised feminine identification.

---

1. The Riddle of Femininity: A Study Group's Inquiry into the Interplay of Primary Femininity and the Castration Complex in Analytic Listening, by Paula Ellman, Ph.D., Elizabeth Fritsch, Ph.D., Harriet Basseches, Ph.D., Susan Elmendorf, C.S.W., Nancy Goodman, Ph.D., Fonya Helm, Ph.D., and Shelley Rockwell, Ph.D. (accepted for publication in *The International Journal of Psychoanalysis*).

David Scharff: We know that we have had to omit many issues in the evolution of psychoanalysis from consideration in our conference. In this closing panel discussion we have an opportunity to discuss issues which you feel we have missed or that you would like to elaborate on. I'm also hoping that people will draw on clinical experience and clinical issues to summarize our experience of being together for these three days to consider the relevance and evolution of analysis.

Stefan Pasternack: While I was here this afternoon, I happened to come across a book that intrigued me by Jessica Benjamin, called *The Bonds of Love*. Thumbing through it, one of the chapters that caught my attention was the chapter on master and slave. The issue has to do with not seeing the patient in the clinical example as black or white, but seeing her as a woman who might be struggling with issues that any woman, or man who is conflicted with the issues of longing to submit versus fear of submission, or the desire to dominate through submission by getting someone else to please you, or getting mixed up in a sado-masochistic enslavement. The master/slave configuration is not always white/non-white or Jew/non-Jew, but may have other universal determinants.

Dorothy Holmes: Stefan is a long-time colleague, and we always have lots of comity between us. I think I agree with you, but I may disagree with you at the same time. Ultimately what you are saying is absolutely correct. But, if the master/slave frame of reference is vivid and important to the patient, the first thing is to be open to understanding it, to appreciate it in the way the patient needs you to if the patient is making reference to race. As I said in my remarks, I am packing that in terms of giving the patient wide latitude to state it any way she wishes, to state it is the first order of business. Keeping in mind that we know racial issues are rich symbolically, and if the matter stayed locked-in only to race, then we would have some concern about the obdurate quality of the defense and would need to see what we could do to help that along.

David Scharff: I thought one thing that the woman I presented did was to be articulate about the developmental tangle of race, issues with her parents, issues of where she grew up, and her struggle to form a relationship with men in an ordinary, committed way. These things in her life are so inextricably bound up together that we should not consider them separately.

Elizabeth Rundquist (New York City): I am part of the International Institute of Object Relations Theory (IIORT) core program here, and I think I am the only art therapist here. I would like to thank Dr. Kuspit for his presentation. I think the job of a therapist as well as an art therapist is to analyze, yes, but not to interpret so as to kill the affect, but to help patients to internalize the affect (however one does that) and make a synthesis in regards to the patient. Your paper on Freud's need to analyze without regard to the aesthetic helped me think about that clinical application. Thank you very much.

Donald Kuspit: Thank you.

Eric Milliner (Rochester, Minnesota): I wanted to highlight one of the comments that was offered briefly by both presenters on race: The dynamics concerning race and ethnicity are by no means limited to reality, even though when they exist in social climates they have tremendous potential for harm. I am currently treating a Scandinavian Lutheran young man who believes me to be German, and both Nazi and Jewish, because those are themes that embody traits within his own character, tendencies toward tremendous aggression and identification with the aggressor, of almost delusional paranoid intensity about retaliation. Those are enacted and played out by him in the transference in ways that have nothing to do with the reality of either his background or mine.

Walton Ehrhardt (New Orleans): I'm a German Lutheran pastor, which is why I want to speak. The element in which I have practiced for more than 30 years has been in the domain of pastoral counseling. I want particularly to thank the last two presenters for helping me to get in touch with what seems to me to be an element that we have alluding to throughout the conference. Freud established for us a rather radical basis of thinking about ourselves as human beings, and about the illusions we claim. These become powerful cultural definitions about who we are as individuals and collectively as groups. We claim them with a great amount of prejudice. Your contributions today have made this weekend so rich that at times it has even been overstimulating. Nevertheless, I regret that we did not make space to think about the way Freud's contribution can help us rethink our approach to religion, faith, and spirituality, elements that are dynamically powerful in the lives of all of our patients in some form or another. So again, thanks.

Stefan Pasternack: It is also interesting to me that Freud never really acknowledged his Jewishness. There is another book on sale here called *Freud's Moses*. In that book the author describes that Freud understood Hebrew and had extensive religious education, because in the Vienna of his day all children had two hours of mandatory religious education after school. Freud never clearly integrated or acknowledged his Jewishness because of his fear that psychoanalysis would then be written off because of stereotypes about Judaism. This is another example of an effect of racism. Racism and its consequences deserve a whole conference of their own.

Cathy Agar (Nebraska): I am not a clinician, I'm an English teacher from Nebraska. What Dr. Holland said about countertransference and its relationship to literary criticism is very important. Matthew Arnold, a nineteenth-century literary critic and poet, wrote a book called *On The Study of Celtic Literature*. He knew almost nothing about Celtic literature and had not read most of it. He characterized the Celtic character almost exclusively on the basis of stereotypes, but one of the things he said was that the Celt partakes of the feminine idiosyncrasy. In that book you can find everything you have described in clinical situations: the attachment of Celticism to the mother, Teutonic to the father, the feminine object versus the masculine object and master versus slave, because you have an analogy of the Celt and Teuton united in the English character as a marriage in which the husband, the Teuton, has to dominate. So, there is an example of how literary criticism can use what you are talking about.

Nell Scharff (New York City): I'm also an English teacher. I have been thinking today about the relationship between individual and social responsibility. I was thinking about the two talks on race in relation to Dr. Volkan's talk about international relations in which he alluded to the way racial and ethnic conflicts erupt into war. I want to link these issues with Dr. Holland's talk about reader response. Reader-response theory emphasizes how each person's individual response to a text is equally valid. This is true despite what the realities might be in the text. There is a social and ethical responsibility to

Closing Panel: Psychoanalysis, Culture, and Society / 301

understand text from the perspective that it comes from, and to extend that to an understanding of people. Reading text is learning how to understand what people mean, and not just a matter of giving in to a solipsistic exercise. My question is, how do you see this connection? You talk about social responsibility and you recommended a book about affirmative action, but then in the clinical examples, the responsibility seems to be to know your own stuff as a way too help the patient explore themselves beyond just race. But where does that meet social responsibility? And how do you think about that in your practice? Those matters also seem relevant to me as a teacher.

Michael Moskowitz: I have a couple of associations. First, in terms of social responsibility, we really have to take on social responsibility within our organizations. I have to say that at the New York University Post-Doctoral Program in Psychoanalysis for many years we took this on as an issue. We developed a committee, of which I was part of for 10 to 12 years, to try to get a more diverse faculty and student body at NYU. We met with a lot of opposition—in the best meaning of opposition. People said, "It's a big problem, what can we do about it?" Fortunately we had a cohesive committee that just kept at it. We ended up adding a number of faculty—Latino and African-American faculty. It was somewhat harder to increase registration in the student body. I think taking a real role in your professional organizations is critical.

Secondly, it's easy to say, as Freud did, "I can reach across any boundary of culture and class because we are all more human than otherwise." To some extent that's true, but there is still a difficult dialectic. You see people falling in love across boundaries of culture, class, and language. Soldiers in foreign countries end up marrying people they can't even speak to. Love can transcend race and prejudice. But there is an issue of trauma that comes up in the treatment of oppressed peoples. I first saw it because in my family there are people who are children of Holocaust survivors, whose analysts didn't even note that fact. Then, things changed in the next generation. If an analysand who was the child of a Holocaust survivor didn't bring it up, it became the analyst's responsibility to introduce it, because it was an unspoken trauma. I think the knowledge of that is important. That also applies to Vietnam veterans who went through years of treatment at the VA without anybody ever thinking, "Vietnam! What was the impact of the war on their lives?" So I think it's one thing to say that we can reach across these boundaries, but unless you can fully understand the fact of racism, it's hard for us who aren't subject to it to fully understand it.

Nevertheless, to whatever extent we can understand it and immerse ourselves in the world of the oppressed other, it helps. It remains a difficult thing to reach across boundaries to understand the suffering and pain caused by the culture in which we live.

Dorothy Holmes: We shouldn't overvalue or underestimate the power of what happens in the consultation room. After all, the people we treat go out into various walks of life. They can have magnificent influence if they are no longer encumbered by these factors. I also agree with Michael: Our organizations are, in the main, woefully inadequate in terms of their response to these issues. We must press on there. Not only to do with race, but also to do with how one's powers can become encumbered by whatever one's conflicts are. We should keep in mind the marvelous story of Mark McGuire. He openly attributes to four years of psychotherapy an important basis in his magnificent success in baseball.

Donald Kuspit: I want to point out something outside my usual bailiwick. The discourse in modernity on master/slave that has been discussed so much here is Hegel. Before Freud there was Hegel. Hegel was a very great psychologist in his own way. We keep using the term "dialectic," which I remind you also comes from Hegel. Hegel pointed out something extremely important that was partly addressed by Professor Holmes: the interdependence of the master and slave. The slave has power over the master, as well as the master having power over the slave, psychologically and social-psychologically. Hegel has one of the first psycho-social models in formulating this dialectic.

I also want to remind you of Pinter's famous play *The Servant*, which is a marvelous example of this dynamic in literature. You have a very peculiar thing happening when the servant takes over the master's situation. I also could point out that Marx's whole bourgeois/proletariat dialectic comes right out of Hegel, as Marx acknowledges. I myself believe, and I have no way of proving this, that certain of Freud's ideas about love of the relationship between object and self come out of Hegel as well. I am sure that Freud was aware of Hegel, indirectly. Freud did acknowledge Schopenhauer, and I would expect behind Schopenhauer there is Hegel, because Schopenhauer was a reaction to Hegel, just as Nietzsche was.

David Scharff: And, of course, object relations comes straight out of Hegel. Fairbairn was closely influenced by Hegel, whose teachings he studied as an undergraduate.

Sandra Snow (Baltimore, Maryland): I would like to hear Dr. Volkan's opinion on this: It seems to me that when you were talking this afternoon, you were illuminating the problem on the national level that we have just addressed on the micro-level. I would just like to comment that no one can be exempt from absorbing all of the "isms" in the culture when they've been so institutionalized. If we think of culture as Dr. Volkan suggested as "mother," then in the service of our need to preserve that parent in order to preserve self, it seems to me that is an intrapsychic struggle we all have. All of us, across class, race, gender, or whatever "ism" there is, engage in such a struggle individually. On a national level it becomes even more complex.

Vamık Volkan: We have a project in a community in Richmond, which is in an area that I think is number one or two as a drug and crime capital in this country. All the people are African-Americans. We have been studying this particular community for about a year and we see the same kind of things we see in international relations. Many unconscious things. For example, if you take look at a map of the backroads of the community, you see that a person from that community cannot take a bus to go two miles away to a museum. It is hard to tell if this isolation is planned consciously or unconsciously, but it doesn't matter really. It is just like prison. The internalization of this situation is such that there are other communities and areas where the children would not go, even though they're not in chains. The inhabitants internalize these kinds of restrictions, so that the most psychoanalytic thing we could do was to buy a bus for them, to rent a driver and a chaperone so that kids could go to a museum whenever they wanted to. That is a psychoanalytic response.

Paula Ellman (Washington, DC): I have been listening to what you are saying about what is inbred in the workings of the city, and the earlier question about what we could do to be more socially responsible. My reaction is in line with Dorothy Holmes's suggestion for self-analysis. We do need to try to be aware of our own aggression. Earlier comments about our discomfort seeing a black woman on videotape, and about the image of master/slave that has been with us this afternoon, may have engendered even more discomfort for us. This causes discomfort because of our own aggression, because in a way we were cast in the role of the master observing this black woman exposing herself and being quite vulnerable. I think that's what the discomfort had to do with, the identification with the master in the master/slave dynamic.

Curtis Bristol: Can I make a comment about the master/slave and return to theory and to Freud? Remember that the mother of love that I spoke about is the idealized, unrealistic love of the mother. There is also the other mother, the mother of hate. The ambivalence that is indigenous to all human beings leads to an externalization of hate onto the available external social receptors. Then the hate is reinforced in the social context that absorbs it. Whether you consider aggression innate, which is Freudian, or self-psychologically aroused within a context, or as narcissistic rage, it's all there to be dealt with by externalization, denial, splitting, projection, projective identification, and fantasy formation. Freud said that this is psychologically intrinsic to all people equally. Everyone has this mechanism.

Charles Ashbach (Philadelphia): I want to follow up Jill Scharff's observation that the pervert attacks differences. The person with a perversion also makes attacks against generational differences and against sexual differences, as well as racial, religious, or cultural differences. But it is not just the person with a perversion who has this potential. Difference itself threatens to annihilate our narcissism. To some extent, a perverse hatred of difference is therefore a permanent feature of the human condition.

David Scharff: As we close this discussion and this conference, I am reminded that the Freud exhibit at the Library of Congress has given us an opportunity to examine our origins and our evolution, to think about what psychoanalysis has to offer the wider world. That's what our discussion today has been about—the application of analysis to the culture, to the arts, to ourselves in our wider sense. It is fitting that we closed with Michael Moskowitz's and Dorothy Holmes's presentations, which have led us to think about the context in which our work exists, a social context to which we must relate fundamentally in order to have any meaningful impact.

I want to end by thanking the panel and all of you as a wonderful audience, as we draw this celebration and examination of Freud's legacy to a close.

19

Epilogue: Freud in Our Time
David E. Scharff

Like most psychoanalysts, I believe Freud is one of the true and abiding geniuses of the modern era, but I also believe we should not accept Freud's work uncritically. He insisted that he had invented a science. Witnessing its evolution over this century, we can no longer say whether our field is more science than craft, more art or philosophy.

A core of Freud's invention has remained. We can still recognize our origins in Freud's clinical examinations, but the theoretical underpinning of our field and the emphasis with which we work has evolved significantly. For many analysts, practice is now so different from that of their teachers and their own analysts that they may wonder if they still work in the same field. In this regard, I think of the incredible silence that characterized the work of many analysts in Britain and America in mid-century, and that seemed to be as different from Freud's own practice as the current emphasis on the analyst's countertransference and co-construction of the analytic experience is both from Freud and from the next generations of analysts.

Notwithstanding his blind spots, Freud is among that small group of wide-ranging geniuses of Western culture to whom we return to study, reinterpret, and to acknowledge the way in which they forever altered our thinking–Homer, Plato, Aristotle, Christ, and—skipping a few centuries—Michaelangelo, Rembrandt, Shakespeare, Galileo, Newton, Mozart, Jefferson, Goethe. In the twentieth century, Freud and Einstein stand out as such intellectual figures; along with James Joyce and Picasso, they are inventors of new orders—not only of a single invention that changed history or culture—but life-long contributors to the way we view the world and the way we think. They have changed who we are!

The ideas that Freud brought to us, like those of Plato and Aristotle, are first principles, likely to be with Western culture for the duration. But as with Plato, Aristotle, and Shakespeare, each age must continually re-examine Freud and psychoanalysis. In addition, since psychoanalysis aims to be a science of the mind, we must expect the evolution characteristic of all science: Yesterday's principles form the foundation on which tomorrow's ideas stand. Few ideas survive unchanged. Some will be refuted by new understanding. All need to be subjected to rigorous examination and modification as we add to our store of knowledge and technique. As Ernst Falzeder demonstrated in his paper, such reexamination is, and always has been, subject to the politics and intellectual agendas of those who claim Freud for their own—or whose agenda is to discredit him.

Not long after Freud's death, W. H. Auden wrote of him:

> For one who lived among enemies so long;
> If often he was wrong and at times absurd,
> To us he is no more a person
> Now but a whole climate of opinion.
>
> (*Collected Poetry*, p. 166)

Throughout this volume, we have been examining Freud's enduring vision of humanity by celebrating, studying, dissecting, and strengthening it. Flawed, sometimes marked by good ideas given exaggerated importance, wrong in places that have hurt, as in his psychology of women, Freud's work emerges as monumental: a climate of opinion, a body of probing, beautifully written thought that is an enduring source of understanding of the human condition.

Index

Abend, S., 252
Abraham, K., 25, 26, 30, 32, 207–208
Abstinence, techniques, 50–51
Achen, C. H., 280
Actuality, reality and, 128
Adaptation, affect theory, 64–65
Adler, 25
Adolphs, R., 64
Adorno, T. W., 200, 270
Aesthetics, psychology of, 198–199, 200, 201
Affects
  centrality of, 42–43
  sexuality, 43
Affect theory
  clinical relevance of, 70–73
  developmental factors, 67–69
  drive theory and, 44, 47–48

Freud, 61, 62–67
  systems theory and, right brain, 73–78
Agar, C., 300
Aggression
  drive theory, 43
  infant research, 47
  underemphasis on, 54
Aichhorn, A., 30
Ainsworth, M. D. S., 119
Alba, R., 271
Allison, G. T., 280
American Psychiatric Association (APA), 282, 283
Amnesia, trauma and, 8–9
Analytic object, Freud, 109–110
Analytic trust, transference, 98–100
Andreas-Salomé, L., 30

310 / Index

Anna O. case (Freud), 17, 149
Anti-Semitism
  Freud and, 259–261, 286
  psychoanalysis and, 271–272, 275–276
Anzieu, D., 285
Apple, R. W., 187
Archeology
  Freud and, xvii–xviii
  psychoanalysis and, xix
Aristotle, 149n3
Arlow, J., 286
Arnold, M., 183, 300
Art. See also Literary criticism
  aesthetics, psychology of, 198–199, 200, 201
  science and, 197
  visual arts, 195–212
Ashbach, C., 304
Association, psychoanalysis and, 6–7
Attachment theory
  affective phenomena, 67–69
  developmental factors and, 45–46
  sexuality and, 44–45
Atwood, G. E., 70
Auden, W. H., 22, 308
Authority
  Freud and, 16–17
  Janet and, 12–13
  psychoanalysis and, 18

Baker, S. C., 67
Balint, M., 26, 40, 104–105, 118
Barbas, H., 72
Barner-Barry, C., 280
Bauer, I. See Dora case (Freud)
Bechara, A., 69

Beebe, B., 119, 217
Benjamin, J., 298
Benowitz, L. I., 64
Bergmann, M. S., 215, 217–222, 225–227, 231–233
Berman, J., 184
Bernal, M., 255
Bernard, V., 253
Bernays, M., xviii
Bernheim, 5, 7, 14, 17
Bettelheim, B., 118
Binswanger, L., 30
Biology
  drive theory and, 48
  mind and, xv–xvi
Bion, W. R., 119, 146n2, 175, 285
Bird, B., 96
Birtles, E. F., 105, 119
Black, M., 103
Blanton, S., 259
Blonder, L. X., 64
Bloom, H., 22
Blum, H., 124, 159n1, 161, 197–198
Blumenthal, J., 171
Body ego, 205
Body involvement, Rosalie H. case (Freud), 154–157
Bollas, C., 105, 184
Bonaparte, M., 182
Bonomi, 26
Borod, J., 64
Botticelli, S., 210
Bouson, J. B., 184
Bowlby, J., 69, 119, 166, 218
Boyer, L. B., 253
Boyer, R. M., 253

Brain, neuropsychology, 37–40. *See also* Biology; Neurobiology; Right brain
Brenner, C., 61, 95, 289
Breton, A., 204
Breuer, J., xv, 5, 6, 110, 117, 146, 148n3, 149
Brill, A. A., 25, 26, 28–29, 30
Briquait, 14
Bristol, R. C., 213, 217, 304
Buck, R., 64
Burke, K., 183
Burton, R., 215
Butts, H., 253

Cancino, R., 255
Capacity for delay, object relations theory, 113–114
Carrol, L., 182
Catullus, 225
Cavalli-Sforza, L., 270
Center for the Study of Mind and Human Interaction (CSMHI), 282–283
Certeau, M. de, 203
Cézanne, P., 210
Chambers, I., xix
Chaplin, C., 190–191
Charcot, J.-M., xviii, 1, 5, 7, 8, 9, 10, 12, 17, 20, 202–203, 204–205
Chasseguet-Smirgel, J., 285
Chebabi, W., 261, 265
Chiron, C., 63
Chused, J., 169, 170, 172, 173–174, 176, 177
Clark, H. A., 168
Clinical practice, psychoanalysis and (panel), 165–177

Coen, S. J., 181, 189
Cognitive-behavioral psychology, psychoanalysis and, 56
Comas-Diaz, L., 253
Condensation, displacement and, hysteria, 140–142
Conflict
  interpersonal relationships, psychoanalysis and, 55–56
  love theory, 231–246
Cooper, D., 172
Countertransference
  love and, 234
  race and, 251–268 (*See also* Race and countertransference)
  techniques, 50–52
Crabtree, A., 9n3
Crews, F., 24, 31, 33, 34
Cristy, B., 168
Culture, psychoanalysis and (panel), 297–305
Cutting, J., 72

Da Costa, G., 253
Damasio, A. R., 62, 65, 141n1, 148n3, 185
Damasio, H., 185
Darwin, C., 141, 167
Davies, E., xviii, 180
Davies, J., 172
Davis, F. B., 204
Davis, R. C., 184
Death instinct, repetition compulsion and, 114–115
de Forest, I., 32n7
Delay, capacity for, object relations theory, 113–114

Derryberry, D., 69
Deruelle, C., 63
Descartes, R., 65, 203
de Schonen, S., 63
Deutsch, H., 30
Developmental factors
 affective phenomena, 67–69
 attachment theory and, 45–46
 infant research, 166
 romantic love, 217, 218–219, 220
Dias, C., 261, 265
Dias, R., 75
Dickens, C., 184, 188, 189
Dicks, H., 111–112
Dillard, J., 255
Diplomacy, psychoanalysis and, 279–295. *See also* Psychoanalysis: diplomacy and
Displacement, condensation and, hysteria, 140–142
Disposition, term of, 148n3
Dolan, R. J., 69
Don Giovanni (Mozart), 198
Dora case (Freud), 90, 94, 125–138, 159, 160, 161–162, 169, 173, 281
 analytic relationship in, 128–132
 background of, 125–126
 case presentation, 126–127
 infantile sexuality, 127–128
 supervisory perspective on, 132–135
 termination of, 135–137
Dostoevsky, F., 182
Dream interpretation
 art and, 200, 202, 203–204
 discovery of, xv

Dora case (Freud), 133–134, 136
 infantile sexuality, 128
Drive theory. *See also* Instinct theory
 affect theory and, 44, 47–48
 biology and, 48
 centrality of, 42–44
 Kernberg on, 47–48
Dupont, 26

Ecevit, B., 282
Edel, L., 183
Edelman, G. M., 141n1, 185
Ego, structural theory, 48–50
Ego orgasm, 199
Ego psychology, Kernberg on, 53–54
Ehrenzweig, A., 208–209
Ehrhardt, W., 299–300
Einstein, A., 286
Eisenberg, L., 68
Eitingon, M., 25, 26, 28, 32, 59, 260
Elaboration process, hysteria, 8–9, 13
Elizabeth (e. of Austria-Hungary), 125–126
Elliott, R., 69
Ellman, P., 303–304
Ellman, S. J., 40, 89, 90, 92n5, 93, 104, 167, 168, 171–174, 176–177
Emde, R. N., 72
Emmy von N. case (Freud), 1, 5–20, 140, 144
Emotion, affect theory, 63. *See also* Affect theory

Emotional processes, systems theory and, 73–78
Erikson, H. E., 128, 129
Esterson, 33
Etzioni, A., 280
Evans, D., 255, 262
Expression, affect theory, 64

Fairbairn, W. R. D., 40, 44, 47, 48–49, 53, 104, 105, 111, 115, 119, 303
Falk, D., 67
Falzeder, E., xvii, 2, 3, 26, 170–171, 172, 308
Federmeier, K. D., 66
Feldman, R., 68
Ferenczi, S., 25n3, 26, 27, 28, 31, 32–33, 50, 118, 171
Fink, G. R., 64
Fiorentino, R., 210
Fischer, N., 253
Fliess, W., 15, 182, 197, 204
Flynn, E. A., 184
Fonagy, P., 119, 175
Forgetting
  Freud and, 16–17
  hysteria and, 8
  memory and, 13, 20
Forrester, J., 31, 33
Fraiberg, L., 195, 198, 199, 201
Francis Joseph I (e. of Austria-Hungary), 125–126
Frank, J., 75
Frau Emmy von N. case (Freud), 1, 5–20, 140, 144
Free association
  concept of, 142–144
  discovery of, xv
Freeman, W. J., 141n1, 148n3

Freud, A., 260
Freud, M., 201
Freud, S., 75, 77
  affect theory, 61, 62–67
  archeology and, xvii–xviii
  collection of, xviii–xix
  contributions of, xv, xvii, 21–22, 37, 307–308
  countertransference, 252
  critics of, xvi–xvii, 23, 24, 33–34
  Dora case, 90, 94, 125–138 (*See also* Dora case (Freud))
  Frau Emmy von N. case, 5–7, 14–20
  free association, 142–144
  group psychology, 284
  historiography and, 23–25
  human nature, 286
  hysteria and, 159–163 (*See also* Hysteria)
  Kernberg on, 41–60
  literature and, 179, 181–194, 195
  love (romantic) and, 215–230
  love theory of, 231–246
  narrative and, 139–140
  neuropsychology and, 39–40
  neuroscience, 142
  object relations theory and, 40, 103–122 (*See also* Object relations theory)
  personal conflicts with, 25–34
  race and countertransference, 259–261
  racism, 286
  Rosalie H. case, 148–157
  semiotic model, 145–148

Freud, S. (continued)
  social issues, 269–270
  transference and, 40, 89–102
  (See also Transference)
  visual arts and, 195–212
Frijda, N. H., 64
Fromm, E., 31, 33n10, 270
Frustration, object relations theory, 113–114

Gabbard, G. O., 73, 217, 253
Galin, D., 62, 76
Garavan, H., 69
Gauchet, M., 11
Gauguin, P., 200
Gay, P., 31
Gazzaniga, M. S., 63
Gedo, J. E., 72
Gellner, E., 22
Genovese, E., 276
George, A. L., 280
Gerhart, R., 171
Geschwind, N., 77
Gibbons, A., 74
Gill, M., 53, 94–95
Gilman, S., 260
Gleick, J., 73
Goethe, J. W. von, 201
Goldhagen, D., 275–276
Goleman, D., 72
Gray, P., 262
Greenacre, P., 182–183
Greenberg, J. R., 65, 96–98, 103
Greenson, R. R., 98, 99
Gross, O., 25
Group psychology
  Freud, 284
  object relations theory, 112–113

Groups, regression in, psychoanalysis and, 56
Guntrip, H. S., 104, 105, 109

Hamilton, V., 171
Hariri, A. R., 72
Hárnik, 25
Harold, F. M., 73
Harrington, A., 10
Harris, J. E., 185
Hartt, F., 210
Hate, love and, 225
Haynal, A., 22, 26
Hegel, G. W. F., 302, 303
Heller, P., 21
Helms, J., 187
Hemingway, E., 188
Hernandez, M., 283
Hillman, J., 175
Historiography
  Freud and, 23–25
  objectivity and, 19
  transference and, 19–20
History, psychoanalysis and, 1–3
Hoffer, A., 33
Hoffman, I., 99, 253
Holland, N. N., 179, 181, 183, 184, 300
Holmes, D. E., 247–248, 253, 262, 272, 273, 298, 302, 304, 305
Homosexuality, psychoanalysis and, 276
Hoppe, K. D., 62
Horace, 187, 188, 201
Hugdahl, K., 71, 77
Human nature, Freud, 286
Hussein, S., 284

Hypnosis
  Charcot and, 10
  Freud and, 15–17
  Janet and, 12–13
  memory and, 7, 9, 12
  suggestion and, 13–14
  trauma and, 10–11
Hysteria, 139–158
  Charcot and, 8–11
  displacement and condensation, 140–142
  Dora case (Freud), 131
  Emmy von N. case (Freud), 5–7, 14–20
  free association, 142–144
  historical context of, 159–163
  Janet and, 11–14
  Rosalie H. case (Freud), 148–157
  semiotic model, 145–148

Id, structural theory, 48–50
Idée fixe, 12
Identification, object relations theory, 115–116
Infantile narcissistic object, Freud, 108–109
Infantile sexuality
  Dora case (Freud), 127–128
  romantic love, 225–226
Infant research
  conditions of, 47
  developmental factors, 166
Instinct theory. *See also* Drive theory
  love and, 233–234
  pleasure principle and, object relations theory, 106–107
  romantic love, 218

Interpersonal relationships
  conflict in, psychoanalysis and, 55–56
  intrapsychic factors versus, object relations theory, 111–113
Intersubjectivity
  countertransference, 252–253
  Kernberg on, 54
Intimacy, romantic love, 217, 222, 223–224, 225
Intrapsychic factors, relational perspectives versus, object relations theory, 111–113
Itzkowitz, N., 282

Jacobs, T. J., 70
Jacobsen, F., 253
Jacobson, E., 49, 105, 167, 218, 238
Jacoby, R., 275
James, W., 151n4, 167, 177
Janet, J., 13n10
Janet, P.-M.-F., 1, 8, 11–13, 17–18, 20
Janis, I. L., 280–281
Jay, M., 202–204
Jervis, R., 280
Johnsen, B. H., 77
Johnson, M., 63, 141n1
Jones, E., 22, 25, 26, 28–32, 182, 259, 260
Joseph, R., 69, 72, 76–77
Joyce, J., 187
Jung, C. G., 25–27, 29, 50, 175–176

Kandel, E. R., 62, 73, 185
Kantrowitz, J. L., 71

Kanzer, M., 90
Kaplan, J., 183
Kaplan-Solms, K., 72
Katharine case (Freud), 146
Kaufmann, S. A., 73
Keenan, J. P., 77
Kernberg, O. F., 37, 38, 41–60, 62, 105, 217, 221, 285
Kiell, N., 181
Kim, 63
Klein, M., 40, 53, 105, 111, 118
Kleinian psychology, 53, 103
Kofman, S., 208
Kohut, H., 75, 92n5, 96, 184, 206–208, 225
Kramer, 26
Krause, R., 47, 174
Kris, E., 183
Kuspit, D., 179–180, 302–303
Kutas, M., 66

Lacan, J., 45, 48, 145n2, 184–185
LaCapra, D., 19
Lakoff, G., 141n1
Language, of art, 198, 199
Laplanche, J., 46, 48
Lazarus, R. S., 64
Lear, J., 215, 217, 224
Leary, K., 254
Lebovici, S., 47
LeDoux, J. E., 62, 64
Leitner, M., 25, 26
Lemlij, M., 283
Leonardo da Vinci, 182, 196–202, 205–209
Levi, D., 169, 170
Lewis, M. D., 73–74
Libido, centrality of, 42–44
Lichtenberg, J. D., 217
Lieberman, 26

Linné, C. von, 141
Listening, Freud and, 17
Literary criticism, 179, 181–194, 195–197, 202–203
  future efforts, 184–186
  past efforts, 182–184
  present efforts, 186–191
Loewenberg, P., 283, 289
Loss, romantic love, 224–225
Lost object, Freud, 110–111
Love
  Freudian theory of, 231–246
  object relations theory, 111–112
  romantic love and, 215–230

Macmillan, M., 23, 24, 33
Madonna-whore split, 220, 236
Magoun, 32n9
Mahfouz, A., 283
Mahler, M., 45, 47, 105, 218, 238
Mahon, E., 252, 265
Mahoney, P., 22n1
Main, 119
Manheim, E., 182
Manheim, L. F., 182
Mann, L., 280, 281
Marcus, D. M., 71
Marcuse, H., 270
Marlowe, C., 184
Marx, K., 302
Masochism, romantic love, 227
Master/slave, 276, 298, 300, 304
Matthis, I., 123, 124, 146n2, 159n1, 160, 167–168, 173, 176–177
Mauron, C., 183
McCrorie, E., 217
McDonald, S., 166
McGuire, M., 302

McGuire, W., 260
McLaughlin, J. T., 62, 76
Megill, A., 22n1
Memory
  Charcot and, 11
  forgetting and, 13
  hypnosis and, 9
  hysteria and, 7
  Janet and, 11–12
  psychoanalysis and, 15, 20
  trauma and, 15
Merezhkovsky, D. S., 199
Mesulam, M.-M., 64, 71, 77
Meynert, 5
Michaelangelo, 180, 196–197, 199–202, 205–210
Michener, J., xvii
Milliner, E., 299
Milner, M., 209
Mind, biology and, xv–xvi
Mind-body connection, affect theory, 65–66
Mitchell, S. A., 65, 103, 117, 159
Mitscherlich, A., 282
Mlot, C., 77
Mnemic symbols, Rosalie case (Freud), 140
Modell, A., 62, 185
Mona Lisa (da Vinci), 196, 201, 206
Montville, J. V., 291
Morality, art and, 201
Morris, J. S., 77
Moser, F., 20
Moses (Michelangelo), 196, 197–198, 199–201, 205–207, 210
Moskowitz, M., 173, 248, 275, 301–302, 305

Motion pictures, 190–191
Mozart, W. A., 198
Multhaup, K. S., 63
Murray, H., 22n1
Music, 196, 198, 206–207

Narcissism
  Freud and, 91, 92
  infantile narcissistic object, 108–109
Narrative, Freud and, 139–140
Natoli, J., 181
Neafsey, E. J., 69
Nersessian, E., 64
Nervous system, Charcot and, 11
Neu, J., 292
Neurobiology
  advances in, 142
  brain, 37–40
  unconscious and, 61–87 (*See also* Right brain)
Nietzsche, F., 303

Oberholzer, E., 25, 27–28
Oberndorf, 25
Object concept, Freud, 107–111
Objectivity, historiography and, 19
Object relations theory, 103–122
  Freud and, 40, 107–111
  instinct theory and pleasure principle, 106–107
  intrapsychic versus relational perspectives, 111–113
  objects (Freudian) and, 107–111
  psychic structure, 113–118
  statement of, 104–106

Oedipal situation
  love and, 219, 220–221, 222, 225–227, 236
  object relations theory, 115–116
  race and, 274
  universality of, 46
Oedipus Rex, 182
Ogen, T., 105
Ohmann, R., 184
One-person psychology, two-person psychology and, 51–52
Ornstein, R., 62, 74, 77
Ovid, 225

Painting
  Freud and, 196
  Mona Lisa (da Vinci), 196, 201, 206
Pally, R., 141n1
Panksepp, J., 70
Passion, 215–230
Pasternack, S., 213–214, 217, 225, 298, 300
Peirce, C. S., 145n2
Penrose, R., 141n1
Perception, affect theory, 63–64
Person, E. S., 216–217, 219
Personality disorders, psychoanalysis and, 55
Pfister, O., 26, 30
Pfluger, M., 66
Phillips, W., 182
Piaget, J., 42
Pinter, H., 302
Pizzagalli, D., 64
Pleasure principle, instinct theory and, 106–107

Poe, E. A., 182
Pontalis, J. B., 14
Porges, S. W., 67
Pribram, K., 62
Price, J. L., 69
Prigogine, I., 73
Primary autism, Freud, 46–47
Psychoanalysis
  archeology and, xix
  association and, 6–7
  authority and, 18
  clinical practice and (panel), 165–177
  culture and society (panel), 297–305
  decline of, 22
  diplomacy and, 279–295
    cooperative possibilities, 283–292
    obstacles to collaboration, 283–290
    overview, 279–283
  evolution of, xx
  future of, Kernberg on, 54–60
  history and, 1–3
  influence of, 21–22
  memory and, 15
  neurobiological research and, clinical relevance of, 70–73
  personal conflicts in, 25–34
  racism and, 269–278
  suggestion and, 7–8
  techniques, Kernberg on, 50–54
  training in, 26–27
  transference and, 17–18
Psychoanalytic societies, Kernberg on, 57–58
Putnam, J. J., 25, 30, 269

Race and countertransference, 251–268
  didactic redress, 255–259
  Freud and, 259–261
  research in, 251–254
  treatment situation and, 261–265
Racism
  Freud and, 286
  psychoanalysis and, 269–278
Racker, H., 51
Ramachandran, V. S., 76
Rank, O., 26, 30, 31, 32, 33, 171
Rat Man case (Freud), 92n5, 169
Reality, actuality and, 128
Reality principle, object relations theory, 113–114
Realpolitik, 280. See also Psychoanalysis: diplomacy and
Recollection. See Memory
Regan, C., xix
Regression
  in groups, psychoanalysis and, 56
  music and, 207
Regulation, affect theory, 66–67
Reich, W., 25, 31n6, 270
Reik, T., 25, 31
Reiser, M., 185
Relational analysis, transference, 96–98
Relational factors. See Interpersonal relationships
Relational perspectives, intrapsychic factors versus, 111–113
Religion, 299–300
Remembering. See Memory
Remington, G., 253

Repetition compulsion, death instinct and, 114–115
Repression, historiography and, 33–34
Rickman, 25
Right brain, 61–87
  clinical relevance of, 70–73
  developmental factors, 67–69
  Freudian affect theory, 63–67
  systems theory and, 73–78
Robinson, R. G., 66–67
Rochau, L. von, 280
Rodgers, T. C., 272, 273
Rogers, C., 171, 172
Rolls, E. T., 69, 72
Romance, defined, 216
The Romance of Leonardo da Vinci (Merezhkovsky), 199
Romantic love, 215–230
Rosalie H. case (Freud), 140, 148–157
  body involvement, 154–157
  traumatic process, 150–152
  treatment, 152–154
Roschmann, R., 70
Rose, G., 183, 202
Rosenwein, R., 280
Ross, E. D., 63
Rotenberg, V. S., 76
Roth, M., xvi, xvii, 1, 2, 3, 15n18
Rudnytsky, P. L., 184
Ruitenbeek, H., 182
Rundquist, E., 299
Rush, F. L., 181
Ryan, R. M., 68, 77

Sachs, H., 25, 31, 32
Sacks, O., 62
Sadat, A., 280, 282

Sadomasochism, romantic love, 220, 227
Sander, L. W., 66, 76
Sandler, A.-M., 47, 70
Sandler, J., 47, 48, 49, 70
Saussure, F., 185
Scalaidhe, S. P., 69
Schachter, D. L., 141n1
Schacter, J., 253
Schapiro, M., 206
Scharff, D. E., 41–60, 73, 104, 105, 112, 117, 119, 166, 298–299, 304–305
Scharff, J. S., 40, 73, 104, 105, 117, 119, 165, 167–169, 170, 173, 175–177
Scharff, N., 300–301
Schelling, F., 203
Schnitzler, A., 201
Scholz-Strasser, I., xix
Schopenhauer, A., 303
Schore, A. N., 37–40, 62, 64, 66–72, 74–77, 119, 172, 173, 175
Schratt, K., 126
Schulman, M. A., 75
Schultz, W., 67, 69
Schwaber, E. A., 70, 75
Schwartz, M. M., 181, 184
Schwarzbeck, C., 166, 176
Schweickart, P. P., 184
Schweiger, E., 65
Science, art and, 197. *See also* Brain; Neurobiology; Right brain
Scott, W., 188
Sculpture, Freud and, 196, 198
Searle, J. R., 141n1
Segantini, K., 207–208

Self psychology, Kernberg on, 54
Semiotic model, hysteria, 145–148, 153
Sexual harassment, psychoanalysis and, 55
Sexuality
  affects, 43
  attachment theory and, 44–45
  Freudian theory of love, 231–246
  libido, centrality of, 42–44
  oedipal situation, 46
  romantic love, 215–230
Shakespeare, W., 182, 183, 187, 201
Sharpston, M., 176
Shevrin, H., 75, 141n1
Sibilla, W., 175
Siffert, G. A., 174
Silver, A., 146n2
Sistine Chapel, 201
Skulsky, S., 175–176
Slade, 119
Slavery, 276, 298, 300, 304
Snidal, D., 280
Snow, S., 303
Society, psychoanalysis and (panel), 297–305
Solms, M., 64, 66, 72, 75, 141n1, 142, 143
Somnambulism, hysteria and, 14
The Sorrows of Young Werther (Goethe), 201
Spence, S., 66
Spitz, R. A., 218
Sroufe, L. A., 68
Stalinism, 31
Stallworthy, J., 215
Starkstein, S. E., 66–67

Stekel, 25, 50, 252
Stengers, I., 73
Sterba, R., 195, 198, 200, 204
Stern, D. N., 71
Stewart, W. A., 90, 91
Stokstad, M., 205
Stoller, R., 218, 238
Stolorow, R. D., 70, 76
Stoltzfus, B., 184
Stone, L., 98, 99
Storfer, 25
Structural theory
  concepts in, 48–50
  object relations theory, 113–118
Suggestion
  Charcot and, 11
  hypnosis and, 13–14, 16
  hysteria and, 14
  psychoanalysis and, 7–8
Sullivan, H. S., 171
Sullivan, R. E., 183
Superego, structural theory, 48–50
Supervision. See Training
Sutherland, J., 49, 104, 105
Swift, J., 182
Systems theory, emotional processes and, right brain, 73–78
Szecsödy, I., 123–124, 159n1, 169–170, 173–175

Tate, C., 286
Tausk, 25
Taylor, G. J., 72, 73
Teasdale, J. D., 72
Techniques, Kernberg on, 50–54
Tennenhouse, L., 183

Ticho, G., 253
Tien, S., 266
Tintoretto (Jacopo Robusti), 210
Tomkins, S., 76
Toulmin, S., 149n3
Training
  Kernberg on, 56–59
  psychoanalysis and, 26–27
  race and countertransference, 255–259
Transference, 89–102
  analytic trust, 98–100
  contemporary perspective on, 94–96
  Brenner, 95
  Gill, 94–95
  Kohut, 96
  countertransference and, 50–52
  Freud and, 40, 90–94
  historiography and, 19–20
  love and, 234
  psychoanalysis and, 17–18
  relational analysis, 96–98
Translation rights, 29
Trauma
  amnesia and, 8–9
  hypnosis and, 10–11
  hysteria and, 6, 8
  memory and, 15
  Rosalie H. case (Freud), 150–152
Tremblay, L., 67, 69
Trevarthen, C., 68
Trust, analytic, transference, 98–100
Tucker, D. M., 67, 69
Tuckett, D., 170
Turkle, S., 269

Two-person psychology, one-person psychology and, 51–52

Unconscious
  centrality of, 41–42
  discovery of, xv
  free association, 142–144
  nature of, xvii
  right brain and, 61–87 (*See also* Right brain)
  romantic love, 219, 220
  transference and, 18
United Nations, 283, 292

Vasquez, J. A., 288
Vinci, Leonardo da, 182, 196, 197, 198, 199, 200, 201, 202, 205, 206, 207, 208, 209
Virgin and Saint Anne with the Christ Child and the Young John the Baptist (da Vinci), 196
Visual arts, 195–212
Volkan, V. D., 248–249, 280, 282, 285, 291, 292, 300, 303

Waelder, R., 281, 284
Watt, D. F., 64
Webster, 33

Weir, 159
Weissman, S., 190
Wells, H. G., 225
Westen, D., 71
Wexler, B. E., 77
White, M. J., 280
Whitehead, A. N., 200
Willbern, D., 181
Williams, A. H., 175
Wilson, E., 183
Winnicott, D. W., 104, 105, 167, 170, 172, 199
Winson, J., 39, 65, 185
Withim, P., 183
Witt, B., 12–13
Wittling, W., 65, 66, 70
Wolf, E., 271
Wolff, C. G., 183
Wolf Man case (Freud), xviii, 92n5
Wollheim, R., 22
Woodward, K., 184
World War I, 113
Wright, E. E., 181

Yalom, I., 171, 172
Young, A., 11n6
Young-Bruehl, E., 201

Zetzel, E. R., 98, 99